VIGILANT CHRISTIAN II PREVENTING AN AMERICAN HIROSHIMA

DAVID J. DIONISI

Order this book online at www.trafford.com
or email orders@trafford.com

Most Trafford titles are also available at major online book retailers.

Printed in the United States of America.

ISBN: 978-1-4669-8814-9 (sc)
ISBN: 978-1-4669-8813-2 (e)

Trafford rev. 04/15/2013

 www.trafford.com

North America & international
toll-free: 1 888 232 4444 (USA & Canada)
phone: 250 383 6864 ♦ fax: 812 355 4082

A key message of this book is "people are destroyed for lack of knowledge."[1] Everything in the Vigilant Christian book series is written to please God by promoting faith, kindness, generosity, nonviolence, and teaching that we should treat everyone as loved members of our family.[2]

<hr/>

[1] Hosea 4:6—"My people are destroyed for lack of knowledge: because thou hast rejected knowledge, I will also reject thee, that thou shalt be no priest to me: seeing thou hast forgotten the law of thy God, I will also forget thy children." Scripture references are available in over 30 versions of the Bible (see www. vigilantchristian.org/accessover30bibleversions.html). Throughout this book the King James Version of the Bible is used unless otherwise noted. The author acknowledges that different versions of the Bible are at times valuable to help deepen understanding.

[2] A summary of the five books in the Vigilant Christian book series is provided in Appendix B and online at www.vigilantchristian.org.

FRONT COVER

The cover picture shows the Hiroshima Peace Park in Japan because the atomic explosion in Hiroshima on August 6, 1945 inspires people around the world to abhor nuclear bombs and work for peace. The center portion of the picture is the former Hiroshima Prefecture Industry Promotion Hall, now known as the Atomic Bomb Dome. The view of the Atomic Bomb Dome is framed by the Cenotaph for the Atomic Bomb Victims. A cenotaph is a monument erected in honor of the dead.

The front cover was created to communicate that the descendants of the people who orchestrated the events leading to World War I and World War II are now hard at work to start a third world war. The photograph of the Cenotaph has been modified with four drawings that appear as if they are engraved on the stone coffin. The drawings are the New World Order Masonic pillars, Awakening Arm, One World Trade Center Building, and Georgia Guidestones.[3] The drawings show the progression of the one-world plan.

---

[3] The Masonic pillars are called Jachin and Boaz. The pillars marked the location for the buried vaults that Freemasons claim were found by Pythagoras and Hermes. Multiple New World Order societies claim the knowledge for their one-world plan is derived from these two pillars and vaults buried beneath them. The Awakening Arm is part of the New World Order monument called The Awakening, located just outside Washington, DC. The symbolic message of this monument is a new species of humans, Homo Noeticus or spiritual enlightened beings, are once again rising. The NWO elite believe that like the phoenix, they are resurrected from fire. The One World Trade Center is a New World Order structure and serves a religious purpose that is explained in the third Vigilant Christian book. The Georgia Guidestones are the Ten Commandments of the New World Order and are further explained in Chapter 10.

FOREWORD

I realize that many people will struggle with the information contained in this book. A cartel of extremely wealthy people are working to make the truth appear as nothing more than a conspiracy theory. I encourage you to open your mind to the possibility that there is something standing between the will of the people and the actions of the United States government. I ask that you think for yourself and do your own research. Following the money spent by the New World Order will lead to answers.

After September 11, 2001, I increasingly noticed people beating the drums about nuclear terrorism, and in 2004 I learned of the first reports of an alleged al Qaeda plan called "American Hiroshima." What I learned motivated me to travel to the Middle East and obtain more information. To communicate what I learned, I wrote five Vigilant Christian books. The books explain that al Qaeda is not responsible for the 9/11 terrorism. More importantly, the books explain that a cartel is working to establish a world government and this group has a third world war planned. World War III is to be prompted by a massive human sacrifice event. This event, a spiritual Hiroshima, can be prevented with education and is discussed in this book.

The first edition of this book was published in February 2005. In 2006, a second edition was published in English and Korean. This 2013 edition corrects mistakes in earlier books and is the product of additional years of research in Belgium, Canada, Egypt, England, Ethiopia, Gaza, Ghana, Indonesia, Israel, Kazakhstan, Liberia, Qatar, Russia, Singapore, Switzerland, the United Arab Emirates, and the United States.

In the years since the first edition, readers have responded that the information has helped deepen their understanding of the world. In 2006, this book led to the creation of the Teach Peace Foundation, a non-profit delivering acts of kindness and peace education.[4] The Vigilant Christian books are endorsed by the Teach Peace Foundation.

---

[4] The Teach Peace Foundation offers life-changing education and acts of kindness helping disabled children live with dignity, providing educational opportunities for children to attend school, and delivering education about the New World Order. A wealth of online resources are available at www. teachpeacefoundation.org.

DEDICATION

Vigilant Christian II: Preventing an American Hiroshima is dedicated to an amazing defender of the defenseless. Her name is Sister Mary Sponsa Beltran.[5] As a Bernardine Franciscan missionary, she has dedicated her life to the poorest of the poor in Africa.

In November 2004, she demonstrated tremendous courage and in the process prevented the slaughter of the disabled Muslim children living at the *Our Lady of Fatima Rehabilitation Center* near Monrovia, Liberia. Mosques and churches were being burned by angry mobs, and the tension between various tribes and faiths escalated out of control. As the attack on the compound for 300 disabled people was about to begin, the Christians separated from the Muslims. Sister Sponsa immediately went to the Christians and said, "What have I taught you? How can you leave your brothers and sisters in their hour of need? Did I not accept all of you in this compound as children of God?"

This amazing woman then went immediately to the attacking force at the compound gate and, putting aside her own safety, began to pray for peace. Her actions mystified the attackers who began to leave. Just then Sister Sponsa's cell phone rang. A former disabled Muslim student, now living in another part of Liberia, called to ask her what she had just done. He explained that he felt God's presence in a powerful way and he knew that she had done something. She responded, "I prayed and experienced a miracle."

Sister Sponsa's call for Christians and Muslims to love each other as Jesus loved us is a key to defeating evil. The New World Order needs people to be divided and fear each other in order to achieve their goals. This is why the September 11, 2001 attacks were designed to divide the Abrahamic religions. Sister Sponsa never let fear rule her life. Her message is to love and serve everyone. Sister Sponsa's life is confirmation that a single person, who never gives up, can make a big difference.

---

[5] Sister Mary Sponsa Beltran was born on March 25, 1925 and lives at St. Joseph's Villa in Reading, Pennsylvania. In 2011, she was awarded the Teach Peace Foundation Lifetime Peacemaker award.

CONTENTS

1

INTRODUCTION

"Now, we can see a new world coming into view. A world in which there is a very real prospect of a new world order." [6] George H. W. Bush

Vigilant Christian II: Preventing an American Hiroshima is the true story of a treasonous plan to undermine the United States with a broader goal of moving toward world government. This book explains how secret societies are part of this occult plan for a totalitarian one-world government. The five books in the Vigilant Christian series can help current and future generations understand how evil is organized and defeated. [7]

While world government may initially sound appealing to some, what is sought by a small but powerful group of people is absolute power. Absolute power in the hands of humans does corrupt absolutely. If not exposed and stopped, this small but powerful group of people will start World War III in their pursuit of world government.

The New World Order and abbreviation NWO are used in this book series as the name for a cartel that seeks to rule the world. If the NWO is a new concept for you or if you seek evidence of its existence, I encourage you to read *Vigilant Christian I: The New World Order*. The first Vigilant Christian book was written to reveal the key NWO leaders, their one-world plan, and physical evidence of their activities. Following the money is all that is needed to see that the NWO is real, although other dimensions, including their construction of symbols, can be eye-opening.

The first Vigilant Christian book provides evidence that the NWO existed before the United States was created. Knowledge of the NWO is necessary to understand much that has happened

---

[6] President George H. W. Bush made this statement in his March 6, 1991 address before a Joint Session of Congress in which he declared the end of the Gulf War.

[7] Proverbs 13:22 - "A good man leaveth an inheritance to his children's children: and the wealth of the sinner is laid up for the just."

and is happening in our world. Seeing what is real takes courage. Fortunately, God made us to be courageous.[8]

Fronts and Bagmen

The NWO uses fronts, often organized as secret societies and corporations, to camouflage their work.[9] The term "NWO agent" or "insider" is used in this book series to identify a person who is knowingly working to advance totalitarian world government.[10] The vast majority of people in one-world front organizations are not insiders and only unknowingly serve the NWO. Often, insiders are the children and grandchildren of people who served the NWO.[11] First-generation secret society members are routinely unaware the NWO is real. In all cases, whether a person is acting with or without knowledge of the one-world plan, they are to be treated with kindness, but held accountable when engaged in criminal activity.

Fortunately, each day, more people are waking up to see that the Bilderberg Group, Council on Foreign Relations, Trilateral Commission and other secretive organizations are NWO fronts. A list of key NWO members is provided in the Appendix section in *Vigilant Christian I: The New World Order*. My sincere hope is that by exposing what the NWO has done in the past and is planning for the future, an American Hiroshima and World War III will be prevented.

One reason that NWO families want banking fronts and bagmen is that violence they initiate sometimes leads to revenge.[12] The story of NWO bagman J. P. Morgan Jr. is one example. On July 3, 1915, J. P. Morgan, Jr. was almost murdered by Frank Holt. Holt wanted to stop the war profiteering that fueled World War I.[13] Morgan survived and Holt's mysterious death before

---

[8] Joshua 1:9—"Have not I commanded thee? Be strong and of a good courage; be not afraid, neither be thou dismayed: for the Lord thy God is with thee whithersoever thou goest."

[9] Like the tentacles of an octopus, multiple cartel names and fronts means when one of the tentacles is exposed, it can be terminated or changed without much long-term damage to the inner circle leadership.

[10] John Pierpont Morgan is an example of a person who served as an NWO agent. J. P. Morgan led one of the largest American banking dynasties. Chernow, Ron. *The House of Morgan: An American Banking Dynasty and the Rise of Modern Finance* (New York, New York: Grove Press, 1990 and preface copyright 2001).

[11] J. P. Morgan's son, J. P. Morgan, Jr., is an example of a son who followed in his father's NWO service.

[12] A bagman is a person who collects or distributes money for racketeers or performs illegal tasks for mob or NWO bosses.

[13] "Man Who Shot J. P. Morgan Twice Admits Setting Bomb At National Capital," *Hartford Courant*, 4 July 1915. "Former German Instructor At Cornell Talks Freely After Third Degree Is Used, and Says He Wanted To Stop Shipment of Munitions To Europe."

trial served to keep the public in the dark about Morgan's effort to drag the U.S. into World War I.[14]

Newspapers across the country reported that "Holt came to his death by a compound fracture of the skull and cerebral hemorrhage caused by a fall."[15] Holt's likely assassination by the NWO was reported both in 1915 and 1942 to fuel hatred for wars.[16] The following is a July 7, 1915 newspaper example which certainly reminded readers to think of the Lusitania which sank on May 7, 1915.[17]

> "It was reported today that Holt had told a detective that he had put fifty pounds of dynamite on board a vessel which had since left New York. Wireless stations along the coast endeavored to reach steamers which had left here since June 29 to warn them of the possibility of an explosion . . . While several of the jail authorities declared Holt killed himself by climbing through the opening at the top of his cell door and then plunging to the narrow court below, Holt's keeper [Jeremiah O'Ryan] said he was positive that the prisoner was killed in his own cell, where he said he found the body. There were many conflicting reports as to the manner in which Holt met his death, but it was definitely established through Dr. Cleghorn, the jail physician, that Holt died of a fractured skull."[18]

The fact Holt's death was used as war propaganda is less confusing to understand with the knowledge that the J. P. Morgan financial empire was created to serve the NWO.[19]

---

[14] Kathleen Burk, "The Diplomacy of Finance: British Financial Missions to the United States, 1914-1918," *Historical Journal 1979 Volume 22 and Issue 2*, 351-372. An abstract of this article is online at http://journals.cambridge.org/abstract_S0018246X00016861. J. P. Morgan organized approximately 2,200 banks for the NWO to float loans estimated at $500,000,000 to fund World War I. Almost all weapons purchased by the U.S. were acquired through a J. P. Morgan company and related funding.

[15] "Frank Holt, Who Shot Morgan, Kills Himself," *The Deseret News*, Salt Lake City, 7 July 1915, 1 and 3.

[16] No writer attributed, "Muenter, Once German Teacher Here, Killed Wife, Shot Morgan, Sabotaged in World War 1," *The Harvard Crimson*, 14 February 1942. Harvard German instructor Eric Muenter changed his name to Frank Holt.

[17] "Frank Holt, Who Shot Morgan, Kills Himself," *The Deseret News*, Salt Lake City, 7 July 1915. The excerpt is on page 1.

[18] Ibid.

[19] The leading NWO financial family is the Rothschild family. The Rockefeller family is an American financial empire that serves the NWO and Rothschild family. The Rockefeller flagship, Chase Manhattan, was merged with J. P. Morgan and renamed J. P. Morgan Chase. In 2000, J. P. Morgan executives assumed the key management positions of J. P. Morgan Chase, which signaled that the Rockefellers are also subordinate to the Morgan family. For additional information on the top NWO families, the first Vigilant Christian book is recommended.

Bombs and More Bombs

Since 1945 the NWO has prompted many countries to fight wars. The NWO influence on the U.S. is one example. The NWO has influenced the U.S. decision to fight or fund combatants in over 65 countries. The following is the list of the countries and the dates of the U.S. interventions since 1945.

- China, 1945-49
- Philippines, 1945-53 and 1970s-1990s
- South Korea, 1945-53 and 1980
- Vietnam, 1945-73
- Soviet Union, 1940s-1960s
- Marshall Islands, 1946-58
- France, 1947
- Italy, 1947-48
- Greece, 1947-49 and 1964-74
- Eastern Europe, 1948-56
- Albania, 1949-53
- Germany, 1950s
- Iran, 1953, 1987 and 2012 to present
- Guatemala, 1953-1990s
- British Guiana/Guyana, 1953-64
- Costa Rica, mid 1950s, 1970-71
- Cambodia, 1955-73
- Middle East, 1956-58
- Indonesia, 1957-58 and 1965
- Laos, 1957-73
- Iraq, 1958-63, 1972-75, 1990s to present
- Haiti, 1959, 1987-94 and 2004
- Cuba, 1959 to present
- Ecuador, 1960-63
- The Congo/Zaire, 1960-65 and 1977-78
- France/Algeria, 1960s
- South Africa, 1960s-1980s
- Brazil, 1961-64
- Dominican Republic, 1963-65

- Ghana, 1966
- Uruguay, 1969-72
- Australia, 1972-75
- Portugal, 1974-76
- East Timor, 1975 to present
- Angola, 1975-1980s
- Jamaica, 1976
- Nicaragua, 1978-90
- Seychelles, 1979-81
- Grenada, 1979-83
- South Yemen, 1979-84
- Afghanistan, 1979-92 and 2002 to present
- Honduras, 1980s and 2009
- El Salvador, 1980-92
- Chad, 1981-82
- Libya, 1981-89 and 2011 to present
- Suriname, 1982-84
- Lebanon, 1983-84
- Fiji, 1987
- Panama, 1989
- Bulgaria, 1990-91
- Peru, 1990s to present
- Mexico, 1990s to present
- Colombia, 1990s to present
- Kuwait, 1991
- Albania, 1991-92
- Somalia, 1993
- Bosnia, 1994-95
- Yugoslavia, 1995-99

- Chile, 1964-73
- Bolivia, 1964-75
- Peru, 1965
- Thailand, 1965-73

- Yemen, 2002 to present
- Venezuela, 2002 to present
- Pakistan, 2005 to present
- Syria, 2012 to present[20]

It is not the protection of U.S. citizens but the NWO's plan for world government that is responsible for the U.S. dropping bombs on many countries. Violence has been and remains a key method to form ten world regions and a world government. In none of the situations where the U.S. Air Force bombed a country did a lasting democratic government develop.[21] For advocates of bombing campaigns, democracies in zero out of over two dozen countries since the end of World War II would suggest to most people that dropping bombs is contrary to bringing about democracy, peace, and prosperity. The truth is that the good derived from violence is temporary and the evil inflicted is permanent.

The next chapter explaining what happened in August 1945 can help prevent an American and ultimately a global Hiroshima. The chapter explains why the first atomic bombs dropped on Hiroshima and Nagasaki were unnecessary for ending World War II, but crucial for advancing a totalitarian world government.

If you ever find yourself losing hope during your process of discovery of how evil is organized, it is helpful to remember evil was eternally defeated when Jesus died for us. Praying that your worries be replaced with trust in God can help. With God, all good things are possible.

---

[20] William Blum, "A Brief History of U.S. Interventions 1945 to the Present," *Z Magazine*, June 1999. Permission for inclusion of text obtained on September 16, 2004. The list compiled by William Blum is supplemented and updated.

[21] Ibid.

2

Uprooting Japanese Christianity

"This is a question I am settling myself." Henry Lewis Stimson's response to the U.S. military's recommendation of atomic bombing targets.[22]

One of the New World Order's best kept secrets is that the first atomic bomb served a much darker purpose. The true story of the two bombs that were dropped on Japan is shared for the first time in this book. The following is a photograph of the Nagasaki atomic bomb detonation.[23]

---

[22] General Leslie M. Groves, *Now It Can Be Told: The Story of the Manhattan Project* (New York, New York: Harper, 1962). Page 273 in the 1983 Da Capo Press edition. Stimson served the NWO and was a high ranking Freemason. General Groves wrote: "When I went over the list for him, he immediately objected to Kyoto and said he would not approve it." Nagasaki was not on the target list presented by Groves.

[23] Courtesy of the U.S. National Archives. U.S. government photograph taken by the 509th Composite Group on August 9, 1945. The 1,500 person 509th, an Army Air Force group, was formed for the sole purpose of delivering atomic bombs. A video of the Nagasaki detonation is online at www.teachpeace. com/nagasaki.htm.

Unnecessary Atomic Bombs

We are instructed by government officials and the media on August 6 each year to believe that we owe a lot to the atomic bomb. The official argument is that the atomic bombs saved lives by bringing an end to the war with Japan. Misinformation intentionally disseminated by NWO agents confuses people into believing the official argument that the first atomic bombs were necessary to save lives. President Harry Truman and top military leaders knew before August 1945 that the atomic bombs were unnecessary to end the war.[24]

Multiple high-level U.S. government officials opposed using atomic bombs. General Dwight Eisenhower wrote to Stimson, "Japan was at that very moment seeking some way to surrender with minimum loss of 'face.' It wasn't necessary to hit them with that awful thing."[25] Admiral William D. Leahy was even stronger in his condemnation of the use of atomic weapons stating: "It is my opinion that the use of the barbarous weapon at Hiroshima and Nagasaki was of no material assistance in our war against Japan. The Japanese were already defeated and ready to surrender . . . Bomb is the wrong word to use for this new weapon. It is not a bomb. It is not an explosive. It is a poisonous thing that kills people by its deadly radioactive reaction, more than by the explosive force it develops. My own feeling is that in being the first to use it, we had adopted an ethical standard common to barbarians of the Dark Ages. I was not taught to make war in that fashion, and wars cannot be won by destroying women and children."[26]

The Manhattan Project name was selected in part because many of the NWO principals lived in Manhattan.[27] To understand the military usefulness of the Manhattan Project, the

---

[24] Michael J. Hogan, editor, *Hiroshima in History and Memory* (Cambridge, United Kingdom: The Press Syndicate of the University of Cambridge, 1996). Page 19 in the 1999 edition. President Truman wrote in his diary that Josef Stalin promised to enter the war against Japan on August 15, 1945 and "Fini Japs when that comes about." Truman's testimony that the atomic bombs were not needed to end the war quickly is often unknown and contradicts claims the atomic bombs prevented a million or more U.S. military deaths.

[25] David Krieger, "From Hiroshima to Humanity," *Nuclear Age Peace Foundation*, August 2005. Available online at www.wagingpeace.org/articles/2005/08/00_krieger_from-hiroshima-to-humanity.htm. The use of the atomic bombs were acts of evil from the perspective of General of the Army Dwight Eisenhower because the mass murders were unnecessary to ending the war.

[26] William D. Leahy, *I was there: Personal Story of the Chief of Staff to Presidents Roosevelt and Truman, Based on His Notes and Diaries Made at the Time* (McGraw-Hill Book Company, 1950), 441. Admiral William D. Leahy (May 6, 1875-July 20, 1959) was the Chairman of the Joint Chiefs of Staff.

[27] The name Manhattan Project was also likely chosen because the NWO has a longer one-world plan for Manhattan. *Vigilant Christian III: The Occult Religion of the 9/11 Attackers* explains the NWO plan for Manhattan. The most visible symbol and a ground zero for the NWO Manhattan plan is the One World Trade Center which is scheduled for completion in 2013.

United States Strategic Bombing Survey interviewed hundreds of Japanese leaders after the war and concluded that Japan would have surrendered in 1945 without the use of the atomic bomb, a U.S. invasion, or Russia entering the war.[28] J. Robert Oppenheimer, known as "the father of the atomic bomb" and the scientific leader of the Manhattan Project, went so far as to personally tell President Truman, "Mr. President, I feel I have blood on my hands."[29] Oppenheimer then went on to oppose the development of the hydrogen bomb.

Why did people like Eisenhower, Leahy, and Oppenheimer feel using the bomb was a horrendous mistake? The answer is that they had access to classified information that the American people would not see for decades. I have reviewed the U.S. intelligence intercepts prior to the first use of atomic weapons, and an analysis of the conditions prior to the atomic bombing of Japan confirms the Strategic Bombing Survey finding that the war would have ended without an invasion of Japan. Since Japan would have surrendered without the atomic bomb being used, the one-half million or more American lives saved rationale is untrue.[30]

---

[28] *United States Strategic Bombing Survey: Japan's Struggle to End the War* (Washington: Government Printing Office, 1946).

[29] Peter J. Kuznick, "A Tragic Life: Oppenheimer and the Bomb," *Arms Control Association*, July/August 2005. Available online at www.armscontrol.org/act/2005_07-08/Kuznick.aspage.

[30] Gar Alperovitz, *The Decision to Use the Atomic Bomb* (New York, New York: Vintage Books, 1996), 7. The chief historian of the U.S. Nuclear Regulatory Commission, J. Samuel Walker, wrote: "It is certain that the hoary claim that the bomb preventing one-half million American combat deaths is unsupportable."

On April 24, 1945, Secretary of War Henry Stimson sent the following letter to Truman requesting a meeting to explain the atomic bomb program.[31]

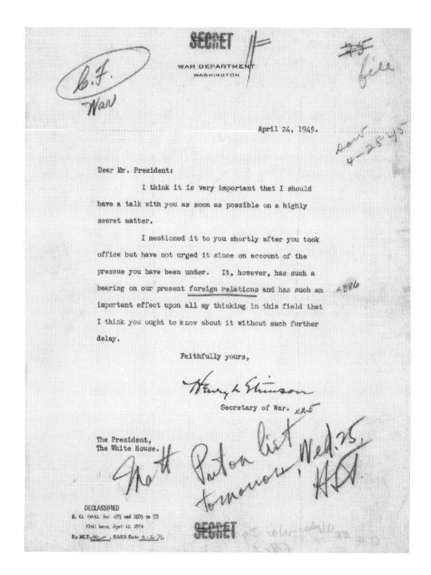

Stimson wrote to Truman for his approval to bomb Hiroshima. Stimson's request was more of a paper trail than it was genuinely seeking approval because both men were high-level

---

[31] Courtesy of the National Archives. Letter from Secretary of War Henry Stimson to President Harry S. Truman on April 24, 1945 and online at www.archives.gov/historical-docs/todays-doc/index.html?dod-date=424.

Freemasons following NWO orders.[32] Truman's handwritten note on reverse of Stimson's once Top Secret communication is shown below.[33]

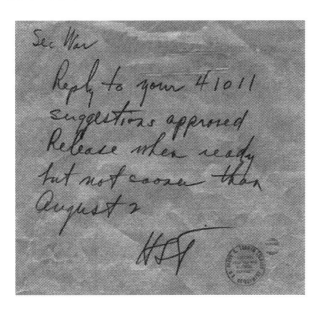

President Truman, an elite Freemason and NWO member, wanted the American people to feel that even though the bombs caused tremendous loss of civilian life, which included innocent children, his actions were justified.[34] Truman realized he had opened a Pandora's Box

[32] The Grand Lodge of Free and Accepted Masons of Pennsylvania provides information about Harry S. Truman (May 8, 1884-December 26, 1972) online at www.pagrandlodge.org/mlam/presidents/truman. html. Truman never obtained a college degree but became the 33rd President of the United States (1945-1953) because of his secret society service. This 33rd degree Freemason was initiated on February 9, 1909 at the Belton Lodge No. 450 in Belton, Missouri. In 1911 he became the first Worshipful Master of the Grandview Lodge No. 618 in Grandview, Missouri. On September 24-25, 1940, Truman was elected the ninety-seventh Grand Master of Masons of Missouri. He was made a Sovereign Grand Inspector General, 33° and Honorary Member of the Freemason Supreme Council in Washington, D.C. on October 19, 1945. On May 18, 1959, Truman became the only U.S. president to be presented with the Masonic fifty-year award.

[33] Courtesy of the Harry S. Truman Library, "Secretary of War to Harry S. Truman with Truman's handwritten note on reverse," *Elsey Papers*, 30 July 1945. Shown is the reverse side only and the front side of the communication is online at www.trumanlibrary.org/exhibit_documents/index.php?tldate=1945-07-30&groupid=3452&pagenumber=1&collectionid=abomb.

[34] President Harry Truman, "State of the Union Address," Washington, DC, 7 January 1953. In his last State of the Union address, he said: "For now we have entered the atomic age, and war has undergone a technological change which makes it a very different thing from what it used to be . . . The war of the future would be one in which man could extinguish the great cities of the world, wipe out the cultural achievements of the past—and destroy the very structure of a civilization that has slowly and painfully

by authorizing the first use of an atomic weapon.[35] To win support for the NWO decision to use the atomic bomb, Truman withheld information and communicated false information to sell people on the idea that mass murdering Japanese civilians was necessary.[36]

The real story of why Nagasaki was destroyed is a prime example of how history can be rewritten. Truman is now portrayed as a good leader, even though it was he who ordered the murder of thousands of Japanese Christians and children. He died in 1972 without any public record of his being asked why he allowed the center of Christianity in Japan to be destroyed.[37]

Hiroshima and Nagasaki Selection

The NWO, intimately involved in every aspect of the atomic program, wanted more than just the defeat of Japan. U.S. General Hap Arnold specifically instructed his generals to keep Hiroshima and Nagasaki undamaged from conventional bombing attacks in order for scientific experiments to be conducted.[38] NWO agents focused the public's attention on the Los Alamos Target Committee as responsible for targeting decisions. This group, led by J. Robert Oppenheimer, never even recommended Nagasaki as a target.[39] Oppenheimer was genuinely surprised when he learned that Nagasaki was where the Fat Man bomb was detonated.[40]

---

built up through hundreds of generations. Such a war is not a possible policy for rational men." His comments are better understood when you remember his role as a NWO insider. Truman knew the atomic bombs were used to "destroy the very structure of" a religion that had "slowly and painfully built up" in Japan.

[35] Pandora's Box is an artifact in Greek mythology that contained the evils of the world. To open a Pandora's box is to create evil that is difficult or impossible to reverse.

[36] The estimate for the number of American lives saved was a number pulled out of the air by General George Marshall. Truman was also provided with a much lower estimate by Secretary of State Byrnes.

[37] Robert L. Messer, "Truman's Decision On The Bomb," *Chicago Tribune News*, 14 August 1985.

[38] Michael Sherry, *The Rise of American Air Power* (New Haven, Connecticut: Yale University Press, 1987), 255. Also Tom Vanderbilt, *Survival City: Adventures Among The Ruins Of Atomic America*, (New York, New York: Princeton Architectural Press, 2002), 73, 300 and 410. On a related note, General Hap Arnold asked General Curtis LeMay in June 1945 when the war was going to end. LeMay, told him September or October 1945, because by then they would have run out of industrial targets to bomb.

[39] Oppenheimer's group recommended Hiroshima, Kokura, Kyoto, Niigata, and Yokohama as possible targets.

[40] After Nagasaki was destroyed, the NWO's misleading focus on the Los Alamos Target Committee for the Nagasaki decision helped to conceal the truth. If the NWO agenda to destroy Christianity became known, the Jewish Oppenheimer was at risk of being falsely blamed as the Jew who targeted Christianity by destroying Nagasaki. Oppenheimer was not accused by NWO agents of trying to destroy Christianity because the NWO role remained hidden throughout the 20th century. The NWO elite hated Oppenheimer for later opposing the hydrogen bomb and destroyed his career by arranging for him to be accused of spying for the Soviet Union.

The cover story that was successfully sold for years was that the city of Kokura was the primary target for the second bomb with Nagasaki being chosen only after Kokura was reported shrouded in smog.[41] Edwin O. Reischauer, a U.S. Army Intelligence Japan Expert on Oppenheimer's team, was falsely credited with having a deciding role in selecting both Kokura and Nagasaki. Reischauer revealed in his autobiography that, as confirmed by the opening quote to this chapter, Freemason Henry Stimson made the decision that had long been attributed to him. The false information about Reischauer served to draw attention away from the anti-Christian secret society members who selected Nagasaki. For this same reason, NWO agents attempted to focus the public's attention on the Catholic and Protestant prayers that were said before the bombing teams departed on their missions.[42]

On August 6, 1945, the first uranium-based atomic bomb was dropped on Hiroshima. An estimated 140,000 people died as a result. The bomb, known as Little Boy, had never been tested before being detonated. The following picture shows a model of the Little Boy atomic bomb.[43]

---

[41] William Craig, *Fall of Japan* (New York: Penguin Books, 1979). The book was first published in 1967 by The Dial Press. Craig documented on page 77 the presence of observers mysteriously added to the Nagasaki mission. William Laurence is reported to be on observer plane, The Great Artiste, on pages 83-84, 86-87, and 102-103. Laurence published a first-hand report after the bombing mission that the Fat Man bomb was dropped by The Great Artiste. The official story is The Great Artiste was the aircraft that was supposed to carry the Fat Man atomic bomb but a change resulted in Bock's Car carrying and dropping Fat Man.

[42] The Catholic chaplain that prayed for the atomic bomb's success was Father George Zabelka. After the war Father Zabelka realized he made a huge mistake by blessing the atomic bomb. He taught nonviolence and opposed militarism for the rest of his life. The Lutheran chaplain, William Downey, also regretted blessing the atomic bomb. He also spent his later years teaching nonviolence. Both men were assigned to the 509th Composite Group.

[43] Courtesy of the National Archives. The photograph identification number is RG 77-AEC.

The plutonium version of the bomb had been tested on July 16, 1945 and was proven to work. The plutonium bomb, called Fat Man, was dropped on Nagasaki on August 9, 1945 killing an estimated 70,000 people.[44] The following picture shows the Fat Man version of the atomic bomb.[45]

---

[44] Edited by The Committee for the Compilation of Materials on Damage Caused by the Atomic Bombs in Hiroshima and Nagasaki, Translated by Eisei Ishikawa and David L. Swain, Hiroshima and Nagasaki: The Physical, Medical, and Social Effects of the Atomic Bombings (New York, New York, Basic Books, Inc., 1981), 115. To obtain a better sense of the widespread devastation, pages 114 and 353 provide additional statistics. For example, Nagasaki's population was 270,000 people on August 6, 1945. In addition to the over 70,000 killed, 74,909 were injured and 120,820 were affected by radiation.

[45] Courtesy of the National Archives. The photograph identification number is RG 77-AEC.

The following is the once classified bombing target map for Nagasaki.[46]

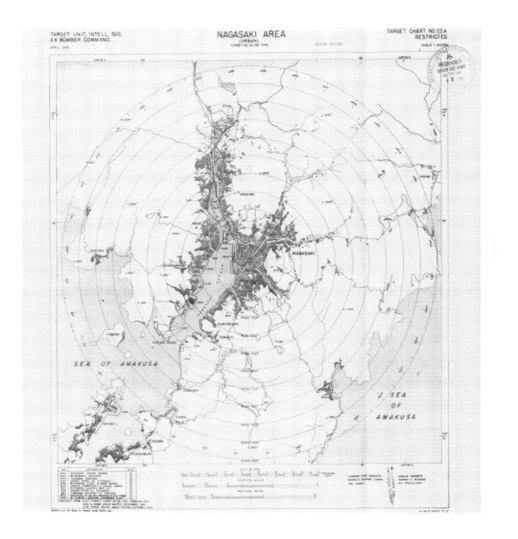

The Nagasaki Catholic Cathedral was the target of the Nagasaki bombing. This sad truth that Christianity was targeted is supported by the fact that the Fat Man bomb exploded twenty-four hundred feet from the Catholic cathedral.[47] Historian William Craig wrote, "Nagasaki was

---

[46] Courtesy of the U.S. National Archives. Map of Target Area 90-36-542, Target Unit, Intelligence Section, XX Bomber Command, April 1945. The U.S. National Archives reports the original Nagasaki target map is missing and is seeking its recovery. More information is online at www.archives.gov/research/recover/missing-documents-images.html.

[47] William Craig, *Fall of Japan* (New York: Penguin Books, 1979), 93. American prisoners of war, held at Nagasaki, were killed by the atomic bomb.

the center of Catholicism in Japan. Our Lady of the Conception was the largest Roman Catholic cathedral in the Far East. It had been built by parishioners as a memorial to the centuries-old quest for religious freedom by converts to the teachings of Saint Francis Xavier, who visited the area in 1549."[48]

Nagasaki was the window through which Christians arrived in Japan and the place where Christianity first began to be exterminated.[49] Toyotomi Hideyoshi was the daimyo (feudal lord) who unified Japan.[50] He banned Christianity in Japan in 1587. Christians were rounded up in Japan and put in large two-wheeled wagons that brought them to Nagasaki much as Jews were rounded up by Hitler in railcars; thousands were persecuted. Hideyoshi's decree led to the famous "execution of the 26 saints" on February 5, 1597.[51] He ordered the public crucifixions in Nagasaki as an example to anyone who dared convert to Christianity. Historian Otis Cary wrote:

> "Death was by crucifixion, a method of punishment said to have been unknown among the Japanese until they heard of it in connection with Christianity. It afterwards became a common form of executing those guilty of heinous crimes. As it was practised by the Japanese, the victim was tied by ropes to a cross and, instead of being left to suffer for a long time, his body was pierced with a spear that was first thrust from the right side upwards towards the left shoulder and then from the left side towards the right shoulder. Thus the heart was usually pierced, causing instant death. It may be that this use of the spear was borrowed from representations that had been seen of the crucifixion of Christ."[52]

In 1619, 1622, 1623, and 1632, Christians were also killed at or near Nagasaki.[53] It was not until 1865, over 200 years later, that descendants of the original Japanese Christians were discovered in the Urakami district secretly practicing their faith. The population for all Christian denominations is difficult precisely to estimate during the periods of Japanese government

---

[48] Ibid., 89.

[49] Samuel Lee, *Rediscovering Japan, Reintroducing Christendom* (Plymouth, United Kingdom: Hamilton Books, 2010). Often Christianity in Japan is reported as beginning with Jesuit missionary Francis Xavier in 1549, although Lee's research supports Christianity reached Japan prior to Xavier.

[50] Toyotomi Hideyoshi was born on February 2, 1536 or March 26, 1537 and died on September 18, 1598.

[51] The twenty-six Christians were crucified at Nagasaki, and died preaching and singing to the end. This information is online at www.newadvent.org/cathen/08297a.htm.

[52] Otis Cary, *A History of Christianity in Japan: Roman Catholic, Greek Orthodox, and Protestant Missions* (New York, New York: Fleming H. Revell Company, 1909), 128.

[53] John Dougill, *In Search of Japan's Hidden Christians: A Story of Suppression, Secrecy and Survival* (North Clarendon, Vermont: Tuttle Publishing, 2012), 97.

persecution prior to 1865 and in the years leading up to World War II.[54] Benchmarks do exist that provide some understanding for the size of the Nagasaki Christian population. For example, the Nagasaki Catholic population in 1885 was 23,000 and by 1910 it grew to 47,104.[55] The Diocese of Nagasaki includes Kiushiu and six neighboring islands.[56]

For the NWO, the history of Christian persecution, the number of Christians in the immediate area, and the presence of the Christian leaders, made Nagasaki their primary atomic bomb target. Years of NWO research have deepened my understanding that the Hiroshima bomb was a diversion to help conceal that Nagasaki was the primary target. The NWO sought to destroy Nagasaki because the approximately 50,000 Christians in and nearby the city threatened the NWO's one-world plans.[57]

Destroying Christianity is a top NWO priority at all times. This fact is explained in *Vigilant Christian I: The New World Order* as well as *Vigilant Christian III: The Occult Religion of the 9/11 Attackers*. With this basic understanding of the NWO, it is not surprising that the center of Christianity in Japan was targeted. Even if the Hiroshima uranium bomb had failed because it had never been tested, it would still have been useful in helping to disguise the NWO agenda.

The NWO is very clever, and its leaders understand the marketing principle called the Law of Leadership. This marketing principle states that people remember the first event in a new category and pay less attention to the second event in the new category. Marketing experts Al Ries and Jack Trout provide an example.[58] Ask yourself who was the first person to fly the Atlantic Ocean solo? Many people can correctly answer the question with Charles Lindbergh. Now ask yourself what is the name of the second person to fly the Atlantic Ocean solo? Fewer people

---

[54] The first Japanese Protestant church was organized in 1872 and inaugurated in 1875. More information is online at www.newadvent.org/cathen/08297a.htm.

[55] The Catholic Encyclopedia reports that prior to the arrival of Christian missionaries in 1569, Nagasaki was an insignificant village. The population statistics are online at www.newadvent.org/cathen/10667c. htm.

[56] Ibid. The six neighboring islands are Amakusa, Goto, Ikitsuki, Tsushima, Oshima, and the Ryukyu (Lu Chu) Archipelago. The total 1910 population was estimated at 7,884,900.

[57] Otis Cary, *A History of Christianity in Japan: Roman Catholic, Greek Orthodox, and Protestant Missions* (New York, New York: Fleming H. Revell Company, 1909), 117, 153, 166, 194, 281, 299, 341, 353, and 371. Cary includes a table on page 371 and page 372 showing the Christian population in Japan in 1908. His source is the 1909 Annual Report of the Société des Missions-Étrangères published in Paris. The 1908 numbers approach 50,000 when all denominations are included. The growth of Christianity from 1908 to 1945 means the estimate of 50,000 Christians at Nagasaki in 1945 may be conservative.

[58] Al Ries and Jack Trout, *The 22 Immutable Laws of Marketing: Violate Them at Your Own Risk!* (New York, New York: HarperCollins Publishers, 1993), 3.

know the answer to this question.[59] Understanding this principle is critical for understanding why Hiroshima, having little connection to destroying Christianity, was the first target.

People in the United States are sometimes surprised to learn that while Christians were persecuted in Japan in the 19th century, before World War II, Japan was a country of religious freedom with multiple Christian Prime Ministers.[60] Japan's most recent Christian Prime Minister was Yukio Hatoyama who was in office from September 16, 2009 to June 2, 2010. In total Japan has had eight Christian Prime Ministers. Christianity is recovering and the 2013 Christian population in Japan is estimated to be 3 million people.[61]

Evil Conceived at the Bohemian Grove

The atomic bomb is officially claimed as "conceived" at a Bohemian Grove planning meeting in September 1942. The Bohemian Grove is in Northern California. Each July NWO members meet for an occult religious ritual called the Cremation of Care.[62] Bohemian Grove religious

---

[59] Ibid. The answer is after Lindbergh's May 20-21, 1927 the next successful solo flight was on June 6, 1927 by Clarence Duncan Chamberlin. The purpose of his flight was different than Lindbergh's because Chamberlin carried a passenger.

[60] Ibid., 315. Cary wrote: "The truth is Japan stands for religious freedom. In Japan a man may be a Buddhist, Christian, or even a Jew, without suffering for it. That is a principle embodied in her Constitution; and her practice is in accordance with that principle." Three Prime Ministers have been Roman Catholic. Hara Takashi, who led the 19th government and was the 10th Prime Minister. Shigeru Yoshida, the leader of the 45th, 48th, 49th, 50th, and 51st governments and the 32nd Prime Minister. Taro Aso, who led the 92nd government and was the 59th Prime Minister. Four Protestant leaders include Viscount Takahashi Korekiyo. He led the 20th government and was the 11th Prime Minister. Tetsu Katayama, led the 46th government and was the 33rd Prime Minister. Ichirō Hatoyama, led the 52nd, 53rd, and 54th governments and was the 35th Prime Minister. Masayoshi Ōhira, led the 68th and 69th governments and was the 43rd Prime Minister. Yukio Hatoyama, led the 93rd government and was the 60th Prime Minister. The only member of the imperial family to be Prime Minister was Prince Naruhiko Higashikuni (December 3, 1887-January 20, 1990). He was the 43rd Prime Minister of Japan from August 17, 1945 to October 9, 1945. Higashikuni played a central role after the atomic bombs to protect the imperial family. To allow Emperor Hirohito to live and avoid being held accountable for war crimes, large portions of the gold and other items stolen from multiple countries were transferred to the NWO. The imperial family crime program, named Operation Golden Lily, is explained in book four in the Vigilant Christian series.

[61] The U.S. State Department's International Religious Freedom Report. The 2007 Bureau of Democracy, Human Rights, and Labor report is online at www.state.gov/j/drl/rls/irf/2007/90138.htm. The 2013 total population in Japan is a little under 128 million people.

[62] Cremation of Care is a Luciferian ceremony using an owl statue to represent Moloch. A documentary called *Dark Secrets: Inside Bohemian Grove* by Alex Jones shows the Cremation of Care ritual. In the summer of 2000, Jones and a cameraman secretly videotaped the occult ceremony. The religious dimension of the NWO is explained in *Vigilant Christian III: The Occult Religion of the 9/11 Attackers*.

rituals suggest an occult ritual was likely performed for the atomic bomb project. This occult ritual is likely one reason why the term "conceived at the Grove" is how Bohemian Grove members describe the atomic bomb when showing new members the Chalet. The Chalet is the building where the NWO met in 1942 to discuss the atomic bomb program.[63]

Even before the Bohemian Grove "conception" meeting, a secretive NWO group called the S-1 Executive Committee was created on June 17, 1942. The official U.S. government story is the S-1 Executive Committee, which was never formally dissolved, became inactive having only an advisory influence on target selection. From inception to the destruction of Nagasaki, NWO agents guided the Manhattan Project.[64]

Manhattan Project Agents

Why do we know now what should have been evident decades ago? Beverly Deepe Keever, a reporter for *Newsweek*, explained one reason why in her 2004 book *News Zero: The New York Times and The Bomb*.[65] She described how, as part of the Manhattan Project's concerted effort to manage the news and cover-up the truth, intelligence agents infiltrated the media. Before Keever's revelation, information about one key individual working directly for the NWO had been published by Eustace C. Mullins.[66] Mullins identified William Leonard Laurence as an agent for the shadow elite. Laurence changed his name from Leib Wolf Siew and he had also used the name Lipman Siew. Mullins wrote:

> "At Harvard, he became a close friend of James B. Conant and was tutored by him. When Laurence went to New York, he was hired by Herbert Bayard Swope, editor of the

---

[63] Peter Martin Phillips, *A Relative Advantage: Sociology of the San Francisco Bohemian Club, 1994* Doctoral Dissertation (1994), 11 and online at http://library.sonoma.edu/regional/faculty/phillips/bohemianindex.php. A second source is Wikipedia and online at http://en.wikipedia.org/wiki/Bohemian_grove. Attending the meeting where the atomic bomb was conceived were physicist Ernest Lawrence, the president of Harvard University, and leaders from Standard Oil and General Electric.

[64] The NWO Briggs Advisory Committee on Uranium first met on October 21, 1939, in Washington, D.C. This group was a result of Roosevelt tasking Lyman James Briggs to secretly organize a team and the Office of Scientific Research and Development (OSRD) created by Roosevelt on May 17, 1941. On July 1, 1941 the ORSD was transformed by Roosevelt to the S-1 project. Led by Vannevar Bush, on June 17, 1942 Roosevelt elevated the S-1 project to the S-1 Executive Committee and tightened NWO target selection control. NWO insiders on the S-1 Executive Committee include Lyman James Briggs, Arthur Compton, Harold Urey, Ernest Lawrence, and Eger Murphree. On a related note, the NWO also had an atomic bomb program in Britain called Tube Alloys.

[65] Beverly Deepe Keever, *News Zero: The New York Times and The Bomb* (Monroe, Maine: Common Courage Press, 2004).

[66] Eustace Clarence Mullins, *The Secret History of the Atomic Bomb: Why Hiroshima was Destroyed*, June 1998 and online at www.whale.to/b/mullins8.html.

New York World, who was known as Bernard Baruch's personal publicity agent. Baruch owned the *World*."

Bernard Baruch, the secret NWO Manhattan Project program leader, selected General Leslie Groves to be the visible day-to-day operational leader. Understanding Baruch's background helps shine light on why he was the secret Manhattan Project director.

Bernard Baruch's father, Simon Baruch, was a doctor from Germany who worked for the Rothschild family.[67] Baruch continued his father's service to the NWO and was rewarded with a great Wall Street fortune. Leading the Manhattan Project was only one of his assignments in the service of the NWO. He previously helped maneuver the U.S. into World War I and was in charge of the War Industries Board in 1918. In 1919, Baruch served the NWO as a staff member at the Paris Peace Conference and as an advocate for the creation of the League of Nations. In 1925, he paid for propaganda books to be written about the Civil War to help cover-up the Rothschild role in funding the Confederacy.[68] Throughout World War II, Baruch provided direction to both President Roosevelt and Secretary of War Stimson.[69] When Roosevelt died, Baruch continued to work closely with President Truman.

Atomic Bill's NWO Mission

William Laurence was placed at the *New York Times* by General Leslie Groves who had been instructed to do so by Bernard Baruch.[70] Groves attempted to conceal Baruch's influence, claiming Jack Lockhart recommended William Laurence.[71]

Eustace Mullin's wrote: "Laurence was the only civilian present at the historic explosion of the test bomb on July 16, 1945. Less than a month later, he sat in the copilot's seat of the B-29

---

[67] During the American Civil War he served as a NWO spy while serving as a Confederate surgeon on Robert E. Lee's staff. Book three in the Vigilant Christian series explains that the NWO orchestrated and funded the Civil War in an attempt to overcome Lincoln's opposition to their controlling the U.S. monetary system.

[68] Bernard Baruch endowed the United Daughters of the Confederacy in 1925 to pay scholars to rewrite Confederate history.

[69] Bernard Baruch's relationship with Henry L. Stimson was a long one. Both men worked for the NWO and successfully helped lead the United States into World War I and World War II. The latter is a key reason Stimson was the Secretary of War from 1911 to 1913 and 1940 to 1945.

[70] William L. Laurence (March 7, 1888-March 19, 1977). Leslie R. Groves, *Now It Can Be Told: The Story of the Manhattan Project* (New York: Da Capo Press, 1962 first edition was reprinted with a new introduction in 1983), 326. Groves wrote: "In discussing arrangements, it seemed desirable for security reasons, as well as easier for the employer, to have Laurence continue on the payroll of the *New York Times*, but with his expenses to be covered by the MED."

[71] Ibid., 325-327.

on the fateful Nagasaki bombing run."[72] In return for embedding an intelligence officer, the publisher and editor of *The Times* were given access to top government officials and "breaking stories." Laurence would become known as "Atomic Bill" for his pro-nuclear propaganda. The first explosion of an atomic bomb in New Mexico was called the Trinity shot. His Trinity explosion press release was crafted to disguise the detonation and resulting radiation.

The name Holy Trinity means the Father, Son, and Holy Spirit or "power of all life." To name a bomb with the power to destroy almost everything Trinity was conceived by the NWO to offend God. In effect, the NWO is stating that they have the power to end what God created.[73] Christians should especially find the name "Trinity site" an abomination, because naming a mass murder device test site after the Father, Son, and Holy Spirit is blasphemous.

Laurence is the only Manhattan Project member that Bernard Baruch allowed to know and see everything. Even Groves could not claim to have observed as much, which is exceptionally remarkable because Laurence was a foreign national who immigrated to the United States from Lithuania.

Laurence's actions provide powerful insights that Hiroshima was meant as a diversion to cover the NWO's true agenda, destroying Christianity in Japan. While Laurence was approved to be on the observer plane that accompanied the B-29 sent to bomb Hiroshima, he claimed he arrived late for the flight and could only watch the bomber depart.[74] Far more likely the truth is his secret Nagasaki mission for the NWO was too important to risk by having him participate in the diversionary, but still lethal, Hiroshima bombing.

William Laurence's attempt to camouflage and suppress Nagasaki mission details started in the days after the bombing. For example, he reported the B-29 that dropped the Nagasaki bomb was The Great Artiste; in truth it was Bock's Car.[75] The presence of Fred Bock and Lawrence

---

[72] Eustace Clarence Mullins, *The Secret History of the Atomic Bomb: Why Hiroshima was Destroyed*, June 1998 and online at www.whale.to/b/mullins8.html.

[73] Explained in greater detail in *Vigilant Christian III: The Occult Religion of the 9/11 Attackers*, is the fact that with the nuclear bomb, the NWO obtained the power to end all human life. For reasons of self-preservation and winning souls for Lucifer, the NWO does not seek total global genocide.

[74] Leslie R. Groves, *Now It Can Be Told: The Story of the Manhattan Project* (New York: Da Capo Press, 1962 first edition was reprinted with a new introduction in 1983), 326-327. Groves wrote Laurence was an eyewitness at the Alamogordo explosion known at the Trinity shot and arrived "just too late to be included in the observation plane for the Hiroshima bombing, but not too late to witness the take-off preparations."

[75] William Laurence, "Eye Witness Account: Atomic Bomb Mission Over Nagasaki," *War Department Bureau of Public Relations*, 9 September 1945 and online at www.atomicarchive.com/Docs/Hiroshima/Nagasaki.shtml.

Johnson, which Laurence reported as on The Great Artiste, may have confused participants in other aircraft.

Bernard Baruch's placement of Laurence on the Nagasaki atomic bomb team enabled him to have Secretary of War Stimson deliver to the pilots orders from levels above the usual military command authority. Laurence's false reports about The Great Artiste support Eustice Mullin's report that he was in the copilot's seat for the Nagasaki bombing run. Regardless of the airplane Laurence traveled in, his presence over Nagasaki when the Fat Man bomb was dropped is important evidence that the one version of the bomb proven to work in the Trinity detonation was used to devastate Christianity.

To prevent the world from seeing the hidden hand of the NWO, the official story attempted to deceive people by claiming Kokura could not be bombed due to smog or other weather related problems. The truth is that the visibility at Kokura was confirmed as good by weather planes that flew ahead of the aircraft carrying the Fat Man atomic bomb.[76] William Laurence would subsequently write, "Destiny chose Nagasaki as the ultimate target."[77] In occult works, the word "Destiny" is often used to communicate with secret society insiders the NWO's active role and responsibility.

After Hiroshima and Nagasaki, Laurence wrote articles designed to make Americans feel justified about mass murdering thousands of children.[78] Laurence continued to report propaganda for many years until his retirement in 1964. He helped dismiss reports from other countries about the "black death" in Japan so that the American people would not know the Japanese people were continuing to suffer and die from radiation long after the initial blast.[79] Laurence's work also aided the U.S. government to deny compensation to thousands of servicemen, production workers, miners, civil defense officials, Pacific Islanders, and others suffering from radiation exposure.[80]

---

[76] Ibid. Once Top Secret meeting notes and documentation pertaining to the atomic bomb target selection are online at www.gwu.edu/~nsarchiv/NSAEBB/NSAEBB162/index.htm.

[77] Ibid.

[78] Ibid. An example of his writing that was designed to win support for mass murdering babies and children from this article is: "Does one feel any pity or compassion for the poor devils about to die? Not when one thinks of Pearl Harbor and of the death march on Bataan."

[79] Amy Goodman and David Goodman, "The Hiroshima Cover-Up," *The Baltimore Sun*, 5 August 2005 and online at www.commondreams.org/views05/0805-20.htm.

[80] The 1979 documentary *Paul Jacobs and the Nuclear Gang* is online at www.linktv.org/programs/paul. The documentary by Jack Willis and Saul Landau and written by Jack Willis and Penny Bernstein exposed the U.S. government suppression of low level radiation health hazards. The film has first-hand interviews with servicemen intentionally exposed to radiation by the U.S. government. By the time this film was released, many of the radiation victims interviewed including Paul Jacobs had died. Jacobs' interview of government scientists, some of whom were fired for revealing the dangers of low-level radiation, sheds light on how nuclear information is successfully suppressed.

The propaganda by Laurence and *The New York Times* successfully sold a false understanding of the atomic bombs. The deception continues to this day, and as a result has robbed humanity in the years since 1945 with the U.S. building cost of 70,000 nuclear bombs exceeding $6 trillion. This is especially insane when you realize this amount far exceeds what it would have cost to end starvation on the planet since the development of the first atomic bomb. In addition, detonating 100 hydrogen bombs is the estimated number needed to create nuclear winter and end life on our earth as we know it.[81]

A Difficult Truth

As difficult as it is for many to hear, atomic bombs were used to uproot Japanese Christianity and help advance a new world order. The war with Japan was set in motion by the NWO when Japan threatened one-world plans by attempting to take over China and all of Southeast Asia. The Japanese royal family was a rival and dynastic power. If able to strengthen its control of occupied land, Japan posed a great threat to the NWO.

NWO agents in the U.S. government were able to orchestrate the passage of a Japanese embargo on scrap iron, oil, and other materials in the summer of 1941. The military response by Japan was both desired by the NWO and recognized in Washington as the likely outcome of the embargo. The Japanese attack was estimated to occur by the end of 1941 because oil was included in the embargo.

Henry Stimson wrote in his diary, "We face the delicate question of the diplomatic fencing to be done so as to be sure Japan is put into the wrong and makes the first bad move—overt move."[82] He also wrote, "The question was how we should maneuver them into the position of firing the first shot."[83] Stimson wanted a trap set and Japan fell into the Pearl Harbor trap. The Pearl Harbor murders served to transform public outrage for mass murdering Japanese children into public applause.

In 1945, the NWO feared their plans for a world government would be frustrated if millions of Japanese converted to Christianity. Millions of Japanese had been brainwashed to believe Emperor Hirohito was a god. With Japan surrendering, the widespread rejection of Hirohito's divinity was a natural outcome. With Christianity in Japan about to expand, the NWO sought to extinguish the Christian leadership concentrated at Nagasaki. The Nagasaki atomic bomb, never needed to end the war or save American lives, was detonated to uproot over three centuries of Christianity in Japan.

---

[81] Nuclear winter is when fires on earth create sufficient smoke to block sunlight from plant life.

[82] John Toland, *Infamy: Pearl Harbor and Its Aftermath*, (Garden City, NY: Doubleday, 1982), 275-276.

[83] Robert A. Theobald, *The Final Secret of Pearl Harbor* (Old Greenwich, CN: Devin-Adair, 1954), 76.

3

No Good War

"And through his policy also he shall cause craft to prosper in his hand; and he shall magnify himself in his heart, and by peace shall destroy many: he shall also stand up against the Prince of princes; but he shall be broken without hand." Daniel 8:25

The true story of the atomic bombs dropped on Japan illustrates how violence is used to advance world government. This chapter builds on the previous chapter with additional examples of how World War II truth has been suppressed.

History is an opportunity to learn and avoid repeating past mistakes. The New World Order fears the truth and funds historians to teach incorrect lessons from history.[84] Norman Dodd explained that in the archives of the Carnegie Endowment for International Peace was the following statement of purpose: "The only way to maintain control of the population was to obtain control of education in the U.S. They [the NWO] realized this was a prodigious task so they approached the Rockefeller Foundation with the suggestion that they go in tandem and that portion of education which could be considered as domestically oriented be taken over by the Rockefeller Foundation and that portion which was oriented to International matters be taken over by the Carnegie Endowment."[85]

---

[84] "Norman Dodd radio interview," May 30, 1977, distributed by *American Opinion*, 395 Concord Avenue, Belmont, MA 02478. The location of the publishing operation changed to 770 N. Westhill Blvd, Appleton, WI 54914. In 1953, Norman Dodd served as the chief investigator for Congressman B. Carroll Reece's Special Committee on Tax Exempt Foundations. In a 1977 interview Dodd said: "They decided that the success of this program lay in an alteration in the manner in which American history was to be presented. They then approached four of the then most-prominent historians -- such as Mary and Charles Beard -- with the suggestion that they alter the manner in which they were accustomed to presenting the subject. They [were] turned down flat, so . . . they decided they [had] to build a coterie of historians of their own selection."

[85] "Norman Dodd video interview," 1982, distribution sponsored by Quantum Communications and online at www.youtube.com/watch?v=YUYCBfmIcHM&feature=related. The Reece Committee found that the American Historical Association was controlled by a secretive elite. This meant that even if concrete

The 1976 U.S. Senate Church Committee revealed that the Central Intelligence Agency published thousands of books to redefine history and suppress the truth.[86] Many of the books were written by historians who twisted history in the service of the CIA and often were unknowingly helping the NWO. Authors are sometimes fooled to write or make changes to manuscripts believing they are helping U.S. national security. Unfortunately, books secretly authored by NWO agents have a profound impact on what many people believe to be true.[87]

Suppressed World War II Information

The NWO selection of Nagasaki explained in the previous chapter can be better understood by seeing through the deception that World War II was a good war. NWO agents in key U.S. government leadership, media, and academic positions continue to suppress knowledge of how the war started. Many people do not know that Pearl Harbor was part of an eight-step plan to provoke Japan into attacking the U.S.[88] The following December 7, 1941 photograph shows the aftermath of the Japanese attack on the USS West Virginia, USS Tennessee, and the USS Arizona.[89]

---

evidence of the NWO shadow government were presented to the American people, agents of the elite working in education would seek to convince people to dismiss this information. The brainwashing includes disabling any mention of the New World Order by labeling it a "conspiracy theory.

[86] The Church Committee of the Senate disclosed in 1976 that "well over a thousand books" had been produced or subsidized by the CIA. A few CIA sponsored books include *The New Class* by Milovan Djilas; *In Pursuit of World Order* by Richard N. Gardner; *The Yenan Way* by Eudocio Ravines; *The Anthill* by Suzanne Labin; *Why Viet Nam?* by Frank Trager; and *Terror in Vietnam* by Jay Mallin.

[87] The Select Committee to Investigate Tax-Exempt Foundations and Comparable Organizations was authorized by House Resolution 561 in the 82nd Congress to be an investigative committee of the United States House of Representatives between 1952 and 1954. The committee was led by Edward E. Cox and B. Carroll Reece. Known as the Cox or Reece Committee, Norman Dodd's official report is online at www.teachpeace.com/Dodd-Report-to-the-Reece-Committee-on-Foundations-1954.pdf.

[88] Robert B. Stinnett, *Day of Deceit: The Truth About FDR and Pearl Harbor* (New York, New York: Simon & Schuster, 2001), 6-11 and 256.

[89] Courtesy of the Franklin D. Roosevelt Library, 4079 Albany Post Road, Hyde Park, NY, 12538. Archival Research Catalog number 196243. Two of the three U.S. battleships were damaged and the USS Arizona sunk.

Only NWO agents and a small number of military personnel needed to process Japanese communications were allowed to see messages called Magic. The Magic program began in 1923 when the codebook Japan's Navy used during World War I was acquired by the U.S. This top secret code was called RED. In 1930, Japan introduced a new code called BLUE which was broken by the U.S. in 1932. In 1939 Japan was assisted by Germany with modified Enigma machines to create the PURPLE code. That same year the Enigma machine was reverse-engineered and a U.S. team led by William Friedman and Frank Rowlett started decoding the messages. By 1940 the American team could produce extremely accurate deciphered PURPLE messages.[90]

Harry Lloyd Hopkins arranged for the Soviet government to receive the U.S. code breaking information. Hopkins was an NWO insider and FDR's chief diplomatic advisor. He was the top U.S. official charged with dealing with Soviet officials during World War II. In the autumn of 1941, a Soviet team led by Sergei Tolstoy was able to replicate the U.S. success in decoding PURPLE messages.[91] Soviet communications intercepts using the PURPLE decoding technology

---

[90] Christopher Andrew and Vasili Mitrokhin, *The Sword and the Shield* (New York, New York: Basic Books, 1999) 95.

[91] Ibid., 95. Soviet cryptanalyst Sergei Tolstoy was credited with breaking the PURPLE code but in light of the information Harry Hopkins was sending to the communists; crediting Tolstoy appears necessary to conceal the NWO hidden hand controlling both the U.S. and Soviet leadership.

resulted in multiple Soviet warnings being sent to the United States that Japan would attack Pearl Harbor.[92]

The confirmation of Soviet foreknowledge of the Pearl Harbor attacks was further supported by the *Mitrokhin Archive* smuggled out of Russia in the early 1990s.[93] KGB Major Vasili Mitrokhin provided the secret Soviet documents that showed decrypted PURPLE messages were shared with President Franklin Delano Roosevelt and contributed to the December 1941 decision by Stalin to reposition troops to protect Moscow.

After World War II ended, the NWO needed to have another credible enemy for people to focus on, so Hopkins sent the nation's atomic bomb blueprints to Stalin.[94] The fact that Freemason FDR gave Freemason Joseph Stalin the information to decipher Japan's communications code and helped advance the Soviet atomic bomb program are two of the NWO's better kept secrets.

Sir John Cecil Masterman, chairman of the British Twenty Committee, ran the Double-Cross System to control German double agents. He revealed that FDR knew Pearl Harbor would be attacked in his 1945 manuscript for the book, *The Double Cross System in the War of 1939 to 1945*.[95] The manuscript was intended to create leverage to manage U.S. leaders who valued keeping FDR's advance knowledge secret, and was limited to a small number of people in 1945.

The British government suppressed publication of Masterman's book for 27 years. In 1972, the book was allowed by the British government to be published with the requirement that at least sixty passages be removed. The 1972 version of Masterman's book includes the Tricycle questionnaire in Appendix 2.[96] Tricycle was the code name for Dušan Popov, a spy from a wealthy

---

[92] Warnings include Soviet agent Richard Sorge's October 1941 notification "that the Japanese intend to attack Pearl Harbor in the next 60 days" which he was told was given to President Roosevelt. Another warning Pearl Harbor would be attacked came from Dušan Dusko Popov. Popov reported that he met with the FBI on August 12, 1941 to share intelligence Pearl Harbor would be attacked. For more information see Sir John Cecil Masterman (12 January 1891-6 June 1977) privately printed 1945 manuscript *The Double Cross System in the War of 1939 to 1945*.

[93] Christopher Andrew and Vasili Mitrokhin, *Mitrokhin Archive: The KGB in Europe and the West* (London, England: Penguin Books, 1992). The *Mitrokhin Archive* has a part II, *The Mitrokhin Archive II: The KGB and the World* that was also published in 2005.

[94] Major George Racey Jordan documented in the book *From Major Jordan's Diaries* that Harry Hopkins directed the shipment of over $11 billion in lend-lease aid to the Soviet Union including the blueprints for the atomic bomb.

[95] John Cecil Masterman (12 January 1891-6 June 1977) privately printed 1945 manuscript *The Double Cross System in the War of 1939 to 1945*.

[96] John Cecil Masterman, *The Double-Cross System: The Incredible True Story of How Nazi Spies Were Turned into Double Agents* (New York, New York: The Lyons Press, 2000), Appendix 2.

Serbian family. The 1972 and later editions of Masterman's book state that Washington was provided Popov's Pearl Harbor information. Masterman wrote, "Another startling example is to be found in Tricycle's questionnaire for America, which contained a somber but unregarded warning of the subsequent attack upon Pearl Harbour."[97]

The NWO efforts to get the U.S. to start a war with Japan were observed even before FDR entered office in 1933. NWO maneuvers to attack Japan include Henry L. Stimson's work to start a war. Stimson was the Secretary of War from 1911 to 1913 and again from 1940 to 1945. The consummate NWO insider, he was a high-level Freemason, Council on Foreign Relations operative, and former Rockefeller attorney. In 1931, Stimson tried to get President Herbert Hoover to agree to attack Japan in return for the NWO ending the Great Depression. Hoover refused Stimson's offer and the NWO used its ownership of the Federal Reserve to continue the Great Depression. Simultaneously, NWO media agents worked to define Hoover as one of the worst of all presidents. During his career Hoover had complied with many NWO demands, but he became an NWO outsider when he refused to attack Japan, which on a related note was at the same time he refused the NWO demand that he take the U.S. off the gold standard.[98]

Unlike NWO outsider Hoover, NWO insider FDR was quick to start promoting war with Japan. The day of his first inaugural address, March 4, 1933, he met with Cabinet designees who would support the one-world plan. Francis Perkins was one of the few non-NWO insiders offered a position and the first woman to hold a Cabinet post. She served as Roosevelt's Secretary of Labor for 12 years. Early on she noticed an agenda to move toward fascism and war with Japan. She reported, "At the first meeting of the Cabinet after the President took office in 1933, the financier and advisor to Roosevelt, Bernard Baruch, and Baruch's friend, General Hugh Johnson, who was to become the head of the National Recovery Administration, came in with a copy of a book by Gentile, the Italian Fascist theoretician, for each member of the Cabinet, and we all

---

[97] Ibid., 79. Masterman used the British spelling "Harbour" for "Harbor."

[98] President Franklin D. Roosevelt instituted actions to move the U.S. off the gold standard to include outlawing the possession of gold coins, bullion and certificates on April 5, 1933. Presidential Executive Order 6102 declared it a crime punishable with ten years imprisonment to hoard gold coin, gold bullion and gold certificates (see www.teachpeace.com/goldconfiscation.htm).

read it with care."[99] In the second Cabinet meeting Postmaster General Jim Farley said, "The new President again turned to the possibility of war in Japan."[100]

General Johnson worked with the War Industries Board that was established on July 28, 1917. He was helped during his career by War Industries Board leader Bernard Baruch. Johnson would eventually discover the NWO influence and oppose Baruch. In 1937 he tried to warn Americans that Roosevelt would send Americans to their deaths in an unnecessary war with Japan.

In 1939 Johnson saw the early signs of the U.S. involvement in World War II. He responded to Roosevelt's desire to repeal the U.S. arms embargo by saying the only hope to avoid war is "the overwhelming popular American determination against getting into a new war."[101] Johnson tried to stop FDR and endorsed Wendell Willkie. Wilkie was the 1940 Republican candidate for president. Regarding Roosevelt's plans to orchestrate a war with Japan he wrote, "I know of no well-informed Washington observer who isn't convinced that, if Mr. Roosevelt is elected [in 1940], he will drag us into war at the first opportunity, and that, if none presents itself, he will make one."[102] Johnson wrote if the U.S. were to get in another war "it is doubtful whether our free economic system could survive the necessary war dictatorship."[103] In the spring of 1941 he published *Hell-Bent for War*, trying to warn the American people that FDR was leading the country to war.[104]

---

[99] David Allen Rivera, *Final Warning: A History of the New World Order* (Joshua Tree, California: Progressive Press, 2010 edition), 197. Rivera is a Christian who had dedicated many years of his life to help save souls by exposing the NWO.

Giovanni Gentile (May 30, 1875-April 15, 1944) was an Italian philosopher and described himself as 'the philosopher of Fascism.' In 1929 he wrote *Origins and Doctrine of Fascism* and in 1932 he ghostwrote *A Doctrine of Fascism* for Benito Mussolini.

For March 4, 1933 schedule see www.bartleby.com/124/pres49.html

[100] Ibid., 197. Rivera provides additional historical information on Roosevelt's plans to orchestrate war with Japan.

Ohl, John Kennedy, *Hugh S. Johnson and the New Deal* (DeKalb, Illinois: Northern Illinois University Press, 1985).

[101] Ibid., 294 and the quote is from the December 13, 1939 *New York World Telegram*.

[102] David Allen Rivera, *Final Warning: A History of the New World Order* (Joshua Tree, California: Progressive Press, 2010 edition), 197.

Ohl, John Kennedy, "Tales Told by a New Dealer: General Hugh S. Johnson," *Montana: The Magazine Of Western History 1975*, Volume 25, Number 4, 66-77. On page 77 Ohl wrote: After leaving the Roosevelt administration, Johnson returned to literary pursuits as a columnist with the Scripps-Howard newspaper chain. There his biting barbs at President Roosevelt and his fervent advocacy of isolationism in the late 1930's gained him a large audience and kept his name before the public until his death in April, 1942.

[103] Ibid., 293.

[104] Ibid, 304.

One of the most detailed accounts of Roosevelt's treason was produced by the legal team defending U.S. Navy Commanders Husband E. Kimmel and Walter C. Short who were being blamed for the tragedy at Pearl Harbor. The NWO had so much success scapegoating Captain William T. Turner for the Lusitania sinking disaster that a repeat scapegoating attempt was made for Pearl Harbor. Roosevelt tried to focus public anger on Kimmel and Short with the first of two presidentially-appointed Roberts Commissions. The commissions were named for the U.S. Supreme Court Associate Justice Owen J. Roberts, who led the attempt to scapegoat Kimmel and Short with charges of dereliction of duty.

Fleet Admiral Ernest King ran the NWO censorship operation and just days before the formation of the Roberts Commission. He had the Director of Navy Communications, Rear Admiral Leigh Noyes, issue on December 11, 1941 a "Destroy all notes or anything in writing" order for evidence confirming that advance knowledge of Pearl Harbor existed.[105] In August 1945, an additional sanitizing effort was initiated for all Navy pre-Pearl Harbor intercepts, making them top secret. Radio operators, cryptographers, and intelligence personnel possessing first-hand knowledge of the Pearl Harbor advance warnings were also ordered to remain silent.[106] NWO clean-up operations routinely involve closely monitoring people with first-hand knowledge and silencing potential problems with blackmail and, if necessary, assassinations. Fortunately, the attempt to destroy all Pearl Harbor foreknowledge evidence failed.

NWO insiders General George Catlett Marshall and Admiral Harold Rainsford Stark failed to respond adequately to difficult joint House-Senate investigation questions, each saying he could not remember details of where he was as the Pearl Harbor bombs began falling. Later it was revealed that Marshall, Stark and Secretary of the Navy Frank Knox were with Roosevelt at the White House waiting for the attack to begin.[107]

The truth that Roosevelt provoked Japan, withheld attack information, and tried to cover the NWO treason resurfaced on May 25, 1999, when the United States Senate passed a resolution exonerating Kimmel and Short. The 1999 resolution concluded the Japanese attacks were "not a result of dereliction of duty" and then found the men were denied vital intelligence that was available in Washington.[108] Senator William V. Roth, Jr. who was in the Army during World War II said,

---

[105] Robert B. Stinnett, *Day of Deceit: The Truth About FDR and Pearl Harbor* (New York, New York: Simon & Schuster, 2001), 255-256 and 384.

[106] Ibid., 256.

[107] Ibid., 203.

[108] Philip Shenon, "Senate Clears 2 Pearl Harbor 'Scapegoats,'" *The New York Times*, 26 May 1999 and online at www.nytimes.com/1999/05/26/us/senate-clears-2-pearl-harbor-scapegoats.html. Multiple members of Congress spoke up in defense of Kimmel and Short. Senator William V. Roth, Jr. (R-DE), said the men were made scapegoats by the Pentagon. Senator Strom Thurmond (R-SC) said Kimmel and Short were *"the two final victims of Pearl Harbor."*

"We're not rewriting history. We're just correcting the record."[109] The amazing Senate resolution went unnoticed by most Americans and completely reversed the official U.S. government position communicated in 1995 when the families of Kimmel and Short sought justice.[110]

The 1999 U.S. Senate finding is now consistent with the documented evidence that the Pearl Harbor attack was known in advance by President Roosevelt. John Toland's book *Infamy* explains in great detail the Pearl Harbor foreknowledge evidence.[111] Robert B. Stinnett, a veteran of World War II, also documented the Pearl Harbor deception in *Day of Deceit: The Truth About FDR and Pearl Harbor*.[112] Stinnett's book drew from more than 200,000 documents and interviews over thirteen years. It provides a source of indisputable evidence that FDR wanted Japan to attack Pearl Harbor. Stinnett's investigative research also discovered the eight-step plan FDR followed to provoke Japan into attacking the U.S.[113] The following is an excerpt from the eight-step plan Lieutenant Commander Arthur H. McCollum wrote on October 7, 1940.[114]

"1. Make an arrangement with Britain for the use of British bases in the Pacific, particularly Singapore.
2. Make an arrangement with Holland for the use of base facilities and acquisition of supplies in the Dutch East Indies.
3. Give all possible aid to the Chinese government of Chiang-Kai-Shek.
4. Send a division of long range heavy cruisers to the Orient, Philippines, or Singapore.
5. Send two divisions of submarines to the Orient.
6. Keep the main strength of the U.S. fleet now in the Pacific in the vicinity of the Hawaiian Islands.
7. Insist that the Dutch refuse to grant Japanese demands for undue economic concessions, particularly oil.
8. Completely embargo all U.S. trade with Japan, in collaboration with a similar embargo imposed by the British Empire.
   If by these means Japan could be led to commit an overt act of war, so much the better. At all events we must be fully prepared to accept the threat of war."[115]

---

[109] Ibid.
[110] Robert B. Stinnett, *Day of Deceit: The Truth About FDR and Pearl Harbor* (New York, New York: Simon & Schuster, 2001), 257.
[111] John Toland, *Infamy: Pearl Harbor and Its Aftermath*, (Garden City, NY: Doubleday, 1982).
[112] Robert B. Stinnett, *Day of Deceit: The Truth About FDR and Pearl Harbor* (New York, New York: Simon & Schuster, 2001).
[113] Ibid., 6-11 and 256. The eight-step plan was declassified in 1994 and an image of the document is online at www.teachpeace.com/eightstep.htm.
[114] Ibid. In addition to www.teachpeace.com/eightstep.htm, the declassified document is online http://en.wikisource.org/wiki/File:McCollum_memo_Page4.png.
[115] Ibid.

The plan to provoke Japan into committing an overt act of war sought to trigger military responses from the two other signers of the Tripartite Pact.[116] FDR implemented all eight steps. The finishing touch of the eight-step plan was not only moving a concentration of U.S. Navy ships from California to Pearl Harbor but positioning ships and aircraft so that they would be easily destroyed.[117] Airplanes at Pearl Harbor were ordered to be put in circles with their propellers facing the center of the circle, making it difficult for the planes to rapidly deploy.[118] Airplanes were also put in lines enabling a single Japanese strafing run to destroy all of them. Older ships built during or before World War I that Roosevelt and his advisors deemed expendable were concentrated at Pearl Harbor. However, the three aircraft carriers the NWO plotters would need to ultimately destroy Japan's Navy were moved out of Pearl Harbor before the attack.[119]

Stinnett's discovery of messages decoded well in advance of December 7, 1941 ends claims that FDR did not know. For example, on November 24, 1941 Admiral Isoroku Yamamoto wrote: "The task force, keeping its movement strictly secret and maintaining close guard against submarines and aircraft, shall advance into Hawaiian waters, and upon the very opening of hostilities shall attack the main force of the United States Fleet in Hawaii and deal it a mortal blow. The first air raid is planned for dawn of X-day" (exact date to be given by later order).[120] Stinnett's findings from a May 2000 Freedom of Information Act release provided conclusive evidence that by mid-November America's radio cryptographers sent messages that Pearl Harbor was the target.[121]

Same day and next day intercepts of Japanese radio communications were available to Roosevelt, Knox, Marshall, and Stark. A Dutch naval liaison reported that U.S. intelligence

---

[116] The Tripartite Pact, or Three-Power Pact and Axis Pact, was signed in Berlin, Germany on September 27, 1940. Adolf Hitler signed the agreement for Germany, foreign minister Galeazzo Ciano signed for Italy, and Ambassador Saburo Kurusu signed for Japan.

[117] Robert B. Stinnett, *Day of Deceit: The Truth About FDR and Pearl Harbor* (New York, New York: Simon & Schuster, 2001), 14. Prior to moving to Pearl Harbor, U.S. Navy ships were concentrated at and near San Diego.

[118] A total of 177 airplanes were destroyed. Had the fighters deployed rapidly the NWO plotters were concerned the Pearl Harbor damage would not be sufficient for the U.S. public to support a war with Japan. Military personnel opposed doing this but were told the orders were to prevent the airplane propellers from being sabotaged. It is important to remember the NWO needed not only a U.S. declaration of war but to fool millions of people to enlist in the military.

[119] The Enterprise left on November 28th for Wake Island, the Lexington left on December 5th for Midway and the Saratoga left for the Pacific Coast.

[120] Robert B. Stinnett, *Day of Deceit: The Truth About FDR and Pearl Harbor* (New York, New York: Simon & Schuster, 2001), 302. The date November 24, 1941 was November 25, 1941 in Tokyo and this is why the intercepted message is dated November 25th. See Vice Admiral Homer N. Wallin, *Pearl Harbor* (Naval History Division, U.S. Government Printing Office, 1968), 86.

[121] Ibid., 261.

officers informed Washington on December 6, 1941 that Japanese carriers were 400 miles northwest of Honolulu.[122] Some of the messages received communicated the precise locations of Japan's ships and the U.S. ships at Pearl Harbor, and stated December 7, 1941 as when the attack would occur. Additional advance warnings of the Pearl Harbor attack came from the U.S. military observer in Java, the Dutch military liaison in Washington, the U.S. ambassador to Japan, a Senator, a Congressman, a Brigadier General, and J. Edgar Hoover who was the director of the FBI.[123]

NWO agents try to hide the truth of what happened leading up to the Pearl Harbor attacks by claiming that messages warning of the attack were not received in time. Due to the American History Association influence on public education described the first Vigilant Christian book, schools rarely teach an eight-step plan to provoke war was followed or that documented warnings were received in advance of the Pearl Harbor attack. Hirohito and FDR share responsibility for the 2,402 people who died at Pearl Harbor as well as a far greater number of people killed from 1941 to 1945.[124]

Pearl Harbor Deception Lessons Applied to 9/11

Just as the public was deceived about Pearl Harbor, it has also been deceived about September 11, 2001. It is important to note that no military officers were court-martialed after 9/11.[125] The NWO learned the danger in trying to court-martial and scapegoat military officers for the Pearl Harbor disaster. This is why no one in the U.S. military was charged with dereliction of duty for not intercepting aircraft in a timely manner and other missteps acknowledged in the Pentagon version of 9/11 events. When after Pearl Harbor the NWO tried to place the blame on Commanders Kimmel and Short, it did not take long for Kimmel and Short to have

---

[122] Ibid., 316.

[123] Ibid. The U.S. military observer in Java was Colonel F. G. L. Weijerman, the Dutch military liaison in Washington was Captain Johan Ranneft, the U.S. ambassador to Japan was Joseph Grew, the Senator was Guy Gillette, the Congressman was Martin Dies, and the Brigadier General was Elliot Thorpe.

[124] While it is commonly known Franklin Delano Roosevelt was a Freemason, it is often less known that many elite Japanese were also Freemasons. Freemasonry was a powerful secret society in Japan until the late 1930s. As Hirohito learned the NWO sought to fight Japan, he ordered a crackdown on Freemasons. By the early 1940s, all Freemason lodges in Japan ceased operations. Hirohito's break with the NWO mirrors Adolf Hitler's actions. Hitler's elimination of Freemasons beginning in 1934 is explained in *Vigilant Christian III: The Occult Religion of the 9/11 Attackers*.

[125] Similar to the 9/11 Commission, FDR appointed a commission packed with Council of Foreign Relations members to investigate the Pearl Harbor disaster. Unlike the Roberts Commission, the 9/11 cover-up team knew it was dangerous to scapegoat military officers who would naturally defend themselves from false charges and in the process expose the NWO 9/11 involvement.

all the documented proof they needed that President Roosevelt and General Marshall had foreknowledge about the attack.

The NWO wanted Japan to attack Pearl Harbor as an overt act of war because they correctly predicted it would infuriate U.S. citizens and help eliminate Japan as an obstacle to a one-world government. The truth suppression of what happened at Pearl Harbor is evidence the NWO has succeeded in misleading the public. NWO control of the media, schools, monetary systems, and politicians is why many people do not see the similarities between the Pearl Harbor and the September 11, 2001 murders.

Nazi Atomic Bomb Program

The NWO has misled the world into believing that Germany's nuclear program was not advanced with the false story that Adolf Hitler dismissed proposals for atomic bombs. This cover story defies common sense when one studies Hitler's fascination with weapons of mass destruction. The documentary, *Copenhagen Fall Out*, is recommended to learn about Werner Heisenberg.[126] Heisenberg was tasked by Hitler in September 1939 to lead Germany's atomic bomb program.[127] Heisenberg's assignment to build an atomic bomb is explained with first-hand accounts in *Copenhagen Fall Out* directed by Howard Davies and aired by the *BBC* on June 13, 2005.

In September 1941, Heisenberg traveled to Copenhagen to discuss the Nazi atomic bomb with his friend Niels Bohr.[128] Bohr warned the British of what Heisenberg told him, and in 1943 British intelligence asked for his help in developing an atomic bomb.[129] After this meeting Bohr traveled to Britain to work on the Tube Alloys Project and then to America to participate in the Manhattan Project.[130]

To repaint the Nazi atomic bomb program as only an insignificant scientific effort, the NWO backed and promoted multiple false books. The fairly successful NWO effort to distort history

---

[126] Howard Davies, *Copenhagen Fall Out* (London, UK: *BBC*, 2005). While most of the documentary is excellent, this *BBC* produced film serves the NWO by attempting to downplay the Nazi atomic bomb program.

[127] Werner Karl Heisenberg (5 December 1901-1 February 1976) is known for asserting the uncertainty principle of quantum theory. The NWO redefinition of the Nazi atomic bomb program was advanced by the Bertrand Russell promoted *Brighter than a Thousand Suns* book by Robert Jungk.

[128] Niels Henrik David Bohr (7 October 1885-18 November 1962) was a Danish physicist who made foundational contributions to understanding atomic structure and quantum mechanics.

[129] Ibid.

[130] Tube Alloys was the code-name for the British nuclear bomb program using the synthetic element plutonium. The Nazi atomic program was focused on uranium.

included a book written by Albert Speer.[131] The books served to support the false claims that Nazi atomic war criminals were really people working to prevent Hitler from acquiring an atomic bomb. In Robert Jungk's *Brighter than a Thousand Suns*, Heisenberg is falsely noted as leading a plot to deny Hitler the bomb. Niels Bohr was offended by Heisenberg's lies.[132] Bohr's unsent letters criticize Heisenberg for providing false information.[133] Bohr was convinced Heisenberg was on a secret mission for the Nazi elite in 1941. He wrote:

> "[I] got a completely different impression of the visit than the one you have described in Jungk's book. I remember quite definitely the course of these conversations, during which I naturally took a very cautious position, when [without preparation, immediately] you informed me that it was your conviction that the war, if it lasted sufficiently long, would be decided with atomic weapons, and [I did] not sense even the slightest hint that you and your friends were making efforts in another direction."[134]

The incorrect statements in *Brighter than a Thousand Suns* helped Nazi atomic scientists avoid being charged as war criminals. Bohr provides conclusive evidence that the Nazi atomic bomb program was in an all out race to be the first with a nuclear bomb. Bohr wrote: "You spoke in a manner that could only give me the firm impression that under your leadership everything was being done in Germany to develop atomic weapons."[135]

---

[131] Albert Speer, *Inside the Third Reich: Memoirs by Albert Speer* (New York, New York: Simon & Schuster, 1997). The first edition in German was published in 1969. This book is filled with fascinating insights on Hitler's inner circle. Unfortunately, NWO manipulation resulted in inner circle occult practices and the truth of the Nazi bomb program being twisted. Combined with *Brighter than a Thousand Suns* and the Operation Bloodstone assassinations, Speer's book deceived people to believe the Nazi leadership was not pursuing an atomic bomb.

[132] Howard Davies, *Copenhagen Fall Out* (London, UK: BBC, 2005). Bohr wrote: "I think that I owe it to you to tell you that I am greatly amazed to see how much your memory has deceived you in your letter to the author of the book." The letter is online at www.nba.nbi.dk/papers/docs/d01tra.htm. Bohr suspected Heisenberg had met with him as part of an official Nazi intelligence gathering attempt to learn if Britain or the U.S. were developing an atomic bomb.

[133] Robert Jungk, *Brighter than a Thousand Suns: Personal History of the Atomic Scientists* (New York, NY: Harcourt, Inc., 1956). By the 1960s, the U.S. and British intelligence that had been shared with Bohr attempted to confuse him about his 1941 conversation with Heisenberg. The NWO tried to lead Bohr to believe that Germany's atomic program was not as serious as Heinsenberg had communicated and this is why Hitler was unable to develop an atomic bomb before the war ended.

[134] The original Bohr letter with this statement is online at www.nba.nbi.dk/papers/docs/d07tra.htm. The set of Bohr letters are available at www.nba.nbi.dk/papers/docs/cover.html.

[135] Ibid. All of the Bohr letters are online at www.nba.nbi.dk/papers/docs/cover.html.

The personal letters of Niels Bohr, withheld by his family until February 2002, confirm that Werner Heisenberg lied about the purpose of his 1941 meeting.[136] For some reason Bohr's Jewish-Danish family was afraid to release his personal letters even for decades after his death. The family may have feared the power and reach of the NWO. Had Bohr's letters been known soon after his death in 1962, it is possible that millions of people would now know why an untested uranium bomb was dropped on the diversionary Hiroshima target and the proven plutonium bomb was saved for destroying Christianity centered in Nagasaki.

Operations Paperclip, Alsos Mission, and Bloodstone

The NWO wanted to safeguard the secret that German war criminals were brought to the U.S. The Office of Strategic Services program to recruit Nazi scientists called Operation Paperclip is no longer a closely guarded secret, but two related programs are still generally unknown. The two highly classified programs, Alsos Mission and Operation Bloodstone, were revealed during the 1976 Church Committee Senate investigation. By keeping both programs secret, the NWO has been able to suppress the truth of why atomic bombs were used in Japan.

Colonel Boris Pash was the chief Manhattan Project counterintelligence officer and in charge of both Alsos Mission and Operation Bloodstone.[137] He was questioned in 1976 by members of the U.S. Senate in one of the rare times the NWO started to lose control of a Congressional investigation. The damage done by the Church Committee was so great that it resulted in NWO insider Gerald Ford authorizing the immediate reassignment of George H. W. Bush from the Chief of the U.S. Liaison Office in the People's Republic of China to lead the CIA.[138]

---

[136] Ibid. Additional information about the Bohr letters is online at www.pbs.org/hollywoodpresents/copenhagen/story/letters.html.

[137] *Church Committee Report, Book IV*, 129. Pash was a NWO secret agent for many years before 1949 and was formally assigned to the CIA on March 3, 1949 and with no formal end date noted.

[138] The U.S. did not have an embassy in China at the time so the title Ambassador was not used. Bush's role is best understood not as the U.S. Ambassador but the NWO Ambassador to China. George H. W. Bush has always falsely claimed he was never in the CIA until he became the Director of the CIA on January 30, 1976. The truth is that Bush joined the CIA in 1948. As background, Bush was in the NWO's Skull and Bones society at Yale University. One of his early NWO assignments was to become a CIA officer and start Bush-Overby Oil Development in 1951 and Zapata Oil in 1953. CIA officer Thomas J. Devine was a key partner. In 1954, Zapata Off-Shore Company was formed as a subsidiary of Zapata Oil. Zapata Corporation split in 1959 into Zapata Petroleum and Zapata Off-Shore. To camouflage Zapata as a front for spies, in 1960, the NWO had Bush create Perforaciones Marinas del Golfo (Permargo) with CIA officer Edwin Pauley. Zapata was more than a CIA-front and operated as a key NWO front performing roles in the unsuccessful April 1961 Bay of Pigs Operation and the 1963 John F. Kennedy assassination. A key FBI document linking George H. W. Bush to the JFK assassination is now part of the public record. To see the FBI declassified memorandum dated November 29, 1963 where George Bush tried to finger the John F. Kennedy NWO assassination on a group of pro-Castro

NWO historians want Pash's work kept unknown for many reasons. Pash was a key person in charge of silencing people who revealed NWO secrets. Pash led the Alsos Mission program to bring Nazi atomic program scientists to the U.S.[139] The assassination program he led, Operation Bloodstone, eliminated uncooperative scientists and other credible people who could expose NWO secrets, including the plan to destroy Christianity in Japan.[140]

A five-person Operation Bloodstone "cleaner team," a reference to assassinations to suppress evidence, was called PB/7.[141] Often, character assassination is the ideal form of NWO assassination. One of Pash's most famous character assassinations was that of Robert Oppenheimer.[142] Author Christopher Simpson noted it was Colonel Pash's testimony "that helped seal the fate of scientist Robert Oppenheimer in the well-known 1954 security case."[143]

Now that the U.S. government's secret programs that brought Nazi scientists to the U.S. are known, the public is told the partial truth that the scientists helped create the NASA program.[144] What has been kept from the American people is the darker truth that when Operation Paperclip is combined with the Alsos Mission and Operation Bloodstone, Nazi war criminals escaped justice and were rewarded with jobs in the CIA and Pentagon developing mind control weapons, chemical weapons, and nuclear bombs for the NWO.

Cubans in Miami go to www.teachpeace.com/BushJFKNov291963document.gif. Bush's role in the Kennedy assassination included creating a disinformation lead from the CIA to the FBI that a James Parrott proposed assassinating John F. Kennedy. James Parrott is believed to be a CIA officer who was easy to prove was not directly involved in the JFK assassination. James Parrott is also believed to be the same person who years later helped run Bush's campaign for president.

[139] Christopher Simpson, *Blowback: America's Recruitment of Nazis, and Its Effects on the Cold War* (New York, New York, Collier Books, 1988), 153.

[140] Joint Strategic Plans Committee, JSPC 862/3. State Army Navy Air Force Coordinating Committee (SANACC) 395, Document 8 State Army Navy Air Force (SANA) 6024: Appointment of Committee, 15 April 1948 and see www.archives.gov/southeast/finding-aids/microfilm/military.html.

[141] Ibid and *Church Committee Report*. PB/7 charter said "PB/7 will be responsible for assassinations, kidnapping, and such other functions as from time to time may be given it . . . by higher authority."

[142] James Reston, "Dr. Oppenheimer is Barred from Security Clearance Though 'Loyal,' 'Discreet,'" *New York Times*, 2 June 1954.

[143] Oppenheimer was unknowingly an NWO pawn. He was accused of being a security risk which effectively ruined his career and disabled his ability to be a credible voice against building a hydrogen bomb.

[144] Nazis recruited in Operation Paperclip included Wernher von Braun, Wilhelm Jungert, Eberhard Rees, Walter Schwidetzky, August Schulze and over a hundred other war criminals. Some of the men were directly responsible for mass murdering Jews.

Historian Shills and German Uranium Shipments

Historians who claim Japan did not have an atomic bomb program have difficulty explaining Germany's delivery of highly enriched weapons grade uranium.[145] Uranium-235 is what was in the Little Boy bomb that detonated over Hiroshima on August 6, 1945. The Manhattan Project may have used Nazi uranium in the Little Boy atomic bomb. Supporting evidence includes a shipment of Uranium-235 that at least one German U-boat delivered to Japan. Uranium-235 is the bomb-grade isotope of uranium, which is known as highly enriched uranium. The delivery of Uranium-235 to Japan contradicts the modern version of history that Germany never developed Uraniam-235 and Japan never worked to develop atomic bombs. The Nazi uranium bomb program may also explain how the U.S. had two very different types of bombs, plutonium and uranium, available to drop on Japan in August 1945.

The German U-boat named the U-234 surrendered to the U.S.S. Sutton on May 14, 1945 as it was carrying uranium to Japan.[146] The official U.S. government story is that the uranium from the U-234 German submarine was only reported to the Manhattan Project but was never sent to Los Alamos. The official story is that the German uranium was stored in a Brooklyn warehouse and not used for the Hiroshima atomic bomb.[147] NWO historians have succeeded in convincing most people that the U-boat 234 carried uranium oxide and not Uranium-235.

The surrender of the U-234 at sea created multiple problems for the NWO because the sub, commanded by Lt. Johann-Heinrich Fehler, carried uranium in gold-lined cylinders. Gold-linings are needed for Uranium-235 to prevent radiation exposure; gold-linings were not used to transport inert uranium oxide, which is the official U.S. government explanation. The gold-lined cylinders are extremely important because uranium oxide does not emit radiation until it is enriched in a fission reactor, and therefore the gold-lined cylinders would not be needed to transport inert uranium oxide. First-hand witness Wolfgang Hirschfeld is quoted in the 1997 book, *Hirschfeld: The Secret Diary of a U-boat*, as saying that he watched the loading of "U-powder" with "U-235" painted on cylindrical shafts.

The German Uranium-235, in U.S. possession before the Uranium-235 Hiroshima bomb, is calculated to have yielded approximately 7.7 pounds of Uranium-235. The official U.S. government position is that the total supply of enriched uranium was insufficient to both test the Little Boy bomb and have enough remaining for the Hiroshima detonation. The fact that Germany sent Uranium-235 via U-boats to Japan reinforces the evidence that Germany had

---

[145] Priit J. Vesilind, "The Last D," *National Geographic*, October 1999. The article is online at http://yamashitatreasures.com/goldsub.html.

[146] Ibid., 134. The article is online at http://yamashitatreasures.com/goldsub.html.

[147] Ibid.

enough fissile material for at least one bomb. The NWO efforts after World War II to rebrand Werner Heisenberg's as an honorable scientist raises the very real possibility that top Nazi nuclear scientists were serving the NWO.

A secret still guarded today concerns the 500 kilograms of uranium oxide and possibly some Uranium-235 that Japan's I-52 submarine was to pick up from Germany and bring back to Japan. The I-52 was built at Japan's Kure Naval Yard in 1943. The submarine was designed to carry 300 tons of cargo 21,000 miles without refueling. In March of 1944, the I-52 commander Kameo Uno left Kure Harbor with a crew of 11 officers and 84 enlisted men plus 14 passengers. The I-52 arrived in Singapore where it was loaded with 54 tons of raw rubber, 2.88 tons of opium, and 3 tons of quinine. The I-52 also carried 2 tons of gold as confirmed by decoded Japanese and German communications.

On June 23, 1944 the I-52 was to rendezvous with the German U-530 commanded by Lt. Kurt Lange.[148] The rendezvous communication was intercepted by U.S. intelligence. The U.S.S. Bogue, commanded by Captain A. B. Vosseller, was sent to launch an air assault on both submarines. Lt. Commander Jesse Taylor flew from the U.S.S. Bogue about 55 miles to find and fire on the I-52 and U-530. The Japanese submarine was hit and sunk in the Atlantic Ocean. The U.S.S. Bogue sent a second attack aircraft commanded by Lt. William "Flash" Gordon.[149] His torpedo hit and sank the U-530. The loss of the I-52 and its gold was confirmed by Yoshikazu Fujimura, who was the Japanese assistant naval attaché in Berlin. He said, "I do not regret losing . . . gold. I regret that we lost about a hundred sailors."

After deep sea salvage expert Paul Tidwell read a declassified document in the National Archives that confirmed the I-52 carried 2 tons of gold, he began an operation to find the ship, which he did in 1995. Salvage efforts are ongoing, but the gold has not been publicly reported as recovered.

---

[148] Ibid., 119. Photos of key individuals and the once top-secret attack plan are online at www.i-52.com/.
[149] Ibid., 124.

4

MASS MURDER

"Our choice, in this age of nuclear bombs, is not between nonviolence and violence, but between nonviolence and nonexistence."[150] Dr. Martin Luther King, Jr.

What are the top reasons for war? At first thought self-defense may come to mind. The truth is war is often planned years in advance by the New World Order to advance a one-world government. Following the money trail illuminates that war is not possible without people profiting financially, and it is often fought for reasons very different from those that are shared with the public.

President George Washington and many other founders of the United States had first-hand experience with secret societies and how elite families in Europe bankrolled military actions. The founding fathers, often lower-level Freemasons, were generally unaware of the darker one-world government agenda advocated primarily by European Freemasons. George Washington did not approve of this form of Freemasonry called Jacobinism and Illuminism. Responding to the Rev. G. W. Snyder's warning about the New World Order threat and insider infiltrations, George Washington replied on October 24, 1798: "It was not my intention to doubt the doctrines of the Illuminati and the principles of Jacobinism had not spread in the United States. On the contrary, no one is more satisfied of this fact than I am."[151] This is why in his farewell address on September 17, 1796, George Washington warned Americans to be on guard against alliances with Europe.

---

[150] Martin Luther King, Jr., the night before he was assassinated, 3 April 1968, Dr. King told thousands of people at the Mason Temple in Memphis, Tennessee, "For years now, we have been talking about war and peace. But now, no longer can we just talk about it. It is no longer a choice between violence and nonviolence; it is nonviolence or nonexistence."

[151] George Washington, *The Writings of George Washington (1745-1799)*, University of Michigan Library, 1931.

Three Planned World Wars and American Hiroshima

In the first Vigilant Christian book, the plan for three world wars was explained. NWO leader Albert Pike taught that three world wars were needed to condition humanity to accept world government.[152] An American Hiroshima event orchestrated by the NWO could mislead people to support killing millions in Iran and in other countries frustrating the one-world agenda.

The list of 20th century involvement by the NWO in promoting wars is long, and includes the Lusitania operation in World War I, funding both Germany and England during World War II, creating the conditions for the Korean War in 1953, the Vietnam War, the 1991 Gulf War, and the war on terrorism. This chapter focuses on the sinking of the Lusitania as one example that the NWO has previously manufactured mass murders to mislead Americans to rush to war. The following World War I poster from 1917 shows how people were misled to participate in mass murders.[153]

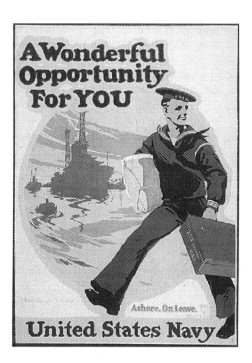

The secret societies, the real power behind the British imperial empire, are very skilled at hiding behind puppet governments. For the NWO to conceal operations in the 20th century,

---

[152] Albert Pike (December 29, 1809-April 2, 1891).

[153] Courtesy of the National Archives and Archival Research Catalog number 512440. The title of this 1917 war propaganda is "Wonderful Opportunity For You. Ashore, On Leave. United States Navy."

new puppets or multiple fronts were needed. The Rothschild banking dynasty is also highlighted in this chapter because it is the leading NWO banking family.[154] The truth of what happened to the Lusitania was kept suppressed for almost a century. The Lusitania truth suppression should prompt us to think before judging people who present evidence the NWO is responsible for other acts of violence, including the September 11, 2001 terrorism.

Four NWO World War I Prongs

World War I was proclaimed to be the war to end all wars. However, a key purpose of World War I was to create front organizations for a one-world government. The NWO elite accomplished this with a four-prong plan to create incredible suffering and debt so that people around the world would increasingly be willing to forfeit national sovereignty.

The first prong of the one-world government attempt, called the League of Nations, failed. The failed first attempt did build momentum and eventually succeed in establishing a one-world framework. The one-world framework, the United Nations, was established by NWO agents in 1945.

The second prong was creating a bank for central banks. The U.S. Federal Reserve private banking cartel enforced by public law in 1913 was replicated on a global scale with the Hague agreements of 1930. The Hague agreements created the Bank for International Settlements (BIS), which claims to be the world's oldest international financial organization.[155] The BIS is one of the NWO front organizations advancing a one-world currency. The privately owned BIS coordinates monetary policies for some 140 central banks or monetary authorities. The total

---

[154] The Rothschild banking dynasty became the leading NWO banking force as a result of Lord Wellington's June 18, 1815 victory at the Battle of Waterloo. The family fortune increased because a Rothschild spy reported Wellington had defeated Napoleon in time for Nathan Rothschild to start a London Stock Exchange rumor that Napoleon had won. As a direct result, stocks plunged and Rothschild was then able to buy up British firms for a fraction of their value. According to the Rothschild endorsed family history by Niall Ferguson, in the years following this event the Rothschild bank became the largest in the world. When a banking family that is Jewish is identified, the incorrect conclusion is the hidden hand is limited to "Jewish bankers." Unfortunately, Jewish people have suffered throughout history from persecution grounded in ignorance and to blame the Jewish community would be as incorrect as to blame the Italian community for the crimes committed by Mafia families. The evidence for this historical event is included in the Jewish Encyclopedia from 1906. This source reveals Nathan Rothschild "made no less than four profits on: (1) on the sale of Wellington's paper, (2) on the sale of the gold to Wellington, (3) on its repurchase, and (4) on forwarding it to Portugal."

[155] Established on May 17, 1930, the Bank for International Settlements is headquartered in Basel, Switzerland. The BIS website has more information and is online at www.bis.org.

currency deposits amounted to 196 billion in Special Drawing Rights.[156] The BIS owners facilitate global monetary control by helping manage Gresham's Law, which states that bad money drives out good. Bad money refers to fiat money that is money not backed by assets. Good money refers to money backed by something of real value, often gold or silver. Gresham's Law is visible in the U.S. as the government has compulsorily overvalued the dollar, and gold has left the country and is being hoarded. The fifth book in the Vigilant Christian series provides more information on gold and the demonetization of the U.S. dollar.

The third prong, the termination of the Austrian royal family's veto power of Catholic popes, was accomplished with the assassination of Archduke Franz Ferdinand in 1914. The Catholic Church for over a thousand years has been on the forward line in combating the NWO affiliated secret societies. Placing an agent in the seat of Peter paid great dividends for the NWO during the crusades and was an NWO objective when Pope Leo XIII died in 1903. The NWO's candidate, Mariano Rampolla del Tindaro (August 17, 1843-December 17, 1913) was about to be elected pope when at the last moment Austrian Emperor Francis Joseph I imposed a veto. The veto during the Conclave came through the agency of Cardinal Jan Puzyna de Kosielsko. When Franz Ferdinand was assassinated the Austrian hereditary veto power, a key obstacle to corrupting the Catholic Church, died with him. This is all less surprising when you remember that we are warned in 2 Corinthians 11:13-15 that religious institutions can at times be infiltrated and controlled by Satan's agents.[157]

The fourth prong was the destruction of the imperial Russian family. The imperial Russian family had frustrated NWO attempts since at least 1613. The destruction of the imperial family took place in two parts. The first part was accomplished when the February Revolution abolished the crown. Nicholas II (May 18, 1868-July 17, 1918), the last Emperor of Russia, abdicated power on March 15, 1917. The second part was his murder, along with his family, after King George V refused to allow him exile in the United Kingdom.

The NWO wanted revenge for Romanov family interference during the United States Civil War. The first book in the Vigilant Christian series provides the details on how Russia's bluewater navy was sent to San Francisco and New York to help the Union during the Civil War. The Civil War alliance between President Abraham Lincoln and Russian Tsar Alexander II is now understood by historians as a key reason the South was defeated.

---

[156] "The BIS in Profile" as of March 31, 2012 and this information is online at www.bis.org/about/profile.pdf.

[157] 2 Corinthians 11:13-15 - "For such are false apostles, deceitful workers, transforming themselves into the apostles of Christ. And no marvel; for Satan himself is transformed into an angel of light. Therefore it is no great thing if his ministers also be transformed as the ministers of righteousness; whose end shall be according to their works."

War is Necessary for Debt Enslavement

The cycle of debt often starts with selling weapons and is accelerated by war. While governments acquire debt through weapon purchases, the weapon manufacturers and lending bankers profit. The leading owners of the weapon manufacturers and banks are often interlocking and the same NWO families. In the 21st century the country that buys the most weapons is the U.S. Total U.S. weapons purchases exceed the combined sum of all other nations. Not surprisingly, government officials, paid experts, and corporate owned media continue to promote the need for more weapons that enslave people in debt.

Creating war debt to advance the NWO is a pattern that has been repeated many times. To see how corporations such as Halliburton play an important NWO role, the documentary *Iraq for Sale: The War Profiteers* is recommended.[158]

President Woodrow Wilson claimed World War I started because a financial elite had too much control over Germany, Russia, and Austria. Lenin also went on record stating that elite banking merchants orchestrated the war.[159] We now know that both Wilson and Lenin were correct. The more precise explanation is that the NWO, cloaked in nationalism, started World War I.

How World War I Started

As with most wars, the seeds of World War I were sown many years before the first shot was fired. In 1870, the Franco-Prussian War resulted in France's defeat by Germany. After that war, a triple alliance was formed consisting of Germany, Austro-Hungary, and Italy. Another contributing factor was the policy of Weltpolitic, or the global imperial policy of Kaiser Wilhelm the Second. The Moroccan crisis of 1905 to 1911 also was a factor that led up to World War I. NWO agents in Germany attempted to use the issue of Morocco's independence to increase frictions between France and the United Kingdom. Regional tension was also fueled by violence in Serbia which led to increased tension with Austria.

On June 28, 1914, the heir to the Austro-Hungarian throne, Archduke Franz Ferdinand, was assassinated in Sarajevo. The Black Hand Serbian secret society, with connections to multiple New World Order fronts including Freemasonry, the British Empire, and French intelligence,

---

[158] Robert Greenwald, *Iraq for Sale: The War Profiteers* (Culver City, CA: Brave New Films, 2006).

[159] *Lenin's Selected Works* (Moscow: Progress Publishers, 1963). Volume 1 was first published in mid-1917 in pamphlet form (1917 pamphlet *Imperialism, the Highest Stage of Capitalism* at www.marxists.org/archive/lenin/works/1916/imp-hsc/).

took credit. World War I ended in 1918 with at least 20 million killed and accomplished most of the four NWO prongs. NWO accomplishments included:

1. A one-world government framework; originally failed with the League of Nations but succeeded after World War II with the creation of the United Nations.
2. A bank for central banks, which was accomplished with the Bank for International Settlements (BIS).
3. Termination of the Austrian royal family's veto power of Catholic popes, which was accomplished with the assassination of Archduke Franz Ferdinand in 1914.
4. Destruction of one of the greatest opponents to the NWO in the early 20th century, the imperial Russian family.

How the U.S. was Manipulated to Join World War I

Citizens of the U.S. were successfully duped to support entering the war in 1917 through a series of cleverly orchestrated efforts. President Woodrow Wilson was directly involved in the deceptions and formally sanctioned U.S. participation through a secret agreement with England on March 9, 1916. We know about this agreement today because it was leaked and confirmed by Sir Edward Grey, Ambassador Walter Hines Page, C. Hartley Grattan, and Colonel Edward Mandell House. Carroll Quigley identifies these important but often unknown men in history as members of what he called the Anglo-American Establishment.[160]

Winston Churchill and Wilson's advisor, Colonel House, both NWO agents, arranged for a shipment of weapons from New York to Liverpool via the Lusitania in May of 1915. In 1915 the U.S. was a neutral country not participating in the war therefore it was against U.S. law to put weapons on a passenger ship traveling to England or Germany.

The Lusitania luxury ocean liner was owned by the Cunard Steamship Line Shipping, a private British company started in 1840 by Samuel Cunard. However, the British government had subsidized the ship's building in 1907 making it officially part of the auxiliary navy. The ship's owners were paid £218,000 a year (£150,000 for reserve military service and £68,000 to carry Royal mail). As an auxiliary naval ship, the Lusitania was under orders from the British Admiralty to ram any German ship seeking to inspect her cargo.

In April of 1915 the Lusitania was docked in New York Harbor preparing for her trans-Atlantic voyage when German dock workers reported seeing weapons being loaded onto the Lusitania; this was reported to the German embassy. In addition, three German spies attempted

---

[160] Carroll Quigley, *The Anglo-American Establishment* (San Pedro, California: GSG Associates, written in 1949 but published posthumously in 1981).

to report that the 90 tons of unrefrigerated butter destined for a British naval base were in reality weapons and ammunition.[161] The spies were discovered at sea and detained on the ship. When the Lusitania sunk, the men went down with the ship.

In an effort to warn Americans from sailing on a ship carrying weapons bound for England, the German Embassy attempted to place the advertisement in 50 East Coast newspapers prior to the Lusitania sailing. The ads were to be printed with a date of April 22, 1915, (nine days before the ship was to set sail from New York) and even without the U.S. involved in the war, NWO agents in the U.S. State Department blocked all the ads except one. George Viereck, the man who placed the ads for the embassy, protested to the State Department on April 26 that the ads were blocked. Viereck met with Secretary of State William Jennings Bryan and produced copies of the Lusitania's supplementary manifests. Bryan, impressed by the evidence that the Lusitania had previously carried weapons, cleared publication of the warning. Someone higher than the Secretary of State, likely NWO agent Colonel House, overruled Bryan. Nonetheless one ad slipped past the State Department censorship. The following shows the single ad that slipped past the government censors and appeared in the *Des Moines Register*.[162]

---

[161] Ballard, Robert D. and Spencer Dunmore, *Exploring the Lusitania* (Warner Books, 1995).

Hickey, Des and Gus Smith, *Seven Days to Disaster* (G. P. Putnam's Sons, 1981).

Preston, Diana. *Lusitania: An Epic Tragedy* (Berkley Books, 2002).

Simpson, Colin, *The Lusitania* (Little, Brown, and Company, 1972).

See http://rmslusitania.info/pages/victualling_crew/leach_jn.html. Below is the text from this source providing additional details about the three German spies.

John Neil Leach, 25, was the British son of a judge in Jamaica. Leach spoke German and lived with Gustav Stahl at 20 Leroy Street. German spy Curt Thummel lived at the same boarding house. Stahl testified under oath that the night before the Lusitania set sail he went aboard the Lusitania with Leach and saw weapons. Leach may have been a German spy. According to Lusitania researcher Peter Engberg-Klarström, the three spies may not have been stowaways but members of the Lusitania crew.

[162] Imperial German Embassy, "Notice! Lusitania Passenger Warning," *Des Moines Register*, 22 April 1915.

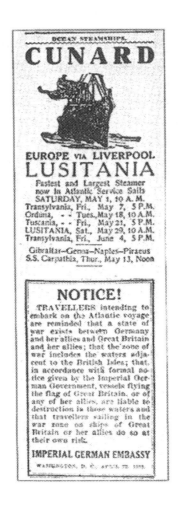

The warning read: "NOTICE! Travellers intending to embark on the Atlantic voyage are reminded that a state of war exists between Germany and her allies and Great Britain and her allies; that the zone of war includes the waters adjacent to the British Isles; that, in accordance with formal notice given by the Imperial German Government, vessels flying the flag of Great Britain, or any of her allies, are liable to destruction in those waters and that travellers sailing in the war zone on ships of Great Britain or her allies do so at their own risk. IMPERIAL GERMAN EMBASSY WASHINGTON, D.C., APRIL 22, 1915."

Captain Daniel Dow, the Lusitania's captain immediately before Captain William T. Turner, had resigned on March 8, 1915 because he was no longer willing "to carry the responsibility of mixing passengers with munitions or contraband."[163] Captain Dow had a close call just two days before he resigned. He was aware the rules of naval warfare changed in October 1914 when

---

[163] Colin Simpson, *The Lusitania* (Boston: Little, Brown & Co. 1972), 87.

First Lord of the Admiralty Winston Churchill issued orders that British merchant ships with munitions or contraband must ram U-boats.[164] Prior to this change by Churchill, both England and Germany adhered to Cruiser Rules. Cruiser Rules enabled crews and passengers to escape in lifeboats before being fired on. Because of the new Churchill ram rules, German U-boats no longer surfaced to issue a warning to their potential targets and fired while still submerged. Churchill explained his ruthlessness.

> "The first British countermove, made on my responsibility...was to deter the Germans from surface attack. The submerged U-boat had to rely increasingly on underwater attack and thus ran the greater risk of mistaking neutral for British ships and of drowning neutral crews and thus embroiling Germany with other Great Powers."[165]

The above combined with the next Churchill quote speaks volumes about what really happened and why.

> "There are many kinds of maneuvers in war...There are maneuvers in time, in diplomacy, in mechanics, in psychology; all of which are removed from the battlefield, but react often decisively upon it...The maneuver which brings an ally into the field is as serviceable as that which wins a great battle."[166]

Winston Churchill, when in charge of the British Admiralty, worked closely with his NWO benefactor Sir Nathan Mayer Rothschild.[167] Nathan Mayer Rothschild was part of a syndicate with J. P. Morgan working to buy up the North Atlantic shipping lines. His intelligence agents in the U.S. warned that Germany, absent a Lusitania-like disaster, would be effective at keeping the U.S. out of the war. Nathan Mayer Rothschild died before the Lusitania sunk. Before his death, Nathan Mayer Rothschild had access to the admiralty reports on German naval operations.

---

[164] Winston Churchill was appointed First Lord of the Admiralty in October 1911. To distance his work for the NWO and orchestration of the Lusitania disaster, he left this position in late May 1915 but remained in the Cabinet as the Chancellor of the Duchy of Lancaster.

[165] Winston Churchill, *The World Crisis* (New York: Scribner's Sons, 1949), 274 -275.

[166] Ibid., 300.

[167] There are a few notable Nathan Mayer Rothschilds in history, so the following is provided to prevent confusion. Nathan Mayer Rothschild (1840-1915) was the nephew of Anthony Nathan de Rothschild (1810-1876) who had no sons but was the son of Nathan Mayer Rothschild (1777-1836). Nathan Mayer Rothschild was the fourth child of Mayer Amschel Rothschild (1744-1812) who founded the Rothschild banking dynasty.

Operation Lusitania

The Lusitania was built for speed, and Captain Dow's previous ability to outrun U-boats appears to be the reason for the highly unusual order from Cunard headquarters to run only three of the ship's four boilers, forcing it to operate at a speed that would increase the chances of a U-boat attack. The reduction in speed resulting from operating with one boiler turned off is a key reason the U-boat attack was successful.

To make sure Captain Turner would not go to full speed in an emergency, he and Lusitania Chief Engineer Bryce were denied the engineering crew to operate the fourth boiler room. Churchill is blamed for sending the Lusitania to a known U-boat location, but it is important to remember he also helped orchestrate sending the Lusitania at a reduced speed. On May 7, the Lusitania entered the Irish Channel. The ship slowed hoping the English escort vessel Juno would arrive. Unknown to Captain Turner of the Lusitania, Churchill, in an effort to maximize American casualties, ordered the British destroyer HMS Juno to return without picking up a single person. The Juno, under the command of Rear Admiral Hood, was so close that Lusitania survivors were able to see the ship approach and leave. Churchill's order left the Lusitania alone and unprotected in a known area patrolled by U-boats.[168]

British Commander Joseph Kenworthy was present in the high-command map room as the Lusitania headed toward a known U-boat position. He had been previously asked by Churchill to write a paper on the political fallout of an ocean liner being sunk with American passengers. In 1927 he wrote *The Freedom of the Seas* revealing, "The Lusitania steaming at half-speed straight through the submarine cruising ground on the Irish coast was incontinently sunk."[169] Colonel House, meeting with King George V just hours before the Lusitania was sunk, discussed the likely American reaction to the King's conjecture: "Suppose they should sink the Lusitania with American passengers on board . . . ."[170]

In the 1981 book *Seven Days to Disaster: The Sinking of the Lusitania,* Des Hickey and Gus Smith reported that one of the crewmen on the U-20 responsible for passing the order to fire to the torpedo room was Charles Voegele. The Lusitania was commonly known to transport

---

[168] Colin Simpson, *The Lusitania* (Boston: Little, Brown & Co. 1972), 119 and www.gwpda.org/naval/lusika04.htm. England had deciphered the German communications code on December 14, 1914. The level of detail known by the British Admiralty was so precise that U-boat names as well as their general locations were known. For example, the British Admiralty knew U-30 left the English coast for Germany on May 4th and that the U-27 also returned to Germany because of jammed blow planes.

[169] J.M Kenworthy and George Young, *Freedom of the Seas* (Plymouth, Great Britain, The Mayflower Press and New York: Horace Liveright, 1927), 72.

[170] Charles Seymour, *The Intimate Papers of Colonel House* (New York, New York: Houghton Mifflin Co., 1926), Vol. I, 432.

U.S. citizens and Voegele refused the order to kill civilians of a neutral country. Upon returning to Germany Voegele was court-martialed and imprisoned for three years. As a result, only one torpedo loaded with 300 pounds of explosives was fired instead of two. Yet, the Lusitania's Captain reported two explosions; the first sounded "like a heavy door being slammed shut" and was followed by a much larger explosion that rocked the ship, which points to a cargo of ammunition blowing up. Captain Turner described in the log "an unusually heavy detonation."[171] The Lusitania sunk 15-18 minutes later.

The following is a 1915 drawing of the Lusitania was distributed by the *New York Herald* and *London Sphere* to reinforce the false information that two torpedoes were fired.[172]

On May 28, 1915, Germany's official response to the U.S. government's protest to the sinking states that the German government had no intention to attack any vessels which were not guilty of hostile acts.[173] The Imperial German government wrote that the Lusitania was of the largest and fastest steamers constructed by the government for the British Navy.

---

[171] The larger explosion was a result of Lusitania contraband including:
- 600 tons of pyroxyline known as gun cotton
- six million rounds of ammunition.
- 1,248 cases of shrapnel shells
- tons of unidentified munitions in containers labeled as cheese, lard and other substances. Additional information is online at www.lusitania.net/disaster.html.

[172] Courtesy of the Library of Congress, Prints and Photographs Division, Washington, D.C. The drawing is online at www.archives.gov/exhibits/eyewitness/html.php?section=18.

[173] Additional information is online at www.firstworldwar.com/source/lusitania_germanresponse.htm.

"It is, moreover, known to the Imperial government from reliable information furnished by its officials and neutral passengers that for some time practically all the more valuable English merchant vessels have been provided with guns, ammunition and other weapons, and reinforced with a crew specially practiced in manning guns. According to reports at hand here, the Lusitania when she left New York undoubtedly had guns on board which were mounted under decks and masked."[174]

The official German government letter also spells out that the Lusitania had 5,400 cases of ammunition that would be used to kill German soldiers. An exceptionally noteworthy section of the letter states the British merchant marine ships received secret instruction in February by the British Admiralty to seek protection behind neutral flags and attack German submarines by ramming them. The German official response that war contraband was on board explains the second explosion.[175]

Despite British and U.S. Denials

The elite families advancing the NWO, even a century later, still fear the repercussions from Americans if a significant percentage ever learn they were tricked into joining World War I.

For decades, the British and American governments have denied that there were weapons on the Lusitania. The wreckage site was declared a protected site, denying divers' access. To further frustrate the ability to determine what the Lusitania carried, since 1946 the Royal Navy has repeatedly dropped depth charges on top of the Lusitania as a site for target practice. Common sense tells us the Royal Navy would not desecrate the bodies of women and children sunk with the Lusitania unless there was more to the story. The Arts and Heritage Ministry did not protest the use of the Lusitania as a target for British depth charges, but it did oppose salvage operations, claiming their opposition "helped" respect the sanctity of the site.

The weapons from Lusitania salvage operations almost a full century after the sinking have confirmed that the German government told the truth and that the NWO agents worked to trick the U.S. into World War I. In 1968, to keep the truth secret, the British Secret Service unsuccessfully attempted to buy the salvage rights to the Lusitania. In 1993 PBS Online visited the wreck and determined previous visitors had tampered with the evidence.[176] One of the more embarrassing confirmations of the Lusitania treachery occurred when Victor Quirke of the

---

[174] Charles F. Horne and Walter F. Austin, *Source Records of the Great War, Volume III* (National Alumi, 1923). Volume III includes the May 28, 1915 official German response by Foreign Minister Gottlieb von Jagow. The letter is also online at www.firstworldwar.com/source/lusitania_germanresponse.htm.
[175] Ibid.
[176] See www.pbs.org/lostliners/lusitania.html.

Cork Sub Aqua Club found 15,000 rounds of .303 bullets in the bow section of the ship in July of 2006.[177]

Churchill's NWO Treachery Confirmed

Prior to the confirmation of weapons on the Lusitania, historians had an extensive body of evidence that 1,201 people were sacrificed to create a reason for the U.S. to enter World War I. Historian Colin Simpson's book fully exposed Churchill's conspiracy to put the Lusitania in danger with the hope of sparking an incident that would bring America into World War I.[178] Many historians including Howard Zinn found proof that weapons were being secretly carried. Zinn wrote in *A People's History of the United States* that the Lusitania carried 1,248 cases of 3-inch shells, 4,927 boxes of cartridges (1,000 rounds in each box), and 2,000 more cases of small-arms ammunition. Patrick Beesly is another historian who supports the claim that Churchill is guilty of mass murder.[179] Beesly wrote: "I am reluctantly driven to the conclusion that there was a conspiracy deliberately to put the Lusitania at risk in the hopes that even an abortive attack on her would bring the United States into the war. Such a conspiracy could not have been put into effect without Winston Churchill's express permission and approval."[180]

Christopher Hitchens' book, *Blood Class and Nostalgia*, directly puts the responsibility on Churchill for his deliberate action to pull America into World War I.[181] History professor and senior scholar of the Ludwig von Mises Institute, Ralph Raico, notes that Churchill wrote in the week prior to the Lusitania sinking that it was "most important to attract neutral shipping to our shores, in the hopes especially of embroiling the United States with Germany."[182]

Churchill worked for the NWO elite and orchestrated the mass murders for the New World Order. Winston Churchill's family members have been NWO-linked Freemasons for generations. A few examples are his father, Lord Randolph Churchill (1849-1895), uncle, George Charles Spencer-Churchill (1844-1892), first cousin, Charles Richard John Spencer-Churchill (1871-

---

[177] On April 2, 2007, Cyber Diver News Network reported the American owner of the Lusitania wreck, F. Gregg Bemis, Jr., won the case to conduct salvage operations.

[178] Colin Simpson, *Lusitania* (London, England: Penguin Group, 1974). The first edition was published by Longman in 1972.

[179] Patrick Beesly, *Room 40: British Naval Intelligence 1914-18* (New York, NY: Harcourt Brace Jovanovich, 1982) and see www.gwpda.org/naval /lusika04.htm.

[180] Ibid., 122.

[181] Christopher Hitchens, *Blood Class and Nostalgia: Anglo-American Ironies* (Farrar Straus & Giroux, June 1990).

[182] See www.lewrockwell.com/orig/raico-churchill2.html. Raico quoted a German historian in his five-part essay on Churchill included in the book *The Costs of War* by John V. Denson.

1934), and ancestor, Lord Henry John Spencer-Churchill (1797-1840).[183] While the discoveries of weapons on the Lusitania as well as insider accounts confirm Churchill's treachery, historians often attribute his orchestration of the Lusitania murders as actions he felt necessary for his country. This argument is Churchill willingly sent women and children to their deaths in order to save even more women and children in England. Unfortunately, saving the lives of people is never an NWO priority, and this private Freemason was advancing a one-world government.[184]

The story of Churchill's resignation from Freemasonry and continued involvement in Freemasonry has left even Freemasons confused as to whether he was or was not a lifetime member.[185] Churchill resigned his Freemason membership as a ploy before World War I to fool the public into believing that his loyalty was to the British people.[186] In the years after his resignation he continued to participate in Masonic affairs and even helped open two new lodges.[187]

Lusitania Propaganda

The NWO did many things to pull America into World War I. NWO insider Churchill attempted to mislead both the British and the American public into believing that the Lusitania sinking was premeditated by Germany. Two of his most effective efforts at deceiving the public were the scapegoating of Lusitania's Captain Turner and the re-creation of a German-made medal designed by Karl Goetz to commemorate the ship's sinking. Captain Turner was successfully blamed for his response to the disaster in order to keep the NWO's involvement hidden. However, Turner deserves little sympathy because he knowingly carried munitions and agreed to the Cunard orders to travel at a reduced speed, making his ship an easy target.

---

[183] Yasha Beresiner, "Winston Churchill: A Famous Man and a Freemason," *Pietre-Stones Review of Freemasonry* and online at www.freemasons-freemasonry.com/beresiner7.html. Beresiner is a high-level Freemason and the Past Master of Quatuor Lodge no 2076.

[184] The *Freemasons Members Journal* No. 3 in 2002 cover page shows in white text "Winston Churchill" and in red text "Public Statesman Private Mason." Winston Churchill was initiated into the Masonic Studholme Lodge 1591 on May 24, 1901 when he was a 26 year old member of Parliament and resigned in 1912 after becoming Lord of the Admiralty.

[185] For an example of the confusion resulting from Churchill becoming an "unattached brother" see *The Churchill Society* letters at www.churchill-society-london.org.uk/lttrs.fmasons.hall.html.

[186] When Churchill resigned from Freemasonry in 1912 the NWO was planning to start World War I with the assassination of Archduke of Austria Franz Ferdinand. This assassination happened on June 28, 1914 in Sarajevo. The Serbian Black Hand assassins responsible had close ties to both British intelligence and Freemasonry.

[187] Yasha Beresiner, "Winston Churchill: A Famous Man and a Freemason," *Pietre-Stones Review of Freemasonry* and online at www.freemasons-freemasonry.com/beresiner7.html.

As for the Goetz medal, copies were distributed by NWO agents in a propaganda effort to rouse English and American sentiment against the Germans. The original medal was designed by Goetz as a condemnation of the NWO and those who put business above peoples' safety; the copies distributed in England were sold with the false message that Germany celebrated the death of women and children. The following picture shows both sides of the Lusitania medal.[188]

Most descriptions of the Goetz medal show only the reverse side depicting the Lusitania sinking and bearing the inscription, "The liner Lusitania sunk by a German Submarine May 5, 1915." Goetz claimed this was an error and corrected the date to May 7, 1915 in a second edition, but the incorrect date was used by Churchill to serve as proof of a premeditated attack on a civilian ship.

An accurate interpretation of the medal requires knowledge of both of its sides. The lesser known front shows a skeleton representing death behind a Cunard customer service window. On the medal the German Ambassador to the U.S., Count Johann-Heinrich von Bernstorff, wears a hat and raises a finger to warn passengers that weapons are on the ship. A person next to him reads a newspaper with the headline "U Boat Danger" representing the warning written by the German government. Above the ambassador's image are the words "Geschaft Uber Alles" which means "Business Above All." The back side of the medal refutes Churchill's claims with the inscription "No Contraband Goods!" and a Lusitania depiction showing weapons falling into the sea.

Churchill's distribution of over 250,000 copies of the Goetz medal in England successfully infuriated people. The public anger roused by this campaign against Germany distracted people

---

[188] Teach Peace Foundation 2013 photographs of the front and back of the Lusitania medal.

from credible reports that Churchill removed the Lusitania's military escort.[189] The Lusitania medal was not intended to celebrate the killing of civilians or reward the sailors involved in murdering civilians. The Lusitania medal was intended to condemn the greed of the NWO elite who orchestrated and profited from the tragedy.[190]

The Zimmerman Telegram

Berlin announced on January 31, 1917 that its submarines would sink all ships aiding Britain. The Berlin announcement, combined with the previous Lusitania sinking, was still not enough for America to enter the war. Churchill served his NWO masters by having the British Intelligence service manufacture another war propaganda bombshell. The success of the Goetz Lusitania war propaganda was followed in the form of a fabricated telegram from German Foreign Minister Arthur Zimmerman to the German Minister to Mexico.[191]

The Zimmerman Telegram was claimed to have been obtained and deciphered by British Intelligence. The deciphered communication was presented to Woodrow Wilson on February 24, 1917, offered Mexico money to attack the U.S. The numerous British propaganda campaigns ultimately proved successful, and on April 6, 1917, the U.S. did declare war on Germany. This technique has been successfully used many times by the NWO who created and controls all United Kingdom intelligence services. This is why in 2002 a British intelligence report falsely reported that "Iraq has sought significant quantities of uranium from Africa." That lie, as had the Zimmerman Telegram almost a century earlier, deceived many Americans into believing Iraq had weapons of mass destruction.[192]

The Seeds for World War II

World War II was born in large part from the NWO's intentionally hostile treatment of the German people in the 1920s, treatment meant to create the conditions for an even greater world war. Sanctions on Germany and forced war reparations successfully produced anger and aggression in the generation following World War I. While kindness begets kindness, the inverse is also true. The anger of the German people grew as the years of poverty and hardship

---

[189] The cover story for the removal of the Juno escort was confusion within the Admiralty about a Gallipoli campaign in the Ottoman Empire. The parallels with the White House claiming confusion even though Donald Rumsfeld was proven to be directly responsible for not scrambling U.S. Air Force fighters to assist alleged hijacked commercial airplanes on September 11, 2001 is noteworthy.

[190] See www.nmm.ac.uk/searchbin/searchs.pl?exhibit=it1135j&axis =1188011907&flash=.

[191] The Zimmerman Telegram is available for viewing at the U.S. National Archives. More information is online at www.archives.gov/locations/why-visit.html.

[192] Mitch Frank, "Iraq: Tale of the Cake," *Time Magazine*, 21 July 2003 and online at www.time.com/time/magazine/article/0,9171,1005235,00.html.

continued. The injustices to the German people created fertile ground for an extremist to appeal to their economic needs with policies of hate. Adolf Hitler and his Nazi party directed the public's anger toward internal and external scapegoats while continuing to build their power over the German people.

The path to World War II was laid by the NWO at the Treaty of Versailles in 1918. The following picture shows Allied and German delegates in the Hall of Mirrors at Versailles on June 28, 1919.[193]

When World War II ended, Freemasons Stalin, FDR, and Churchill all met at the Tehran Conference between November 28 and December 1, 1943. The NWO secret society agents met a

---

[193] The German delegation accepted the terms of the Treaty Of Versailles which formally ending World War I. This photograph taken in Versailles, France on June 28, 1919, is courtesy of the National Archives and Records Administration in College Park, Maryland.

second time at the 1945 Yalta Conference to discuss Europe's NWO post-war reorganization.[194] The following photograph shows the three leaders at the Yalta Conference.[195]

The Freemason control of the three NWO fronts or "Big Three" powers as they were called at the time, was further made transparent at the Potsdam Conference when another Freemason replaced FDR.[196] FDR had died on April 12, 1945 and high-level Freemason Harry S. Truman continued the one-world march.

The Potsdam Conference ended on August 2, 1945 and a week later the Nagasaki atomic bomb was detonated. The pictures of the Tehran Conference, Yalta Conference and Potsdam Conference tell the real World War II story. All of the "Big Three" leaders were serving their

[194] The Yalta Conference was codenamed the Argonaut Conference and held on February 4-11, 1945 in the city of Yalta in Crimea.

[195] Photo by the U.S. Army Signal Corps. Courtesy the FDR Library Photo Collection. Picture taken on February 9, 1945. From left to right the photo shows Winston Churchill, Franklin D. Roosevelt, and Joseph Stalin Roosevelt at the Livadia Palace during the Yalta Conference.

[196] The Potsdam Conference was held from July 16, 1945 to August 2, 1945 in Potsdam, Germany. The "Big Three" powers are the NWO and Freemason allied leaders of the United States, the United Kingdom, and the Soviet Union.

NWO masters and had been since they were very young men. British Prime Minister Winston Churchill, U.S. President Harry S. Truman, and Soviet Leader Josef Stalin, all initiated into one or more NWO secret societies.[197]

After Germany lost World War II, the Soviet Union provided the U.S. with a constant reminder that things could be worse. The contrast between prosperous free people in the West and impoverished state-controlled people in East Germany did not go unnoticed. Sadly, the NWO is repeating the harsh policies shown to contribute to starting world wars. The NWO U.S. led sanctions on Japan in World War II, post-Gulf War sanctions on Iraq, and current economic sanctions on the Palestinian people are three examples. The NWO seeks to start World War III at some point in the 21st century. For this reason, repeating a policy that will promote a world war is perceived as necessary in order to condition people to accept world government.

This chapter began with a quote from Dr. Martin Luther King, Jr. He taught evil must be aggressively opposed, but not with more evil. Advice from Dr. King ends this chapter.

> "Darkness cannot drive out darkness; only light can do that. Hate cannot drive out hate; only love can do that. Hate multiplies hate, violence multiplies violence, and toughness multiplies toughness in a descending spiral of destruction . . . The chain reaction of evil—hate begetting hate, wars producing more wars must be broken, or we shall be plunged into the dark abyss of annihilation."[198]

> "If you succumb to the temptation of using violence in your struggle, unborn generations will be the recipients of a long and desolate night of bitterness, and your chief legacy to the future will be an endless reign of meaningless chaos."[199]

---

[197] In *Vigilant Christian I: The New World Order*, a photograph taken on July 25, 1945 by the U.S. Army Signal Corps is on page 54. The Truman Library also makes the Potsdam Conference photograph available online at www.trumanlibrary.org/photographs/view.php?id=13342.

[198] Martin Luther King, Jr., *Strength to Love* (New York, Harper & Row, 1963).

[199] Martin Luther King, Jr., sermon in Montgomery, Alabama, Nov.6, 1956.

5

THE REAL TERRORISTS

"My Brother, you desire to unite yourself to an Order which has laboured in silence and secrecy for more than five hundred years with a single end, in which it has as yet only partially succeeded, and to which, if you join us, you must devote yourself. You have been partially prepared for this in some of the degrees that you have already taken." Albert Pike[200]

The New World Order has been creating terrorism for a long time. Understanding modern terrorism requires knowing that in the 16th to the 20th century soldiers from Great Britain frequently fought New World Order wars in foreign lands. Britain used the word "emergencies" for systematic planned violence rejecting imperialism. The American Revolution is an example of one of these emergencies, and America's founding fathers were considered terrorists by King George III.[201]

After World War II, the U.S. military became the primary NWO manipulated fighting force to be deployed in foreign lands. From 1945 to 2013, the NWO has used the U.S. to bomb over two dozen countries including: China 1945-46 and 1950-53, Korea 1950-53, Guatemala 1954, 1960 and 1967-69, Indonesia 1958, Cuba 1959-60, Congo 1964, Peru 1965, Laos 1964-73, Vietnam 1961-73, Cambodia 1969-70, Grenada 1983, Libya 1986 and 2011, El Salvador 1980s, Nicaragua 1980s, Lebanon 1983, Panama 1989, Kuwait 1991, Iran 1987, 2012 and 2013 (includes

---

[200] Albert Pike's *Magnum Opus or The Great Work of the Ancient and Accepted Scottish Rite of Freemasonry* first published around 1869 and on page 61 in the 2010 Kessinger Publishing edition. Pike acknowledged "The Great Work" is ancient. The five hundred years in Pike's quote is referring to the elimination of his secret society as a world power when the Knights Templar Grand Commander Jacques de Molay was punished with the death penalty in 1314.

[201] "Kings and Queens of the United Kingdom: George III," *The Official Website of The British Monarchy*, accessed 5 December 2004. The online address is www.royal.gov.uk/output/page111.asp. George III was born on 4 June 1738 in London. He became heir to the throne on the death of his father in 1751, succeeding his grandfather, George II, in 1760. He died at Windsor Castle on 29 January 1820, after a reign of almost 60 years - the second longest in British history.

covert operations), Syria 2012 and 2013 (includes covert operations), Iraq 1991 to 2013 (includes bombs dropped during economic sanction enforcement and covert operations leading up to the 2003 invasion), Bosnia 1994, Sudan 1998, Afghanistan 1998 and 2001 to 2013, Yugoslavia 1999, Yemen 2002 to 2013, and Pakistan 2004 to 2013.[202]

People who focus all accountability for U.S. government wrongdoing on the CIA and not on NWO infiltrators in the U.S. government perform an important service for the NWO. Noam Chomsky and Edward Herman are generally viewed as anti-establishment writers. In 1979 the two men wrote *The Washington Connection and Third World Fascism*, which provides a detailed account of the United States' key role in the military takeovers of 18 Latin American countries between 1960 and 1976.[203] Chomsky and Herman consistently attribute imperial actions to U.S. foreign policy and not to the NWO. When you understand this point, their work should rightly be deemed valuable; however, do not expect to receive helpful insights on the September 11, 2001 attacks or any other issue directly exposing the NWO's hidden hand.

Iran 1979 Uprising

Reviewing acts of terror against Americans is eye-opening once you add the NWO dimension. One example of violence prompted by the NWO seeking control of oil is the 1979 Iranian uprising, which was a reaction to the 1953 NWO conquest of Iranian oil resources. Secretary of State Madeline Albright acknowledged this once highly classified CIA operation.[204] The operation was also documented in 1954 by one of the coup's chief planners, NWO insider Dr. Donald N. Wilber. This document details how a powerful elite used both the Central Intelligence Agency and the British Secret Intelligence Service to overthrow Iran's elected prime minister.[205] While the 1953 coup was classified and kept relatively unknown in the United States, the operation was, and is commonly known by Iranians.

The planning for the Iranian coup began in 1952 because the NWO feared an independent Iran would frustrate its one-world agenda. NWO insiders who were in key U.S. and British

---

[202] William Blum, "A Brief History of U.S. Interventions 1945 to the Present," *Z Magazine*, June 1999. Also Chapter 17 of William Blum's book, *Rogue State: A Guide to the World's Only Superpower*, published in 2000. Permission for inclusion of information from his research was obtained on September 16, 2004. The list compiled by Mr. Blum is supplemented and updated to the date this book was published.

[203] Noam Chomsky and Edward Herman, *The Washington Connection and Third World Fascism* (New York, NY: South End Press, 1979).

[204] RFE/FL Iran Report Volume 3, Number 13, "Hostile Official Reaction to Albright Speech," *Radio Free Europe/Radio Liberty*, 27 March 2000. Available online at www.globalsecurity.org/wmd/library/news/iran/2000/13-270300.html.

[205] James Risen, "Secrets of History: The C.I.A. in Iran," *The New York Times*, 16 April 2000. Available online at www.nytimes.com/library/world/mideast/041600iran-cia-index.html.

leadership positions wanted to stop Iran from nationalizing its oil industry.[206] As illustrated by Venezuala's nationalization of oil to retain more oil profits, NWO controlled international oil corporations will kill to regain lost profits.[207]

CIA efforts to topple Iran's Prime Minister Mohammed Mossadegh had become serious in early 1953. On April 4, Allen Dulles, a long-time high-level NWO insider and director of the CIA, approved one million dollars to be used in any way that would bring about the fall of Mossadegh.[208] The CIA selected retired General Fazlollah Zahedi to replace the Prime Minister. In early August 1953, Iranians working for the CIA posed as communists and harassed religious leaders in a campaign to turn the country's Islamic religious community against Mossadegh's government.[209] Shah Mohammed Riza Pahlavi, the reigning monarch in Iran at the time, feared overt involvement and he refused to sign the CIA-drafted royal decrees to dismiss Mossadegh and empower General Zahedi.[210] Zahedi was an NWO insider largely motivated by bribes. The Central Intelligence Agency arranged for the Shah's twin sister, Princess Ashraf Pahlavi, and General H. Norman Schwarzkopf to influence the Shah to sign the decrees.[211] On August 13, 1953, the Shah did sign.

The coup, which started on August 15, 1953, was initially thwarted when just hours before a planned attack it was prematurely revealed to General Taghi Riahi, Mossadegh's chief of staff. Pro-Shah soldiers were sent to attack Mossadegh's home but having lost the advantage of surprise they were captured by soldiers loyal to the prime minister. The following morning Iranians learned on the radio that a coup against the government had failed.

---

[206] Ibid.

[207] James Petras, "CIA Venezuela Destabilization Memo Surfaces," *Venezuala Analysis,* 28 November 2007 and online at http://venezuelanalysis.com/analysis/2911.
The Revolution Will Not Be Televised documentary by Kim Bartley and Donnacha O'Brian is recommended. The battle against the New World Order is shown by two independent filmmakers who were inside the Venezuelan presidential palace during the April 11, 2002 coup attempt. More information about this documentary is online at www.teachpeace.com/therevolutionwillnot.htm.

[208] Roosevelt, Kermit, Jr., *Countercoup, the Struggle for Control of Iran* (New York, NY: McGraw Hill, 1979).
William Blum, *Killing Hope: U.S. Military and C.I.A. Interventions Since World War II* (Monroe, ME: Common Courage Press, updated in 2008).

[209] James Risen, "Secrets of History: The C.I.A. in Iran," *The New York Times,* 16 April 2000. Available online at www.nytimes.com/library/world/mideast/041600iran-cia-index.html.

[210] Ibid.

[211] Herbert Norman Schwarzkopf (August 28, 1895-November 25, 1958) was the lead investigator on the 1932 Lindbergh baby kidnapping and became a Major General in the U.S. Army. He is the father of Norman Schwarzkopf who was born with the name Herbert Norman Schwarzkopf, Jr. (August 22, 1934-December 27, 2012). Norman Schwarzkopf served the NWO by leading the Coalition forces for Operation Desert Shield/Storm in the 1991 Gulf War.

The Shah fled the country and went to Baghdad and later to Rome. On August 17, 1953, the CIA organized a "council of war" with General Zahedi, Iranian CIA operatives, and Iranian army officers at the U.S. embassy in Iran. The people at this meeting decided to enlist a leading cleric from Tehran to call for a holy war against communism. These same religious people the CIA attempted to manipulate would years later declare the United States "the Great Satan." The secret meeting at the U.S. embassy concluded with an agreement that another coup would begin in two days. On August 19, 1953, General Zahedi succeeded and Mossadegh was overthrown.[212] The CIA covertly funneled five million dollars to General Zahedi's regime on August 21, 1953.[213] The Shah once again returned to Iran and ruled until February 11, 1979.[214]

Terrorist Attacks Against the United States

The following list is a compiled, condensed, and corrected summary of notable terrorist acts against the United States from the Frontline *Target America*[215] and Frontline *The Man Who Knew* timelines. The list highlights that al Qaeda never existed as a terrorist organization and that Israel's occupation of Palestine fuels terrorism.[216]

> November 4, 1979: Fifty-two American citizens were taken hostage at the U.S. embassy in Tehran when students of Islam stormed the U.S. embassy in Tehran. The hostages were released just hours after Ronald Reagan's presidential inauguration on January 20, 1981 after 444 days in captivity.

The 80 Iranian students that took over the United States embassy feared that the events of 1953 were going to be repeated.[217] In 1979 the Shah was in first-class exile from Iran, traveling to

---

[212] Ibid. After the coup Mossadegh was sentenced to three years in prison. Following his release he spent the rest of his life under house arrest. Mossadegh died in 1967.

[213] James Risen, "Secrets of History: The C.I.A. In Iran," *The New York Times*, 16 April 2000. Available online at www.nytimes.com/library/world/mideast/041600iran-cia-index.html.

[214] A circa August 1953 Top Secret U.S. government document that was declassified provides additional insights. The document is available online at www.gwu.edu/~nsarchiv/NSAEBB/NSAEBB21/docs/doc02.pdf. Many of the documents revealing the CIA was working for the NWO were destroyed after former CIA Director and NWO agent James Woolsey ordered their destruction in the 1960s. The George Washington University National Security Archive reports some surviving files remain locked away from public view on the grounds that their declassification would damage the national security.

[215] "Target America," *Frontline*, timeline aired October 2001, and "The Man Who Knew: Al Qaeda's Global Context," *Frontline*, 3 October 2002 and updated in 2004.

[216] National Commission on Terrorist Attacks upon the United States, "The 9-11 Commission Report, Final Report of the National Commission on Terrorist Attacks Upon the United States," *Official Government Edition*, 24 July 2004, 362.

[217] Ibid.

Assuan, Egypt, Morocco, the Bahamas, and Mexico. He suffered from gallstones and demanded medical treatment in the United States. On October 22, 1979, the NWO's David Rockefeller and Henry Kissinger pressured President Jimmy Carter to allow the Shah to receive surgical treatment at the Weill Cornell Medical Center in New York.[218] The Shah's arrival in the U.S. led to public protests in Iran. The students specifically feared that the gallstone operation was a cover story for the Shah to plan his return to the throne.[219] The key point in understanding the 1979 kidnappings is it was a direct result of the NWO using the CIA to intervene in the affairs of Iran in 1953. The following letter written by President Jimmy Carter was sent to Iran's Ayatollah Khomeini on November 6, 1979.[220]

---

[218] Rothbard, Murray, "Why the War? The Kuwait Connection," *LewRockwell.com*, May 1991 and online at www.lewrockwell.com /rothbard/ir/Ch27.html.

[219] David Farber, *Taken Hostage: The Iran Hostage Crisis and America's First Encounter With Radical Islam* (Princeton, New Jersey: Princeton University Press), 2005, 13.
Other good resources for additional information are: David Harris, *The Crisis: The President, the Prophet, and the Shah—1979 and the Coming of Militant Islam* (New York, New York: Little, Brown and Company), 2004.
Like most historical events, there were numerous motivations for the Iranian hostage crisis. Certainly the hostages were held in part as an act of retaliation against the United States' support for the Shah and to demonstrate that the new Iranian government was capable of opposing the United States. Reza Aslan in "Days of Rage" published in the December 13, 2004 issue of *The Nation*, has noted that the crisis was also very much about an internal struggle between Iran's religious and secular forces.

[220] Courtesy of the Jimmy Carter Library, 441 Freedom Parkway, Atlanta, GA, 30307. Archival Research Catalog number 593939 and online at www.teachpeace.com/carternov61979.htm.

THE WHITE HOUSE
WASHINGTON

November 6, 1979

Dear Ayatollah Khomeini:

Based on the willingness of the Revolutionary
Council to receive them, I am asking two dis-
tinguished Americans, Mr. Ramsey Clark and Mr.
William G. Miller, to carry this letter to you
and to discuss with you and your designees
the situation in Tehran and the full range of
current issues between the U.S. and Iran.

In the name of the American people, I ask that
you release unharmed all Americans presently
detained in Iran and those held with them and
allow them to leave your country safely and
without delay. I ask you to recognize the
compelling humanitarian reasons, firmly based
in international law, for doing so.

I have asked both men to meet with you and to
hear from you your perspective on events in
Iran and the problems which have arisen between
our two countries. The people of the United
States desire to have relations with Iran based
upon equality, mutual respect, and friendship.

They will report to me immediately upon their
return.

Sincerely,

Jimmy Carter

His Excellency
Ayatollah Khomeini
Qom, Iran

DECLASSIFIED

Jimmy Carter's NWO service and participation in the one-world Trilateralist Commission front is explained in the first Vigilant Christian book.

April 18, 1983: The U.S. media reported an Iranian-backed Hezbollah suicide bomber supported by Syria drove a pickup truck with explosives into the U.S. embassy in Beirut, Lebanon.

The media in the Muslim world reported the attack was a Mossad false flag operation. Sixty-three people were killed, including 17 Americans.

October 23, 1983: A suicide bomber detonated a truck full of explosives at a U.S. Marine barracks located at Beirut International Airport. The attack killed 299 American and French servicemen. The U.S. media blamed Hezbollah while in Lebanon the Mossad was understood to be the responsible group. Author Jack Bernstein wrote, "By instigating the attack on the Marine base, Israel's 'hawks' hoped that it would turn the American people against the Arabs, and that the U.S. would be drawn into the war and further help Israel in its aggression against the Arabs."[221]

December 12, 1983: Members of al Dawa or "The Call," alleged to be both an Iranian-backed group and by others a Mossad operation, bombed multiple targets in Kuwait. Targets included the U.S. Embassy, the French Embassy, the control tower at the airport, the country's main oil refinery, and a residential area for employees of the American Raytheon corporation. Five people died in addition to the suicide bomber.

The 1983 al Dawa terrorist attacks in Kuwait were believed to be motivated by President Ronald Reagan's support of Saddam Hussein. Members of al Dawa supported the Islamic Revolution in Iran. During the Iran-Iraq War, Iran funded al Dawa in Iraq to oppose Saddam Hussein.

March 16, 1984: Hezbollah kidnapped and later killed CIA Station Chief William Buckley. Eventually, 30 westerners would be kidnapped during the 10-year-long Lebanese hostage-taking crisis that ended in 1992.

September 20, 1984: A truck bomb in Aukar, northeast of Beirut, exploded outside the U.S. Embassy annex, killing 24 people. Hezbollah has claimed that this is a Mossad false flag operation.

December 3, 1984: Hezbollah's Imad Mughniyah planned the hijacking of Kuwait Airways Flight 221. Two American officials from the U.S. Agency for International Development were killed. On the sixth day, Iranian security forces stormed the plane and released the remaining hostages. Iran arrested the hijackers and then allowed them to leave the country.

---

[221] Jack Bernstein, *The Life of an American Jew in Racist, Marxist Israel* (Newport Beach, California: Noontide Press, 1984), 29.

June 14, 1985: Hezbollah hijacked TWA Flight 847 as the plane departed Athens for Rome and was forced to land in Beirut, Lebanon. Robert Dean Stethem, a U.S. Navy diver held hostage on the plane, was shot and his body dumped on the airport tarmac.

October 7, 1985: The Palestine Liberation Front and Libya collaborated to highjack the Achille Lauro. The ship was hijacked off the coast of Egypt by four gunmen demanding the release of Palestinian prisoners. Leon Klinghoffer, an American tourist, was killed by Magid al-Molgi.

December 27, 1985: Libya was claimed to have exploded bombs in the Rome and Vienna airports killing 20 people.

April 5, 1986: Libya was claimed to have sponsored the La Belle Discotheque bombing in Berlin, wounding over 190 people and killing an American soldier and a Turkish woman. On April 15, 1986, President Reagan ordered retaliatory air strikes on Tripoli and Benghazi, killing 37 people and injuring 93 others. Two days after the U.S. retaliatory operation, the Arab Revolutionary Cells, a pro-Libyan group of Palestinians, executed three men in retaliation.

December 21, 1988: Libyan intelligence officers were claimed to have destroyed Pan Am Flight 103 over Scotland, killing 270 people. Significant evidence contradicting accusations against Libya were revealed subsequently but remain generally unknown to most people.[222]

Al Qaeda Deception

The third and fourth books in the Vigilant Christian series comprehensively explain the al Qaeda deception. A brief version is that informed intelligence officers know that al Qaeda is the name for the database that the CIA maintained to monitor jihad fighters who were recruited by Pakistan, Saudi Arabia, Britain, and the U.S. during the 1980s to fight the Soviet Union in Afghanistan.[223] Muslim leaders know al Qaeda is not real. Imam Abdul Alim Musa was asked on January 5, 2010 if America played a role in the 9/11 terrorism.[224] He responded:

---

[222] William Blum, "The Bombing of PanAm Flight 103 Case Not Closed," 2001 and online at http://killinghope.org/bblum6/panam.htm.

[223] Robin Cook, "The Struggle Against Terrorism Cannot Be Won by Military Means," *The Guardian*, 8 July 2005 and online at www.guardian.co.uk/uk/2005/jul/08/july7.development.
Produced by Thomas Torelli, *Zero: An Investigation into 9/11* documentary was broadcast in 2009 to millions of people in Europe and Russia. The documentary is online at www.youtube.com/watch?v=O-YqET96OO0. The documentary features Gore Vidal and Nobel Prize winner Dario Fo. See 1 hour and 15 minutes and 30 seconds to 1 hour and 16 minutes and 15 seconds.

[224] Imam Abdul Alim Musa, "Memri TV Project Interview," *Press TV*, 5 January 2010 and available online at www.dailymotion.com/video/xbzaal_just-a-man-speaking-the-truth_news?ralg=meta2-

"Yes, definitely. This is our belief . . . Now, I'm saying this because I go to Pakistan, I've been to Afghanistan, I go to Iran. I have been knowing the people for thirty years that are involved in the Islamic movement . . . I talked with one of the main brothers here in the area, an Arabic-speaking brother. I said: "Do we know any al Qaeda?" He said: "I ain't never seen one." And I asked him, because we had been to conferences all over the world. Neither one of us know any al Qaeda, and we are supposed to be the most revolutionary Muslims in the United States. I have never seen them . . . And we look at the pattern of behavior. Who has done this before? Who broke every treaty with the Indians? It was the American government. The Israelis and the Americans."[225]

Serious 9/11 researchers also know that many former CIA officers have stepped forward to denounce the U.S. government 9/11 deception.[226] In late November 2007, former Italian President Francesco Cossiga made Italian headlines when he revealed that the 9/11 attacks were run by the global elite using the CIA and Mossad. Cossiga's explosive news was ignored by the U.S. media even though it was published in Italy's most respected newspaper, the *Corriere della Sera.*[227]

Our understanding of al Qaeda in the years leading up to 9/11 was shaped by New World Order agents. Almost everything that we have been told by the U.S. government about al Qaeda is false, including that it was led by Osama bin Laden. The alleged al Qaeda attacks, conducted by the Mossad before 9/11, served to set the stage for 9/11. Prior to 9/11 and for at least the decade after 9/11, al Qaeda never existed as an international organization with sleeper cells in the United States.[228]

The following alleged al Qaeda acts of terrorism were not by al Qaeda. The fact that an act of terrorism occurred is not questioned. The question is: How did al Qaeda, which did not exist, have anything to do with the attacks? The answer is that starting in 1992, in order to make al Qaeda a credible threat, acts of terrorism were falsely attributed. NWO agents created the illusion that al Qaeda was real. The false labeling continues even now as acts of terrorism around

---

only#from=playrelon-4.

[225] Ibid.

[226] In late 2004, intelligence officers sent a letter to Congress expressing their concerns about omissions and major flaws in the *9/11 Commission Report.* One of the signers, 27-year veteran of the CIA Raymond McGovern, said: "I think at simplest terms, there is a cover-up. The 9/11 Report is a joke." William Christison, a 28-year CIA veteran, said: "I think you almost have to look at the *9/11 Commission Report* as a joke and not a serious piece of analysis at all." More information on this subject is presented in *Vigilant Christian IV: 9/11 - The Secret War.*

[227] A translation of Francesco Cossiga's statement is online at www.rockcreekfreepress.com/CreekV2No1-Web.pdf.

[228] The video at www.teachpeace.com/informedintelligenceofficersknow.htm provides a concise explanation how informed intelligence officers knew the al Qaeda threat was manufactured.

the world are frequently immediately attributed to al Qaeda and the subsequent investigations repeatedly finding no al Qaeda involvement are routinely ignored.[229] Fabricated al Qaeda attacks are summarized below.

- December 29, 1992: The first attack attributed to al Qaeda took place when a bomb exploded at a hotel in Aden, Yemen, killing two Austrian tourists. The 1992 attacks were designed to be traced to the fictitious terrorist group, laying the groundwork for implicating them in the much more devastating September 11, 2001 attacks.
- February 26, 1993: The first alleged al Qaeda act of terror in the United States was the cyanide truck bombing in the garage of the World Trade Center. Osama bin Laden was used by the NWO as a bogeyman. However, the links to the Mossad began to surface with this operation when dual American-Israeli citizen and future Department of Homeland Security leader Michael Chertoff defended Dr. Magdy Elamir, who was accused of sending money to Osama bin Laden.[230] When victims' families sued, it was not bin Laden who was found responsible, but it was proven in court the U.S. government provided the bomb. FBI informant and Egyptian intelligence officer Emad Salam said he participated in a sting operation where the FBI was supposed to supply him with a harmless powder instead of real explosives.[231] Salam saved himself from being branded as an al Qaeda agent by secretly recording his conversations with his FBI handlers. As a result the jury assigned the majority of the bombing liability to the Port Authority because it put the public at risk by allowing the FBI to use a real bomb.[232] Nonetheless, the NWO-controlled media continues to falsely report Osama bin Laden made the bomb that was actually made by the FBI.

---

[229] Paul Harris and Ed Pilkington, "Underwear bomber was working for the CIA," *The Guardian*, 8 May 2012. This and other major news reporting crimes alleged to al Qaeda were not committed by al Qaeda often receive little notice by many people.

[230] Prior to 2001 Michael Chertoff served as a private attorney with highly unusual assignments that are now suspected to be helping the Mossad make the fictional al Qaeda organization appear real.
Ibid. *The Record* is also called *The Bergen Record* or *The Record of Hackensack* is a daily newspaper in Bergen County, New Jersey that reported on June 20, 2000 that Michael Chertoff defended Dr. Magdy Elamir who was sued by the State of New Jersey for $16.7 million dollars. The court proceedings revealed over $5.7 million went "to unknown parties . . . by means of wire transfers to bank accounts where the beneficial owner of the account is unknown." On the NBC *Dateline* August 2, 2002 program, Rep. Ben Gilman (R-NY) was quoted as saying that Dr. Magdy Elamir had "financial ties with Osama bin Laden for years." Elamir also had mysterious connections with the first World Trade Center bombing in 1993.

[231] Ralph Blumenthal, "Tapes Depict Proposal to Thwart Bomb Used in Trade Center Blast," *The New York Times*, 28 October 1993 and online at www.nytimes.com/1993/10/28/nyregion/tapes-depict-proposal-to-thwart-bomb-used-in-trade-center-blast.html.

[232] Anemona Hartocollis, "Port Authority Liable in 1993 Trade Center Attack," *The New York Times*, 30 April 2008 and online at www.nytimes.com/2008/04/30/nyregion/30bombing.html?ref=nyregion.

- October 3-4, 1993: Trained Islamic followers attacked U.S. soldiers in Somalia. The "Black Hawk Down" violence resulted in the deaths of 18 U.S. soldiers and of an estimated 500 local people caught in the crossfire. Al Qaeda was falsely blamed for the response of a Somali warlord resisting capture.

- April 19, 1995: The Alfred P. Murrah Federal Building in Oklahoma City was bombed. Timothy McVeigh was convicted and executed. False reports by *Fox News* reporter Jayna Davis claimed Osama bin Laden was working with McVeigh and was therefore responsible.[233]

- June 26, 1996: The al Qaeda organization was claimed to have exploded a gasoline tanker in Dhahran, Saudi Arabia, killing 19. From this point in time forward, any violent response by Saudi citizens to oppose the dictatorship was labeled an act of al Qaeda terrorism.

- August 7, 1998: Al Qaeda was claimed to have partially destroyed the U.S. embassy in Nairobi, Kenya. Evidence by Jamal al-Fadl was shown to be false.[234] Jamal al-Fadl would become the single most important first-hand witness to reveal the origin and organizational structure of al Qaeda. He subsequently confessed he provided false information about al Qaeda for money. More information about Jamal al-Fadl is provided in Chapter 10. The people responsible, suspected to be the Mossad, were never identified.

- October 12, 2000: Al Qaeda in Yemen was blamed by the U.S. government in the attack on the U.S.S. Cole that killed 17 sailors. U.S. investigators sent to find the al Qaeda connection were frustrated and returned home. The leader of the U.S. investigation, John O'Neal, complained about U.S. ambassador Barbara Bodine interfering with the investigation. O'Neal returned to the U.S. wondering if al Qaeda was responsible and Bodine blocked his reentry into Yemen. O'Neal left the FBI the following year, and on August 23, 2001, he started working as the head of security for the Twin Towers. He was killed on 9/11.[235]

- December 14, 2000: Continuing to set the stage for September 11, 2001, Ahmed Ressam is duped by foreign intelligence officers to enter the United States from Canada with a car full of explosives. Ressam was convicted in 2001 of planning to bomb the Los Angeles

---

[233] Jayna Davis, "The O'Reilly Factor: Was Osama Bin Laden Involved in the Oklahoma City Bombing?," *Fox News*, 20 March 2001 and online at www.jaynadavis.com /fox_bo1.html and the online video report is at www.youtube.com/watch?v= z9Q3L6x9PjU.

[234] "The Power of Nightmares: Baby It's Cold Outside," *BBC News*, 14 January 2005. The full documentary is online at http://polidics.com/cia/top-ranking-cia-operatives-admit-al-qaeda-is-a-complete-fabrication.html.

[235] John Patrick O'Neill (February 6, 1952-September 11, 2001) was the subject of the 2002 Frontline documentary, "The Man Who Knew."

International Airport on New Year's Eve. The London-based Algerian is serving a 37 year imprisonment in Colorado. Al Qaeda is blamed.[236]

September 11, 2001: Al Qaeda was blamed for three World Trade Center buildings collapsing into their footprints and an attack on the Pentagon. The public was told suicide hijackers were responsible, even though some of the reported suicide hijackers were alive after 9/11.[237] The smoking gun of 9/11, the Salomon Building, continues to create a huge problem for the New World Order. The 47-story Salomon Building was not hit by an aircraft and was destroyed in a classic controlled demolition.[238]

The above drawings show the Salomon Building which collapsed on 9/11.[239] From start to finish, the violence on 9/11 was designed as an occult religious ritual. The third and fourth books in this series, *Vigilant Christian III: The Occult Religion of the 9/11 Attackers* and *Vigilant Christian IV: 9/11—The Secret War* are recommended to learn more about this NWO orchestrated terrorism.

Don't be fooled into thinking that the current wars must be fought in order to defeat terrorism. By understanding the NWO's lead role in sponsoring terrorists, justice can be brought to criminals and injustices can begin to be addressed.

Sows Seeds to Create Terrorists

Using foreign militias and economic sanctions to fight terrorists may sound like a good idea, but in practice this can be especially disastrous because of blowback, unintended consequences,

[236] Craig Pyes, "Canada Adds Details on Algerians' Suspected Bomb Plot," *The New York Times*, 21 January 2000.

[237] Produced by Thomas Torelli, *Zero: An Investigation into 9/11* documentary, 2009. The documentary is online at www.youtube.com/watch?v=O-YqET96OO0.

[238] On September 11, 2001, three steel-framed buildings turned to dust. Prior to 9/11, there had never been a steel-framed building that collapsed or turned to dust from either an airplane crashing into it, or from a long-lasting fire.

[239] Teach Peace Foundation drawing showing the Salomon Building collapsing. A video showing the Salomon Building collapse is online at www.teachpeace.com/911salomonbuilding.htm. The Salomon Building is also known as World Trade Center 7 and Building 7.

and NWO influence. In August 2004, the Bush administration asked Congress to provide $500 million to fund militias around the world.[240] U.S. Deputy Secretary of Defense, Paul Dundes Wolfowitz, was a key architect of the policy to fund foreign fighters.[241] This NWO insider presented the reasoning for this new strategy in the war on terror.[242] His supporting argument was that local militias could win wars that conventional American armed forces could not.

Funding foreign militias is neither a new idea nor a good one. During Wolfowitz's presentation to Congress, he failed to mention that the United States armed and funded fighters in Afghanistan in the 1980s. The fighters were tracked with a CIA database called al Qaeda, which is the source for the al Qaeda name. Wolfowitz failed to mention that militias often have local enemies that they have been trying to eliminate for hundreds or even thousands of years. As a result, the local agenda of the U.S. officials, even ones with good intentions, quickly fall to the side as local militias pursue their own agendas.

In 1987 to 1988, while in the U.S. Army, I served on a rapid deployment team with special training to intervene in Central America. At that time, the School of the Americas in Fort Benning, Georgia was training Central and South Americans who fought for their governments and in local militias under the direction of the CIA. Since its inception the CIA has been a tool of the NWO.[243] In countries like Honduras, which was a staging ground for the war in Nicaragua, religious leaders and others who disagreed with the Nicaraguan government were routinely assassinated by graduates of the School of the Americas.

In Honduras, a military intelligence unit called Battalion 316 was secretly supported by the Reagan administration. On March 9, 1981, Ronald Reagan signed a presidential finding to "provide all forms of training, equipment, and related assistance to cooperating governments throughout Central America in order to counter foreign-sponsored subversion and terrorism." On December 1, 1981, he ordered the CIA to work primarily through "non-Americans" against the Sandinistas in Nicaragua and leftist insurgents in El Salvador. United States military aid to

---

[240] Editorial, "Washington Should Promote the Rule of Law, Not Lawless Militias," *The Daily Star in Beirut, Lebanon*, 13 August 2004.

[241] Richard Clarke, statement on National Public Radio, 22 September 2004.

[242] Scott Lindlaw, "Bush Suggests War on Terror Cannot Be Won," *Associated Press*, 30 August 2004. The funding of foreign fighters accompanied statements by President Bush and military leaders that the war on terrorism would not end.

[243] To help downplay the slaughter and torture of innocent people from graduates of the U.S. Army's School of the Americas, the program was renamed the Western Hemisphere Institute for Security Cooperation. The Fort Benning, Georgia program continues to produce graduates with deadly skills. These graduates are ultimately outside the U.S. system of justice and military command structure.

Honduras jumped from $3.9 million in 1980 to $77.4 million by 1984, three years after Battalion 316 started in 1981.[244]

The stories of torture by Battalion 316 are horrifyingly similar to what would occur 20 years later in Iraq when the U.S. military held prisoners at the Abu Ghraib prison. Prisoners in Honduras were hooded, with nooses tied around their necks and wires for shock treatment attached to their bodies. The previously-classified CIA manual used in Honduras provides the details confirming the testimony of Ines Consuelo Murillo Schwaderer[245] Her torture is significant because she was able to identify specific Honduran military officers who tortured people, and the identity of a participating CIA officer. She testified in 1987 before the Inter-American Court of Human Rights, which led to the verdict that the Honduran military systematically tortured people. Many of the techniques in the CIA's 1983 Human Resource Exploitation Training Manual remained unchanged, as illustrated by Abu Ghraib.[246]

A brief review of Abu Ghraib also helps illustrate the convergence of two very different interrogation standards. One is the NWO or CIA standard and the other is the U.S. military standard. The U.S. military standard prohibits torturing people. The fact that the U.S. military has taught soldiers not to torture people is something I know well because I taught soldiers how to interrogate battlefield prisoners when I served as an Army Intelligence Officer. By contrast, the CIA has for years practiced interrogation techniques that torture people. After September 11, 2001, the U.S. military started adopting the CIA interrogation standard, and the Abu Ghraib scandal has effectively branded both the CIA and U.S. military as organizations that torture people. The reason Americans never realized the CIA has tortured people for decades is that the CIA has done a better job than the U.S. military in keeping their operations unknown. In addition, with rare exceptions, CIA interrogation methods were exclusively performed by citizens of other countries.

In Abu Ghraib, Donald Rumsfeld authorized torture in a highly secret operation called Copper Green.[247] The torture was never directed at finding al Qaeda operatives but for darker

---

[244] Gary Cohn and Ginger Thompson, "Unearthed: Fatal Secrets," *The Baltimore Sun*, 11 June 1995. The article is online at www.baltimoresun.com/news/local/bal-negroponte1a%2C0%2C 3704648.story.

[245] James LeMoyne, "Testifying to Torture," *The New York Times Magazine*, 5 June 1988 and online at www.mayispeakfreely.org/nodev/index.php? gSec=doc&doc_id=98.
Gary Cohn and Ginger Thompson, "A Survivor Tells Her Story." (Third of a four-part series.), *The Baltimore Sun*, 15 June 1995 and online at www.baltimoresun.com/news/maryland/bal-negropnote3a,0,556680.story.

[246] The leaked classified torture training manual is online at www.teachpeace.com/CIAHumanResExploitA1-G11.pdf.

[247] Seymour M. Hersh, "The Gray Zone: How a Secret Pentagon Program Came to Abu Ghraib," *The New Yorker*, 15 May 2005.

reasons explained in *Vigilant Christian III: The Occult Religion of the 9/11 Attackers.* The NWO needs torture to be accepted by the general public in order to achieve one-world government. One way to do this is to use the widely supported brand of the U.S. military as the means of delivering torture. Another useful tool for creating support for torture includes television shows and movies where the hero routinely brutalizes people.

Prior to the 2003 invasion of Iraq, Donald Rumsfeld had authorized torture in the Guantanamo detention center to support the false notion that al Qaeda was a real organization. He ordered General William Boykin to develop a program to "migrate the coercive techniques" from Guantanamo to Iraq. The order to start torturing prisoners in the Abu Ghraib prison was significant because it was the first time Regular and National Guard Army personnel would officially participate in torture.

In addition to General Boykin, the Undersecretary of Defense for Intelligence, Stephen Cambone, was a key Copper Green architect. General Richard Myers and Major General Geoffrey Miller were also key Cooper Green leaders. In total, fewer than two hundred people were granted a need-to-know for Copper Green. This type of program is called a Special Access Program, or SAP. Alberto Gonzales, the Attorney General who replaced John Ashcroft in President Bush's second term, helped provide the legal guidance for the physical coercion and sexual humiliation of prisoners. Ashcroft may have been replaced because of a four part *Fox News* report by Carl Cameron on Israeli espionage in the U.S. After the *Fox News* report, Ashcroft's role in releasing Israeli spies arrested on September 11, 2001 became a very sensitive subject. The mysterious release of Mossad agents is explained in *Vigilant Christian IV: 9/11—The Secret War.*[248]

To assist President Bush's desire to use "coercive techniques," Gonzales issued a memo saying that the Geneva Convention, as well as treaties signed by the United States banning torture, do not apply to combatants or terrorists. Donald Rumsfeld reportedly ran with the legal approval from Gonzales with reported statements to U.S. operatives such as "the rules are, grab whom you must. Do what you want."[249] As a result of this memo written before he became attorney general, Gonzales had to pledge during his confirmation for attorney general that he would no longer support torture.[250]

To change from the U.S. military interrogation standard prohibiting torture to the CIA standard allowing torture, General Boykin ordered Major General Geoffrey Miller to Iraq. Not

[248] David J. Dionisi, *Vigilant Christian IV: 9/11 - The Secret War* (Bloomington, Indiana: Trafford, 2012).
[249] Seymour M. Hersh, "The Gray Zone: How a Secret Pentagon Program Came to Abu Ghraib," *The New Yorker*, 15 May 2005.
[250] Brian Dominick, "Opposition Builds Against 'Torture Apologist' Gonzales," *The New Standard*, 5 January 2005.

coincidentally, Miller was the leader of the detention and interrogation center at Guantanamo. In short order he transferred the Guantanamo methods to Abu Ghraib. The internal Army report on the abuse charges, written by Major General Antonio Taguba, quotes Miller as ordering that "detention operations must act as an enabler for interrogation."[251] Taguba testified that Miller influenced the commanders in Baghdad to place intelligence officers in charge of the prison who would oversee the torture program.

President Bush misled the country about his authorization of torture in his State of the Union Speech on January 27, 2005. He said, "Torture is never acceptable, nor do we hand over people to countries that do torture." Just a month later, on February 28, 2005, Michael Scheuer confirmed that he was one of the authors of a CIA program that performed what they called "extraordinary renditions."[252] He said that he and other members of the CIA knew that they were sending people to countries, such as Egypt and Syria, that employed torture in their prisons.[253] Under this secret rendering program, people can and have been seized by the U.S. around the world, without charges or evidence, for export to a country that practices torture. This also means that any person can be taken from the U.S. and sent to countries that practice torture.

A CBS investigation found that a jet used by the CIA for the extraordinary renditions program had made at least 600 flights to 40 countries since September 11, 2001. Uzbekistan was visited 10 times, Jordan 30 times, Afghanistan 19 times, Morocco 17 times, and Iraq 16 times.[254] In January 2002, State Department Counsel William Howard Taft IV objected to the presidential directive that Alberto Gonzales and John Yoo had helped create for the president while serving as Department of Justice officials. Jane Mayer reported that Taft urged Gonzales and Yoo to warn the president that he would "be seen as a war criminal by the rest of the world" if he did not abide by the Geneva Conventions. Gonzales and Yoo disagreed. Jane Mayer, in an article she wrote for *The New Yorker*, noted that she spoke with Yoo and he said Congress "can't prevent the president from ordering torture during a war. It's the core of the Commander-in-Chief function."[255]

---

[251] Seymour M. Hersh, "The Gray Zone: How a Secret Pentagon Program Came to Abu Ghraib," *The New Yorker*, 15 May 2005.

[252] Jane Mayer, "Outsourcing Torture," *The New Yorker*, February 14 and 21, 2005 80th Anniversary Issue, 106. Also Michael Scheuer responded to a question at the February 28, 2005 World Affairs Council meeting in San Francisco confirming his role as one of the authors of the extraordinary renditions program.

[253] Ibid. Mayer reported that the most common destinations for rendered suspects are Egypt, Morocco, Syria, and Jordan, each of which is known to use torture in interrogations. People have also been sent to Uzbekistan.

[254] Tim Reid, "Flight to Torture: Where Abuse Is Contracted Out," *Times Online*, 26 March 2005.

[255] Jane Mayer, "Outsourcing Torture," *The New Yorker*, February 14 and 21, 2005 80th Anniversary Issue. Mayer also writes that William Howard Taft IV, the State Department's counsel, sent a memo to Alberto

The CIA became concerned that ordinary and "good" soldiers would expose the torture. They feared a widespread investigation that would reveal that these practices have been part of U.S. covert operations for decades. Donald Rumsfeld, in an ongoing saga of poor judgment, did not anticipate the very predictable dynamic that would explode when ordinary soldiers observed obvious Law of Land Warfare violations.

A 15-month investigation by the Guardian and BBC Arabic revealed President Bush had General David Petraeus implement a $2 billion torture program.[256] U.S. Colonel James Coffman reported directly to Petraeus and partnered with U.S. civilian James Steele to oversee torture centers in Iraq. Steele is a veteran of multiple New World Order wars using the U.S. military, including Vietnam, El Salvador, and Nicaragua.[257] Steele's role included training U.S. funded special police commandos who operated the Special Action Program torture centers and death squads.[258]

Special Action Programs operations are covert, which is different from clandestine. Clandestine is an operation meant to be undetected. Covert means that the U.S. government denies its responsibility or—said more directly—lies. America's democracy would be stronger if Americans made all covert operations illegal and did not permit the government to lie. Under U.S. law, a covert action is subject to very strict legal requirements. Specifically, covert action must be authorized by the president with prompt notification of the senior leaders of both parties in the House and Senate. In other words, Copper Green, the top secret program for torture, had both President Bush's approval and limited congressional oversight.

Lawmakers have attempted to learn more about secret intelligence teams and SAPs.[259] The Pentagon sent its top intelligence official in January 2005 to address concerns from Congress that congressional oversight had been bypassed. Larry DiRita, chief spokesman for Defense Secretary

Gonzales and John Yoo in January 2002, warning them that their legal advice to the president—that he had almost unfettered latitude in his prosecution of the war on terror—was "untenable," "incorrect," and "confused."

[256] Narrated by Dearbhla Molly, "U.S. Special Forces veteran links General Petraeus to Torture in Iraq," *The Guardian*, 6 March 2013. The documentary is online at www.guardian.co.uk/world/video/2013/mar/06/james-steele-america-iraq-video.

[257] Ibid.

[258] Ibid. The documentary provides a ten year review of the 2003 Iraq invasion and includes first-hand accounts about death squads that murdered at one point in the conflict about 3,000 people each month.

[259] Robert Burns, "Pentagon Tries to Explain Spy Unit," *Associated Press*, 24 January 2005. Also, William Arkin, a former Army intelligence officer and author of the book, "*Code Names: Deciphering U.S. Military Plans, Programs and Operations in the 9-11 World*," noted that the DIA unit may be a permutation of a secret intelligence unit known as Gray Fox.

Donald Rumsfeld and Stephen A. Cambone, the Undersecretary of Defense for Intelligence, misled Congress.[260] They correctly acknowledged the existence of the Strategic Support Branch that is managed by the Defense Intelligence Agency's Human Intelligence Service. Lawmakers were told the Strategic Support teams were previously called Humint Augmentation teams.[261] Lawmakers were misled because covert Special Action Programs were used to bypass Congress. Senator Dianne Feinstein, a member of the Senate Intelligence Committee, sent a letter to Donald Rumsfeld seeking an explanation and requesting a hearing. She and other Democrats were effectively ignored, as the comments provided by DiRita and Cambone were deemed sufficient by Congress.

Another way to say this is that Strategic Support teams obtain their priority information requirements from the Defense Intelligence Agency through the military command structure. SAP teams obtained their priority information requirements directly from Donald Rumsfeld. By using the military for covert operations, Donald Rumsfeld had the military performing operations normally performed by the CIA. When the protocols for covert operations are not followed, specifically obtaining approval from Congress, these operations are illegal. Without congressional oversight or any other checks and balances on SAPs, Rumsfeld could have initiated a variety of secret missions, including the assassination of an American citizen, with little risk of anyone finding out.

Illegal intelligence operations, like Copper Green, extraordinary renditions, or Battalion 316 in Honduras, sow the seeds for the abuse of innocent civilians. The NWO plan calls for a world where the fear of being tortured helps them maintain their grip on absolute power. The Abu Ghraib-like torture in 1983 of Ines Consuelo Murillo Schwaderer, a 24-year-old Honduran woman, exemplifies what people are being desensitized to accept.[262]

In June 1988, Richard Stolz, the CIA Deputy Director of Operations, testified before the Senate Select Committee on Intelligence that a CIA officer had visited the jail where Battalion 316 held and tortured Murillo, whom they believed to be a subversive. *The Baltimore Sun* confirmed that Michael Dubbs, a CIA officer, was stationed in Honduras at the time. The CIA did not confirm or deny that Dubbs was the "Mr. Mike" who visited Murillo while she was imprisoned. The point in making the connection between a CIA officer and a prison that was visibly torturing people is that the CIA absolutely knew that people there were being tortured.

---

[260] Barton Gellma, "New Espionage Branch Delving Into CIA Territory," *Washington Post*, 23 January 2005, A01.

[261] Humint means human intelligence and is a standard military intelligence specialty.

[262] What is unique about the torture of Ines Consuello Murillo is that her story was reported by *The Baltimore Sun* and discussed by the 1988 Senate Select Committee on Intelligence.

This lends some credibility to claims by Hondurans that the torture was at the request of the CIA and performed by locals trained by the CIA.[263]

There are many sad stories in Central America like that of Ines Consuelo Murillo. The aid workers and missionaries I work with in Honduras vividly recall the numerous assassinations and disappearances during the 1980s. Much of the violence in Central America during the 1980s was related to the secret war the NWO influenced the U.S. to start with Nicaragua. A quick refresher on the specifics of the war with Nicaragua may be helpful.

In 1978, the United States attempted to install a new leader in Nicaragua. That country's former president, Anastasio Somoza, wrote a book exposing how the Carter administration and CIA had deposed him. The book, *Nicaragua Betrayed*, includes the transcripts of tape recordings Somoza made of visits by U.S. officials.[264] However, the planned transfer of power between Somoza and a new leader the United States supported became irrelevant after the Sandinista rebels seized the capital.

On July 19, 1979, when the Sandinistas marched victoriously into Managua, the United States did not have a rapid deployment military unit in place to help arrange for the NWO-backed candidates to seize power. Due to underestimation of the rebels, it was believed that all that was needed to turn the tide against the Sandinistas was for a U.S. battalion to be inserted within the first 48 hours of the take-over, which was to be followed by a much larger force, a division, over the next 72 hours.[265] However, it became clear after only a few weeks that a much bigger military intervention would have been necessary to set things straight. But with the memory of the Vietnam War still fresh, an invasion of this magnitude was unlikely to be supported by the American people. The military division I was assigned to, the 7th Light Infantry or "Light-Fighter" Division, was created in direct response to what happened in Nicaragua. As a result, in the mid-1980s, the United States could deploy a battalion anywhere in Central America within 48 hours and a division within a week. Under the pretext of the U.S. fighting communism, the NWO pursued its one-world-shaping foreign policies and undermined America's credibility in Central America.[266]

---

[263] Gary Cohn and Ginger Thompson, "Unearthed: Fatal Secrets," *The Baltimore Sun*, 11 June 1995.

[264] Anastasio Somoza, *Nicaragua Betrayed: As Told to Jack Cox by Former President Anatasio Somoza* (Western Islands, 1980).

[265] A battalion size ranges between 300 and 1,200 soldiers and often there are three to six battalions in a brigade with two or more brigades in a division.

[266] Christopher Dickey, *With the Contras: A Reporter in the Wilds of Nicaragua* (New York, NY: Simon & Schuster, A Touchstone Book, 1 May 1987).
The situation in the Middle East deteriorated because President Reagan's illegal weapon transfers to Iran increased the anger of Iraq toward the United States. Other Arab nations also viewed this event as another example of the United States selling weapons of death in the Middle East.

The secret war in Nicaragua became less secret with the passage of the first of three Boland Amendments in 1982. The Boland Amendments between 1982 and 1984 were written to limit U.S. assistance to fund war with Nicaragua. The NWO used the CIA to mine Nicaragua's harbors in 1984, which brought the conflict to the attention of many Americans. The Reagan administration imposed a full trade embargo against the Sandinistas in 1985. In 1986, the extent of the Reagan administration's secret war, exposed almost to its NWO orchestration, was shown when illegal weapon transfers to Iran were revealed to the world. President Reagan's backing and funding for the Contras, the U.S.-formed and supported militia fighting the Sandinistas, resulted in torture, deaths, and unnecessary suffering in Central America.

Economic Sanctions

More seeds for future acts of terror were planted following the first Gulf War when economic sanctions against Iraq were led by the NWO and enforced by the United Nations. The United Nations adopted sanctions in its 1945 charter as a tool to maintain global order. The NWO is a fan of sanctions that include denying essential health and welfare supplies because this type of sanction makes innocent people suffer. To fully understand this dimension I encourage you to read *Vigilant Christian III: The Occult Religion of the 9/11 Attackers*.[267]

Iraq's sanctions were unique in that they were comprehensive; every aspect of the country's imports and exports were controlled. If Americans had understood the NWO agenda and the economic sanctions against Iraq in the 1990s, then they would not have been surprised by the ever-expanding insurgency in Iraq. The ineffectiveness of sanctions is demonstrated with the continuing decades-old U.S. economic sanctions against Cuba. These sanctions, still in place because of hatred for Fidel Castro, have only strengthened this dictator's hold on Cuba.

So why do sanctions usually work *against* promoting justice, freedom and, ultimately, peace in the world? In the case of Iraq, the comprehensiveness of its sanctions meant that obtaining even basic necessities was obstructed. Since 1990, the United Nations estimated that at least 500,000 Iraqi children under the age of five have died because of economic sanctions.[268] In 1996,

---

[267] David J. Dionisi, *Vigilant Christian III: The Occult Religion of the 9/11 Attackers* (Bloomington, Indiana: Trafford, 2013).

[268] Dr. Joy Gordon, "Cool War: Economic Sanctions as Weapons of Mass Destruction," *Harper's Magazine*, November 2002. The United Nations Children's Fund (UNICEF) reported the half-million children and toddlers killed were a direct result of the sanctions. Richard Garfield, a critic of the 500,000 number, concluded the rise in the mortality rate was between a minimum of 100,000 and a more likely estimate of 227,000 excess deaths among young children from August 1991 through March 1998. He attributed one-quarter of the deaths to the Gulf war and the remaining excess deaths as primarily associated with economic sanctions. His work is available at www.cam.ac.uk/societies/casi/info/garfield/dr-garfield. html.

Madeleine Albright, then the U.S. Secretary of State, was asked on national television what she felt about the fact that half a million Iraqi children had died as a result of U.S. economic sanctions. She replied that it was "a very hard choice," but that all things considered "we think the price is worth it."[269] It is noteworthy that this number of fatalities far exceeds the death toll from the atomic bombs dropped on Japan.

Iraq's sanctions were enforced by the Security Council 661 Committee through the Office of Iraq Program. The Office of Iraq Program operated the Oil for Food Program. The Oil for Food Program was first offered in 1991 and went into effect in 1996. The Oil for Food Program was a $62 billion initiative that allowed Iraq to sell oil to pay for humanitarian goods. Documents surfacing as recently as late 2004 show that Iraq used the system to buy political support from the United Nations and other well-placed world officials. The scandal exposed United Nations corruption.[270]

According to Joy Gordon, a professor of philosophy at Fairfield University, beginning in 1991 the U.S. sanction strategy in Iraq was to withhold a single essential element, rendering the approved items useless. For example, Iraq was allowed to purchase a sewage-treatment plant but was blocked from buying the generator necessary to run it. As a result, tons of raw sewage poured into Iraq's rivers. The estimate is that 300,000 tons of sewage flowed into Iraq's rivers each day.[271] This policy was instituted as a means to seek revenge for Saddam Hussein's outspoken criticism of the U.S. and its support of Israel.

Hussein, oddly enough, actually benefited from economic sanctions while his people suffered. Even so, the people of Iraq focused their frustration and hatred on the U.S. and Britain for imposing the sanctions. A population distracted by survival needs, such as clean water, is in a very weak position to build opposition to a bad government. In addition, Saddam Hussein was able to reach out to the Arab world for sympathy because of the Iraqi suffering that was broadcast throughout the Middle East as a result of these sanctions. It is generally known in the Middle East that before the Gulf War, the majority of Iraq's population had access to clean water and

---

[269] Arundhati Roy, "The Algebra of Infinite Justice," *The Guardian*, 29 September 2001. Online at http://humanrightsonline.net/algebra.html.

[270] Economist Magazine, "Toward a More Relevant United Nations," *Economist.com*, 1 December 2004. Benon Sevan, the former head of the Oil for Food Program, allegedly took oil vouchers from Saddam. The U.N. Secretary-General's son, Kojo Annan, received payments as recently as 2004 from one of the firms that won an Oil for Food Program contract from the United Nations. Kojo Annan worked for the Swiss firm Cotecna inspecting goods at border crossings until December 1998. The fact that Kojo Annan continued to receive payments until 2004 surprised and embarrassed his father.

[271] Dr. Joy Gordon, "Cool War: Economic Sanctions as Weapons of Mass Destruction," *Harper's Magazine*, November 2002.

health care. Iraq's social programs in the two decades prior to the Gulf War brought health care to 93% of the country's people.[272]

In 1990 the UN established the 661 Committee to oversee sanctions. The committee is operated by consensus with every member country having veto power. The U.S. and Britain routinely vetoed proposals by France, China and Russia attempting to approve shipments to Iraq. Between the spring of 2000 and 2002, the holds on humanitarian goods tripled.[273] Goods blocked by the U.S. included dialysis equipment, water tankers, milk production equipment, and dental supplies. While some items, like water tankers, could arguably provide a means to move chemical weapons, the U.N. arms experts confirmed that water tankers lacked the necessary lining to be useful for military purposes and therefore were not on the restricted "1051 list." Delegates from Argentina, France and other nations pleaded with the U.S. representative to approve flour because it was an essential element of the Iraqi diet.[274] The U.S. representative, Eugene Young, argued that "there should be no hurry to move on this request." Britain agreed that the flour should be blocked and the request did not go forward.

On March 20, 2000, Anupama Rao Singh reported to the 661 Committee that 25% of the children in the south and central regions suffered from chronic malnutrition.[275] She also reported that child mortality rates had more than doubled since the sanctions were imposed in 1991. Many members of the Security Council have been critical of the U.S. decisions to block humanitarian contracts. In April 2000, the U.S. informed the 661 Committee that $275 million in humanitarian holds had been released. As of September 2001, nearly a billion dollars in medical-equipment contracts were on hold because the U.S. had not reviewed the contracts.[276] No matter how you look at this, people were dying unnecessarily.

Key items that the United States blocked included water pipes and the earth-moving equipment to install them. This is critical to note because the number one killer of children and adults in Iraq was the lack of clean water. Prior to 1990, at least 90 percent of all urban households had access to potable water.[277] After the start of the Gulf War, diseases that had been largely eradicated skyrocketed and dysentery killed thousands of children. The mortality rate in 1980 for children under five years old was 50 per thousand. In 2002, the mortality rate

---

[272] "The Health Conditions Of The Population In Iraq Since The Gulf Crisis," *World Health Organization*, March 1996. Available online at www.who.int/disasters/repo/5249.html.

[273] Dr. Joy Gordon, "Cool War: Economic Sanctions as Weapons of Mass Destruction," *Harper's Magazine*, November 2002.

[274] Ibid.

[275] Ibid.

[276] Ibid.

[277] "The Health Conditions Of The Population In Iraq Since The Gulf Crisis," *World Health Organization*, March 1996. Available online at www.who.int/disasters/repo/5249.html.

was 130 per thousand.[278] For the most part, the children died as a direct or indirect result of contaminated water.

In early 2001 the U.S. placed holds on $280 million in medical supplies.[279] Blocked medical supplies included treatments for hepatitis, tetanus, diphtheria, and infant vaccines. Even infant incubators and cardiac equipment were blocked. It was quite certain that preventing child vaccines from entering Iraq would result in the deaths of thousands of babies. To address the negative publicity and international public outcry against the ban on infant vaccines, a new program in 2001 was created called "smart sanctions." In June 2001, the U.S. announced that key contracts would be unblocked.[280] The net effect of this new program was to actually slow down the approval process. Staff for the new "smart sanctions" program needed to be hired and the new rules learned. The clock kept on ticking and children kept on dying.

A potentially dangerous item in water purification is chlorine, but chlorine was one of the few items approved to ship to Iraq. Every canister of chlorine for water purification was tracked through arrival, installation, and disposal. Why was the most threatening element allowed and humanitarian goods excluded? Does this have anything to do with who was selling the goods? Items sold by the United States or Security Council members had a much greater chance of being authorized and not blocked. The only countries that blocked goods were the U.S. and Britain.

The United States and Britain made the situation worse by introducing retroactive pricing. Iraq's basic ability to sell oil was undermined because the price of the oil was established by the 661 Committee. By delaying approval until after the shipment occurred, the U.S. and Britain could establish the price after the sale. The effect of retroactive pricing was to undermine the entire Oil for Food Program. Buyers did not want to take the risk of knowing the price only after delivery.

With over 500,000 children dead (and a far higher death toll if adults were counted), the average Iraqi on the street was extremely angry at the United States and Britain for the economic sanctions.[281] The massive preventable deaths and suffering were known by President George W. Bush. The Iraq invasion—sold to the U.S. citizens as an effort to liberate Iraq from Saddam Hussein—was not greeted with cheers from the average Iraqi citizen. The huge number of deaths incurred under years of sanctions is a key reason why projections that the invading American

---

[278] Dr. Joy Gordon, "Cool War: Economic Sanctions as Weapons of Mass Destruction," *Harper's Magazine*, November 2002.
[279] Ibid.
[280] Ibid.
[281] Hassan Ibrahim in the documentary *Control Room*, directed by Jehane Noujaim and released by Magnolia Pictures in 2004.

force would be welcomed by the Iraqi people were simply lies to help sell the war.[282] Senior military commanders who readily realized the resistance U.S. forces would face in Iraq and projected the realistic requirement of at least 500,000 U.S. ground forces were quickly forced into retirement to protect the lie.

Imagine the size of the resistance in Iraq today if there were just one insurgent fighter for every child under the age of five who died from economic sanctions. The reality is that every person murdered comes back to life in the form of multiple insurgents. The same is true for the adults who died from military operations. If the U.S. government revealed the classified estimate for insurgents in Iraq, the number would likely far exceed one million people.

TWA 800

To understand intentional NWO acts of terror it is helpful to acknowledge that sometimes American citizens are killed in military accidents. When this happens the government will usually seek to bury the truth so that the public can continue to be brainwashed into supporting everything connected to the military. Serious inquiries into military accidents as illustrated by the 1996 TWA Flight 800 disaster are also denied because inquiries have the potential to disclose classified technology or frustrate an upcoming false flag operation.

In the TWA 800 disaster, the public was told by the National Transportation Safety Board (NTSB) that the crash is an unsolved mystery. Soon after the crash, an animated video was produced by the CIA using professional narration and dramatic music in an effort to dismiss over 96 eyewitness accounts that a missile originating from the surface of the water hit TWA 800.[283] People should have at least found it suspicious that the CIA was involved in trying to explain a domestic air accident.

The NWO-controlled major media corporations replayed the CIA disinformation and marginalized or ignored the eyewitnesses who provided first-hand accounts from beaches, boats, and aircraft. According to the CIA and NTSB, an airplane defect may have led to an explosion.

---

[282] U.S. Secretary of Defense Donald H. Rumsfeld, "Rumsfeld gave a briefing on situation in Iraq," 11 April 2003. He said, "And I think it's increasingly clear that most welcome coalition forces and see them not as invaders or occupiers, but as liberators. The images of thousands of cheering Iraqis, celebrating and embracing coalition forces, are being broadcast throughout the world, including the Arab world."

[283] The CIA acknowledged spending $40,000 to produce the TWA 800 disaster video. The video is online at www.youtube.com/watch?v= eskcDKI5WGc. The NWO does work with governments to break and block revealing information. If the link for this animation or any other link in this book stops working, enter the key words in a search engine to find alternative supporting information. In addition to the 96 eyewitnesses, another 659 eyewitnesses reported seeing a missile or flare of light in the sky (see http://flight800.org/radar9.htm).

The official deception campaign focused the public attention on a fuel tank explosion from a spark that ignited gas fumes. Since the spark was never real, no spark source was identified, and for over a decade Boeing was not required to take measures to eliminate the fictional spark source. This obvious sign that the spark was never real would not fade away, and awareness of the TWA 800 shoot down increased. To help the cover-up appear credible, in 2008, Transportation Secretary Mary Peters announced that a device would be added to prevent airplane fuel tanks from exploding.[284]

The CIA and NTSB told a lie and helped sell it with a video. Today, many people believe the CIA explanation that the steep climb of the main wreckage immediately after forward fuselage separation accounted for what over 755 eyewitnesses described as a "streak of light" or "missile" rising upward. There are many problems with the CIA and NTSB explanation, beginning with the fact that it is inconsistent with the actual flight path of TWA 800 provided by radar.[285]

What really happened on July 17, 1996 is that the final test of a U.S. Navy surface-to-air missile went terribly wrong. TWA 800 departed about an hour later than scheduled and flew into the test area at exactly the worst time. The Long Island airspace was selected for this final military test due to the heavy air and ground traffic. The high level of traffic was needed to stress test the system, especially because an earlier version of the AEGIS system was involved in the 1988 shoot down of Iran Air Flight 655 by the USS Vincennes which killed 290 people.[286]

In the July 17, 1996 test, the Navy's AEGIS radar and target management system malfunctioned resulting in the missile losing the target lock. TWA 800 was then acquired as the new target and destroyed.[287] A Navy missile with a dummy warhead was used because the missile guidance system was being tested. The dummy warhead also makes analyzing the actual missile strike more accurate. The missile that entered the TWA 800 fuselage several feet below the passenger

---

[284] Joan Lowy, "Jet fuel-tank protection ordered," *The Associated Press*, 16 July 2008 and online at www.seattlepi.com/business/article/Jet-fuel-tank-protection-ordered-1279529.php.

[285] "The NTSB and CIA Simulations of the Official Crash Sequence of TWA Flight 800," Flight 800 Independent Researchers Organization, 2000 and online at http://flight800.org/radar9.htm.

[286] Iran Air Flight 655 was shot down on July 3, 1988. The U.S. never apologized to Iran for the mass murders. John Barry and Roger Charles in the article "Sea of Lies," published by *Newsweek* on July 13, 1992, claimed that USS Vincennes commander Captain Will Rogers III was overeager for combat, that he started the fight with Iranian gunboats, and he illegally entered Iranian territorial waters. In 1990, Rogers was awarded the Legion of Merit by President George H. W. Bush "for exceptionally meritorious conduct" from April 1987 to May 1989.

[287] The AEGIS Combat System name has significance in Greek, Egyptian, Nubian and Norse mythology. In Greek mythology the name can mean a protective shield which is what the AEGIS is supposed to deliver for the U.S. Navy.

cabin made a clean exit hole. The destructive power of the missile resulted in a catastrophic structural failure of TWA 800 including the fuel tank explosion.[288]

Fortunately, the government cover-up of TWA 800 is documented in *The Downing of TWA Flight 800* by James Sanders.[289] He wrote: "There was no instant explosion, as the dummy warhead missile sliced through the huge plane as a sheet of paper, depositing a trail of reddish-orange residue in its wake. It roared through the fuselage and exited through the left side of the plane, just forward of the left wing, where it left a hole . . ."[290] Sanders' book shows a photograph of reddish-orange missile fuel stains on recovered seats. The fact that the Navy was conducting tests in the area that night was too hard to conceal, and the Navy tests are confirmed by government documents. For people wishing to learn more about this military accident that killed 230 people, Sanders' book is recommended.[291]

Operation Gladio and Operation Northwoods

Operation Gladio and Operation Northwoods are very different from the TWA 800 accident. Both classified programs sought to kill civilians and blame terrorists. While proof of Operation Gladio in the U.S. and confirmation by multiple European governments has been established for decades, most people have little or no knowledge of it.[292]

My research has never found an instance where the U.S. military knowingly participated in an Operation Gladio-like event to kill U.S. civilians without the operation being an NWO operation. Yes, previously classified programs that have been declassified prove that top government officials can plan and do kill U.S. citizens. The point is that direct NWO involvement is visible every time American citizens are killed intentionally. Understanding why Operation Northwoods remained on paper and was eventually shared with the public is important.

---

[288] The finding of the Flight 800 Independent Researchers Organization and online at http://flight800.org/probable_cause.htm. The group concluded a missile hit TWA 800 but did not know the warhead was a dummy warhead. The group finding is: "The combined destructive power of the missile and the fuel tank explosion caused catastrophic structural failure of TWA Flight 800."

[289] James Sanders, *The Downing of TWA Flight 800: The Shocking Truth Behind the Worst Airplane Disaster in U.S. History* (New York, New York: Zebra Books, 1997). It is noteworthy that Sanders was unaware that in 1988 even more people were killed by the USS Vincennes using the AEGIS system. A total of 230 people died on TWA 800 and 290 people died on Iran Air 655. Sanders' book title also ignores the American Airlines Flight 191 Chicago disaster killing 273 people in 1979.

[290] Ibid., 23-24.

[291] Ibid.

[292] Daniele Ganser, *NATO's Secret Armies: Operation Gladio and Terrorism in Western Europe* (New York, New York: Frank Cass, 2005). On a related note, Ganser's book was written to help justify the "stay behind army" concept and it is the parts where he confirms civilian terrorism naming the specific people doing the killing that is most valuable.

Operation Northwoods was proposed by the Joint Chiefs of Staff to Secretary of Defense Robert McNamara on March 13, 1962.[293] This plan to kill U.S. civilians was never implemented. The proposal for "massive casualty producing events" by terrorists was to create a false justification for a U.S. invasion of Cuba. The plan presented options of pretending to or actually attacking a passenger plane, a refugee boat, a U.S. warship, and other acts of terrorism. The following image is a page from the once Top Secret plan to kill U.S. citizens.[294]

~~TOP SECRET SPECIAL HANDLING NOFORN~~

THE JOINT CHIEFS OF STAFF
WASHINGTON 25, D.C.

13 March 1962

MEMORANDUM FOR THE SECRETARY OF DEFENSE

Subject: Justification for US Military Intervention in Cuba (TS)

1. The Joint Chiefs of Staff have considered the attached Memorandum for the Chief of Operations, Cuba Project, which responds to a request of that office for brief but precise description of pretexts which would provide justification for US military intervention in Cuba.

2. The Joint Chiefs of Staff recommend that the proposed memorandum be forwarded as a preliminary submission suitable for planning purposes. It is assumed that there will be similar submissions from other agencies and that these inputs will be used as a basis for developing a time-phased plan. Individual projects can then be considered on a case-by-case basis.

3. Further, it is assumed that a single agency will be given the primary responsibility for developing military and para-military aspects of the basic plan. It is recommended that this responsibility for both overt and covert military operations be assigned the Joint Chiefs of Staff.

For the Joint Chiefs of Staff:

L. L. LEMNITZER
Chairman
Joint Chiefs of Staff

SYSTEMATICALLY REVIEWED
BY JCS ON _____
CLASSIFICATION CONTINUED

1 Enclosure
Memo for Chief of Operations, Cuba Project   EXCLUDED FROM GDS

EXCLUDED FROM AUTOMATIC
REGRADING; DOD DIR 5200.10
DOES NOT APPLY

~~TOP SECRET SPECIAL HANDLING NOFORN~~

---

[293] The Operation Northwoods document is available at www.teachpeace.com/OperationNorthwoods.pdf.
[294] Ibid.

Operation Northwoods was inspired by the NWO's success with the "Remember the Maine, to Hell with Spain!" event.[295] The February 15, 1898 operation was successfully used by the NWO as the excuse to start the Spanish-American War. A monument in Havana, Cuba is dedicated to the 266 sailors who are "the victims of the Maine and were sacrificed for imperialist greed in its fervor to seize control of the island of Cuba."[296]

Operations Northwoods was created by people directly linked to the NWO, but the plan died on the drawing board because President John F. Kennedy refused to approve it. The bombshell evidence that the U.S. Chiefs of Staff had recommended killing U.S. citizens was declassified just three months before the September 11, 2001 attacks. By declassifying the document, which had previously been kept classified past its original release date, the NWO avoided having this bombshell evidence announced as part of the post 9/11 inquiry.[297]

Unlike Operation Northwoods, Operation Gladio was implemented with over 200 acts of terrorism and is an example of the NWO using the CIA to kill people. Gladio is one of the most historically confirmed examples of false-flag terrorism. Gladio originally referred to the Italian branch of the program but is often used as the name for the entire program. Most of the victims, including children, were European, and this NWO program was designed to create fear and eliminate people who were frustrating the attainment of a one-world government. The documentation, confessions, and convictions made NWO attempts to conceal Gladio impossible.

An example of an Operation Gladio false flag mass murder is the Piazza Fontana Bombing on December 12, 1969. A bomb exploded at the headquarters of Banca Nazionale dell'Agricoltura

---

[295] James Bamford, "Operation Northwoods plan," National Security Archives, 30 April 2001. Available at www.gwu.edu/~nsarchiv/news/20010430/doc1.pdf.

[296] The Cuba Maine monument inscription is, "A las victimsas de el Maine que fueron sacrificadas por la voracidad imperialista en su afan de ap derarse de la isla de Cuba. 15 de Febrero de 1898 - 15 de Febrero de 1961."
On January 18th, 1961 NWO agents were able to modify the original monument inaugurated on March 8, 1925. An eagle and the busts of William McKinley, Theodore Roosevelt and Leonardo Wood were removed. McKinley was the president who declared war with Spain, Wood was the first administrator of the island and Roosevelt was the NWO representative who both behind the scenes and with his "Rough Riders" led the charge for war.
Lucia Newman, Cynthia Tornquist and *Reuters*, "Remembering the Maine," *CNN*, 15 February 1998 and online at www.cnn.com/US/9802/15/remember. the.maine/.

[297] Neil Doyle, *Terror Tracker* (Edinburgh, London: Mainstream Publishing, 2004), 100. When Operation Northwoods was finally made public, the NWO insiders in the U.S. government knew that America was in the countdown phase for the 9/11 attacks. For more information to reinforce what was known by the U.S. government prior to 9/11, read Paul Thompson's, *The Terror Timeline*, published by HarperCollins Publishers Inc. in 2004.

in Milan, Italy. The CIA terrorism killed 17 people and wounded 88.[298] Another example of Operation Gladio terrorism is the 1980 Bologna massacre. On August 2, 1980 the Bologna, Italy Central Station bombing killed 85 people and wounded more than 200. Seven children under the age of 15 were murdered. Several people were convicted of crimes, including Operation Gladio key insider Licio Gelli and the leader of the CIA-connected Propaganda Due Masonic lodge.[299]

The origins of Gladio are anti-Communist organizations dating back to 1948. These organization were over time increasingly focused to serve the NWO. By the 1960s the CIA was engaged in widespread civilian terrorism. Funding for Operation Gladio came from illegal CIA drug sales and gold the U.S. secretly acquired in the Philippines which allowed the CIA to bypass congressional oversight.[300] The gold from Japan's Operation Golden Lily hidden in the Philippines during World War II funded multiple NWO false-flag operations in the 1950s and 1960s. The Golden Lily program is explained in *Vigilant Christian IV: 9/11—The Secret War*.

Italian Judge Felice Casson discovered Operation Gladio in the course of his investigations into right-wing terrorism. He reported the existence of the secret operation, and on October 24, 1990, Italian Prime Minister Giulio Andreotti reported Operation Gladio had committed acts of terror in multiple countries. Casson helped identify 622 Gladio members, including two people who served as prime minister and president. The CIA with help from British intelligence agents and NWO infiltrators in NATO operated in Italy, France, Spain, Portugal, Germany, Belgium, the Netherlands, Luxemburg, Denmark, Norway, Sweden, Finland, Switzerland, Austria, Greece, and Turkey. The last known meeting of Operation Gladio leaders was in October 1990 in Brussels.

As a direct result, parliamentary inquiries were launched in Belgium, Italy, and Switzerland. On November 22, 1990, the European Parliament passed a resolution for a full investigation of the Gladio crimes. NWO insiders have successfully stalled investigations, but the disclosed evidence of the illegal operations is extensive. One of the more comprehensive studies of Operation Gladio was completed by Swiss historian Daniele Ganser. In 2005 he published *NATO's Secret Armies: Operation Gladio and Terrorism in Western Europe*.[301] Professor Jussi Hanhimaki observed, "Dr. Ganser's findings raise fundamental questions about the nature of the cold war and the role of intelligence organizations in democratic societies."[302]

---

[298] Also on December 12, 1969 the CIA detonated three more bombs in Rome and Milan plus one bomb was found undetonated.

[299] In 1981 the public learned that Licio Gelli was the Venerable Master of Propaganda Due or P2.

[300] An excellent source to learn more about CIA illegal drug operations is *The Politics of Heroin: CIA Complicity in the Global Drug Trade* by Alfred W. McCoy. The 1972 edition was published by Harper and Row.

[301] Daniele Ganser, *NATO's Secret Armies: Operation Gladio and Terrorism in Western Europe* (New York, New York: Frank Cass, 2005).

[302] Ibid., back cover.

General Gerardo Serravalle, who commanded the Italian Gladio from 1971 to 1974, revealed the NWO leadership and lesser roles played by the CIA and NATO officials. He wrote: "in the 1970s the members of the CPC (Coordination and Planning Committee) were the officers responsible for the secret structures of Great Britain, France, Germany, Belgium, Luxemburg, the Netherlands and Italy. These representatives of the secret structures met every year in one of the capitals . . . At the stay-behind meetings representatives of the CIA were always present. They had no voting rights and were from the CIA headquarters of the capital in which the meeting took place . . . members of the US Forces Europe Command were present, also without voting rights."[303] Serravalle clearly distinguishes the difference between the CIA and the NWO elite. The CIA literally served the NWO, and only the NWO people had voting rights.

COINTELPRO

NWO programs are often linked with government secret programs to discredit people who are threatening the NWO or frustrating accomplishment of an objective. An example is the U.S. Federal Bureau of Investigation (FBI) program against peaceful U.S. citizens called COINTELPRO, which is an acronym for Counter Intelligence Program. In this 1956 to 1971 program, FBI agents made up crimes to blackmail, character-assassinate, and convict people by planting false information, forging evidence, and attributing acts of violence. Operation CONINTELPRO included wrongful imprisonment, extralegal violence, and assassination.

In 1976 the investigation by the Select Committee to Study Governmental Operations with Respect to Intelligence Activities of the United States Senate or "Church Committee" concluded COINTELPRO exceeded statutory limits on FBI activity.[304] FBI Director J. Edgar Hoover had issued COINTELPRO directives ordering FBI agents to "expose, disrupt, misdirect, discredit, or otherwise neutralize" the activities of peaceful people including Dr. Martin Luther King, Jr.

The COINTELPRO program shines a light on the domestic assassinations. The assassination of Dr. Martin Luther King, Jr. was proven to be an act of state by William F. Pepper's thirty year investigation and his successful 1999 civil action suit on behalf of the King family.[305] Pepper's work, exonerating James Earl Ray and fully supported by Coretta Scott King, identifies the key conspirators by name.[306] The NWO, using many of the same fronts as were used to assassinate

[303] Gerardo Serravalle, *Gladio* (Rome, Italy: Edizione Associate, 1991), 78-79.
[304] The Church Committee Reports were published in 1975 and 1976. The reports are provided online by the Assassination Archives and Research Center at www.aarclibrary.org/publib/contents/church/contents_church_reports.htm. The name of the committee comes from its chairman, Senator Frank Church (July 25, 1924-April 7, 1984) of Idaho.
[305] William F. Pepper, *An Act of State: The Execution of Martin Luther King* (New York, New York: Verso, 2003).
[306] Ibid., 62-77, 92-96, and 204-211.

John F. Kennedy, succeeded in shutting down a social change movement by executing its leader. Today, a more aggressive version of COINTELPRO is believed to be underway by the classified version of the Patriot Act revealed by Senator Ron Wyden.[307]

2002 Venezuela Failed Coup

In 2002, President George W. Bush instructed the CIA to overthrow the democratically elected government of President Hugo Chavez. Leaked classified documents show that the U.S. government orchestrated the military coup. Bush press secretary Ari Fleischer attempted to convince the media that the Bush administration was not involved in the turmoil.[308]

President Bush's Venezuela fiasco did not even rate as an issue in the 2004 U.S. presidential election. On March 5, 2005, President Hugo Chavez presented evidence that the United States was trying to assassinate him.[309] Chavez, along with other leaders in South America opposing the NWO, did develop and die from cancer.[310] Chavez said: "Would it be so strange that they've invented the technology to spread cancer and we won't know about it for 50 years?"[311] Chavez was 58 years old when he died on March 5, 2013 from cancer.[312]

---

[307] Spencer Ackerman, "There's a Secret Patriot Act, Senator Says," *Wired Magazine*, 25 May 2011, online at www.wired.com/dangerroom/2011/05/secret-patriot-act/. Ronald Lee "Ron" Wyden is the senior United States Senator for Oregon, serving since 1996, and a member of the Democratic Party.

[308] Mark Weisbrot, "CIA Documents Cast New Light on Washington's Role in Venezuela," *Center for Economic and Policy Research*, 10 December 2004.
On 12 April 2004, White House spokesman Ari Fleischer gave the coup leaders' version of events - that violence at the demonstrations had led to Chavez' "resignation," and that the government was responsible for the violence. "The results of these events are now that President Chavez has resigned the presidency. Before resigning, he dismissed the vice president and the cabinet, and a transitional civilian government has been installed." The documents are available at www.venezuelafoia.info/CIA/CIA-index.htm and show that the White House knew that there were detailed plans for a coup in April.

[309] "Chavez: Evidence proves Washington murder plot, U.S. denies," *ChinaDaily.com*, 6 March 2005. "We have enough evidence . . . if anything happens to me, the person responsible will be the president of the United States."

[310] Tom Phillips, "Hugo Chavez hints at US cancer plot," *The Guardian*, 29 December 2011 and online at www.guardian.co.uk/world/2011/dec/29/hugo-chavez-us-cancer-plot.
Chavez found it odd very beneficial to the forces seeking to privatize key resources in South America that many of the leaders opposing the NWO in the region, including Argentina's president Cristina Fernández de Kirchner, had been diagnosed with cancer.

[311] Ibid.

[312] Caitlin Dewey, "Maduro promises to investigate Chavez 'assassination'," *The Washington Post*, 5 March 2013. Venezuela's new President Nicolas Maduro promised on state television that a "scientific commission" would investigate Chavez's death and the possibility that his "historical enemies" had induced his cancer.

2011 Libya War

On March 19, 2011, the U.S., France, and Britain started bombing Libya. The unconstitutional bombing followed a United Nations resolution authorizing this violence.[313] The United Nations resolution violated the U.S. Constitution as the President did not consult Congress.[314] The public was told by all the major corporate media services that the violence would only be used to enforce a no-fly zone to prevent civilians from being attacked by Libya's fighter jets. Arab League Secretary-General Amr Moussa said, "What is happening in Libya differs from the aim of imposing a no-fly zone . . . And what we want is the protection of civilians and not the shelling of more civilians."[315]

The major news services did not report to U.S. viewers that Libyan leader Muammar Qaddafi's was in the progress of introducing an alternative monetary system based on gold to replace the U.S. dollar system.[316] On March 27, 2011, just 8 days after the war with Libya started, the new oil contracts with the rebel government were disclosed. On March 29, 2011 the NWO-created rebel government established a central bank that rejected Libya's alternative monetary system. Even before the UN authorization to bomb Libya was passed, the NWO used Egypt to deliver weapons to the Libyan NWO-organized rebels.[317]

If a dictator in Bahrain, Yemen, Saudi Arabia or any other oil rich country in the Middle East announces they are killing civilians, at most words of condemnation will flow from the NWO-controlled United Nations. If any country in the world tries to introduce an alternative monetary system, the NWO will arrange for the bombs to start falling.

The 2011 NWO war with Libya will hurt nuclear non-proliferation efforts. This is because the international community promised in 2003 not to attack Libya if it terminated its nuclear bomb program. In 2009, Qaddafi's threat of using nuclear bombs ended with his compliance and delivery to the U.S. of casks of highly enriched uranium.

---

[313] "UN Security Council Approves No-Fly Zone Over Libya," *Voice of America News*, 17 March 2011 online at www.voanews.com/english/news/africa/UN-Security-Council-Approves-No-Fly-Zone-Over-Libya-118204324.html.

[314] Ewan MacAskill, "Libyan bombing 'unconstitutional', Republicans warn Obama," 22 March 2011, online at www.guardian.co.uk/world/2011 /mar/22/libyan-conflict-unconstitutional-obama-warned.

[315] "Arab League leader opposes Libya attack," *UPI World News*, 20 March 2011 online at www.upi.com/Top_News/World-News/2011/03/20/Arab-League-leader-opposes-Libya-attack/UPI-17551300655960/.

[316] "Motivation for allies may be black gold, not humanitarian mission," *RT News*, May 2011, online at www.youtube.com/watch?v= TB6MJnzhMYY.

[317] "Libya crisis: Egypt shipping arms across border to aid rebels," *The Telegraph*, 18 March 2011, online at www.telegraph.co.uk/news/worldnews/africaandindianocean/libya/8390521/Libya-crisis-Egypt-shipping-arms-across-border-to-aid-rebels.html.

Iran War?

The NWO seeks to finish military actions in Syria to prepare for a much larger war with Iran. War with Iran would be bad for U.S. national security and create unnecessary tremendous human suffering. The "March to War" timeline documents how the very good relationship with Iran in the early 1950s deteriorated by design to the point where war could start at any moment.[318] The truth is Iran has not initiated an attack against another country in more than 200 years. The claims the U.S. must attack Iran to prevent another 9/11 are based on the lie that Muslims are responsible for 9/11.

The public is presented with predictive programming messages to produce the idea that going to war with Iran is both necessary and the only option. Articles with titles such as "Israel, U.S. Discuss Triggers for Military Strike on Iran"[319] and "U.S. Navy: We Will Not Allow Iran to Stop the Flow of Oil"[320] are published almost on a daily basis. Assassinations and false flag attacks by Israel in Iran have already occurred.[321] Mark Perry disclosed that "a series of CIA memos describes how Israeli Mossad agents posed as American spies to recruit members of the terrorist organization Jundallah to fight their covert war against Iran."[322] Laura Rozen expanded on Perry's exposure of Israel's false flag operations noting "Israeli intelligence officers posed as CIA spies to recruit members of a Sunni Baluch militant group which has carried out numerous attacks against Iranian security forces, civilians, journalists."[323]

A U.S. attack on Iraq and Iran was proposed in 1997 by the Project For A New American Century (PNAC), a neo-conservative group. The PNAC document, written by Cheney, Rumsfeld and other neo-conservatives, called for pre-emptive attacks so that the U.S. would remain the dominant military and economic arm for the NWO in the 21st century. The cornerstone of this strategy focused on keeping a rising China and a united Europe subordinate by putting U.S. weapons in space and managing access to strategic resources in Central Asia and the Middle East. To achieve military and economic dominance, neo-conservatives, often not realizing they

---

[318] The "March to War" timeline is online at www.teachpeace.com/Iran2012Timeline.pdf

[319] Eli Lake, "U.S., Israel Discuss Triggers for Bombing Iran's Nuclear Infrastructure," *The Daily Beast*, 28 December 2011 and online at www.thedailybeast.com/articles/2011/12/28/u-s-israel-discuss-triggers-for-bombing-iran-s-nuclear-infrastructure.html.

[320] Reuters, "U.S. Navy: We will not allow Iran to stop flow of oil," *Haaretz*, 28 December 2011 and online at www.haaretz.com/news/middle-east/u-s-navy-we-will-not-allow-iran-to-stop-flow-of-oil-1.404172.

[321] Mark Perry, "False Flag," *Foreign Policy*, 13 January 2012 and online at www.foreignpolicy.com/articles/2012/01/13/false_flag?page=full.

[322] Ibid.

[323] Laura Rozen, "Israel used "false flag" operation to recruit anti-Iran militants, report alleges," *Yahoo! The Envoy*, 14 January 2012.

served the NWO, endorsed invading Iraq and repeatedly sought and continue to seek to initiate war with Iran.

Soon after President Bush was inaugurated, the secret 2001 Energy Task Force was organized with Vice President Dick Cheney collaborating with officials from Exxon Mobil, Conoco (before its merger with Phillips), Shell Oil, and BP America. Cheney called this meeting to discuss peak oil and how the U.S. military would secure oil resources in Iraq and Iran. Cheney fought to prevent the American people from learning the details of the meeting. In the spring of 2002, the U.S. Department of Energy released to Natural Resources Defense Council over 13,000 pages relating to the previously secret Bush administration's energy task force. [324] While some meeting information is still secret, we now know that NWO infiltrators in the U.S. government coordinated with energy industry leaders to invade oil-rich countries.

To save today's teenagers from becoming tomorrow's casualties in another NWO orchestrated U.S. fought and funded illegal war, we must be voices for peace. If we are silent, the NWO will orchestrate war with Iran and World War III. We should also remember the standard false flag formula, as epitomized by September 11, 2001, is to scare people into supporting wars and make people who oppose violence appear as disloyal. The truth is that opposition to attacking Iran is often coming from former soldiers, myself included, who care about people.

The Lesson of Custer's Last Stand

Time has a way of helping people understand that terrorists and heroes can be the same people, depending on which side of a war you are supporting. In 1876, after Custer's famous "last stand," Americans clearly saw the Lakota chief Sitting Bull as a person committing acts of terror. Officers in the U.S. Army's 2nd Infantry Division wear a patch of an Indian on their uniforms in memory of the "successful" Indian wars. Many officers, including myself, have been given tomahawks upon joining this military unit. The holder of the tomahawk is the "victor," as this was the weapon used by native Americans. Few members of the military are offended or even take a moment to realize that the tomahawk is really a symbol of the genocide of thousands of children, women, and men. An analogy would be for Rwanda's soldiers to be given machetes in the next century to acknowledge the success of the Rwanda genocide.

Many Americans now see Sitting Bull as a hero and General Custer as a destroyer of families. As Americans have come to understand that the genocide of Native Americans was unjust, the

---

[324] The Natural Resources Defense Council provides many of the Cheney Energy Task Force records online at www.nrdc.org/air/energy/taskforce/tfinx.asp.

perception of Sitting Bull and Native Americans in general has changed.[325] As illustrated by Sitting Bull and General Custer, there is clarity when we step back from the economic drivers of war and the calls to hate other people, which can brand anyone a terrorist.

Defining Christians as Terrorists

U.S. led wars and the Abu Ghraib prisoner abuse scandal created hate for both Americans and Christians around the world.[326] Many other examples of hate messages from NWO-initiated operations appear routinely. Americans will increasingly notice the NWO is devaluing the U.S. dollar to fuel global anger at all things American. Less noticeable is that the NWO is working to fool U.S. citizens to believe Christians are terrorists.

Changing public perception to see Christians as violent and mass murders will take the NWO at least a few decades and likely most of the 21st century. The reason for this lengthy transition is because approximately 75% of Americans define themselves as Christian.[327] In 1948, the first year Gallup began tracking religious identifications, 91% of Americans defined themselves as Christian. By 1971 the number was down to 89% and by 1997 at 79%. The ultimate NWO goal is to drive the number to 0%.

In order to redefine a group of people who are opposed to murder as people who advocate murder requires two things: moral deterioration in the people themselves and the creation of a false association of Christians with terrorism. This strategy has worked well for the NWO as many in the Middle East are now conditioned to see Christianity as a religion supportive of murdering Muslims. For the years 2012 to 2030, domestic false bogeymen are needed by the NWO to replace al Qaeda bogeymen. The pattern will be to stage mass murders and put the blame on Christians. NWO sponsored violence of horrific crimes by people claiming to be Christians will serve to both paralyze one-world opposition with fear and trick people into hating Christians.

Transforming U.S. and European public opinion to believe Christians are terrorists is beyond comprehension for many Christians. However, many Israelis and Arabs were successfully conditioned to believe that Christians are terrorists by the Crusades and World War II Holocaust.

---

[325] "The West: New Perspectives on the West," *PBS*, September 1996. This documentary is an eight-part series on the genocide of native Americans. Available online at www.pbs.org/weta/thewest/places/states/montana/mt_littlebighorn.htm.

[326] The American public learned in 2004 that in 2003 U.S. Army personnel were torturing prisoners in Iraq. Eleven military personnel were convicted in 2005 of abuse crimes by Army courts-martial.

[327] Frank Newport, "This Easter, Smaller Percentage of Americans Are Christian," *Gallup Poll*, 10 April 2009 and online at www.gallup.com/poll/117409/Easter-Smaller-Percentage-Americans-Christian.aspx.

The U.S. bombing operations in 1991 in Iraq, and during the decade after September 11, 2001 in multiple Islamic countries, has solidified the notion that Christians are terrorists. NWO efforts to deceive people into hating Muslims, Jews, and Christians have been and will continue to be extensive. The events of September 11, 2001 have redefined, albeit incorrectly, the understanding of Islam as a religion of violence.

The NWO has used the United States to fight in over 65 countries since 1945 but has never once fought to defend the American people. Blinded by the false justification of needing oil, fighting communism, or fighting terrorism, the U.S. public has supported assassinations, human rights abuses, and the overthrow of democratically elected leaders. The real terrorists are the agents of the NWO.

6

ALLIANCES WITH KILLERS

"The people can always be brought to the bidding of the leaders. That is easy. All you have to do is tell them they are being attacked and denounce the pacifists for lack of patriotism and exposing the country to danger. It works the same way in any country."[328]
Hermann Göring

This chapter explains the shocking reality of how the United States worked with both Saddam Hussein and Osama bin Laden in the 1980s. There was never a relationship between Saddam Hussein and al Qaeda but there was a relationship between Hussein and the New World Order. The Reagan administration, used U.S. tax dollars to help Iraq fight Iran. They also used taxpayer money to fund the mujahedeen, including Osama bin Laden, to fight the Soviets in Afghanistan.

Saddam Hussein as Ally

Saddam Hussein will no doubt be remembered in history as one of the leading mass murderers of our time. His human rights violations were overlooked because the NWO wanted Iraq and Iran to fight in the 1980s so that neither nation would be a military force to challenge Israel. U.S. leaders also wanted Iraq to inflict as much damage on Iran as possible to seek revenge for the 1979 Iranian hostage crisis. NWO insiders arranged for the U.S. to give Saddam Hussein the key ingredients to make chemical and biological weapons to use against Iran. The 1980-1988 Iran-Iraq War was, in many ways, the catalyst for Iraq's 1990 invasion of Kuwait. The invasion of Kuwait resulted in the Gulf War that started on January 17, 1991, which in many respects continued with the 2003 Gulf War.

The official U.S. policy during the 1980-1988 Iran-Iraq War was pure evil: keep both sides fighting for as long as possible since both were threats to U.S. interests. The U.S. started

---

[328] From an interview on 18 April 1946 with Gustave Gilbert in Göring's jail cell. The statement was recorded and published in Gilbert's 1947 Nuremberg Diary.

supplying Iran with weapons, as revealed by President Reagan's Iran-Contra Affair. This betrayal by President Reagan greatly upset Hussein, as Iraq was in a life-and-death struggle with Iran. A million people died in the Iran-Iraq War, and economic development for both countries was set back decades.

Understanding the interdependencies between these wars requires understanding how Kuwait was created. The border between Kuwait and Iraq has been tense ever since the British Colonial Office serving the NWO established Kuwait as a separate country in 1961. Historically, during the Ottoman rule, Kuwait was a district of Iraq. Kuwait was split from Iraq for profit and strategic advantage because of its oil resources and Persian Gulf waterfront boundary (hence the name Kuwait, which is a diminutive of an Arabic word meaning fortress built near water).[329] Reuniting Kuwait with Iraq has been a policy of Iraqi leaders since the 1960s.

Following is a refresher on the Iran-Iraq War, sometimes referred to as the first Persian Gulf War. The war was fundamentally a war over the Shatt al-Arab waterway, which is important for the oil exports of both Iraq and Iran. Following the 1979 Iranian Revolution, Iran was a tempting target for Saddam Hussein as it was clear that the United States would not intervene in any conflict there. To start the war, Saddam Hussein accused Iran of attempting to assassinate Foreign Minister Tariq Aziz. Hussein started the conflict on September 22, 1980. In June of 1982, a successful Iranian counter-offensive recovered all Iraqi-held Iranian territory. This war ended on August 20, 1988.

Concerned that Iran might win the war, the NWO used the U.S. to support Iraq with biological and chemical weapons.[330] Donald Rumsfeld met with Saddam Hussein in 1983 as President Reagan's Middle East envoy, with a mission to provide biological, chemical, and intelligence capabilities.[331] The fear of the NWO was that if Iran won, the country would become stronger and more difficult to force into their one-world framework.

As part of the program to assist Saddam Hussein, the U.S. Centers for Disease Control and Prevention sent anthrax, the bacteria that produces botulinum toxin, and the germs to create gas gangrene to Iraq's biological weapons labs in the 1980s. The receipts for supplying Iraq with the

---

[329] "Kuwait History," *Arabic German Consulting*, 17 September 2004. The online address is www.arab.de/arabinfo/kuwaithis.htm.

[330] "Iraq got seeds for bioweapons from U.S.," *Baltimore Sun* and *Associated Press*, 1 October 2002 and online at www.baltimoresun.com/bal-te.bioweapons01oct01,0,2387930.story.
Kenneth R. Timmerman, *The Death Lobby: How the West Armed Iraq* (New York, NY: Houghton Mifflin Company, 1991).

[331] Ibid.
Duelfer, Charles, *Comprehensive Report of the Special Advisor to the Director of Central Intelligence on Iraq's Weapons of Mass Destruction*, 30 September 2004, Volume III.

key ingredients for weapons of mass destruction are part of a 1994 Senate Banking Committee report. Iraq immediately went to work to make weapons from all of the materials supplied by the United States under President Reagan and Vice President Bush.[332]

Iraq informed the United Nations in 1991 that it had been successful in making anthrax, botulinum toxin, and gas gangrene weapons. Iraq disclosed that all biological and chemical weapons had been disposed of in the summer of 1991 as demanded by the United Nations after the Gulf War.[333]

President George W. Bush would know unmistakably that his father and President Reagan had given Saddam Hussein the deadly ingredients. Rumsfeld lied when he told the world he knew exactly where the weapons of mass destruction were located.[334] Bush and Rumsfeld knew all of the weapons of mass destruction storage sites were destroyed during the 1991 Gulf War.

In 2012 the public would learn the U.S. bombing of these sites in January 1991 released deadly gas that was a major contributor to what later came to be called the Gulf War Syndrome.[335] The study revealed that U.S. troops were told chemical alarms went off by mistake, but researchers Robert Haley and James Tuite published proof U.S. troops were exposed to sarin gas in the journal *Neuroepidemiology*.[336] Both men may have been surprised that Iraq actually had destroyed, as

---

[332] Matt Kelly, "U.S. Supplied Germs to Iraq in '80s," *Associated Press*, 30 September 2002. The deadly exports by the Centers for Disease Control and the American Type Culture Collection were cleared by the Reagan Administration Commerce Department and are detailed in the 1994 Senate Banking Committee report.
"U.S. Chemical and Biological Warfare-Related Dual Use Exports to Iraq and their Possible Impact on the Health Consequences of the Persian Gulf War, Senate Committee on Banking, Housing and Urban Affairs with Respect to Export Administration," report of May 25, 1994, page 11 (in the stand-alone report) or page 239 in Senate publication S. Hrg. 103-900.

[333] Ibid. Also, "Report of the Secretary-General on the activities of the Special Commission established by the Secretary-General pursuant to paragraph 9 (b) (i) of resolution 687 (1991)," *United Nations*, 6 October 1997.

[334] Secretary of Defense Donald H. Rumsfeld, Secretary Rumsfeld Remarks on ABC "This Week with George Stephanopoulos," *United States Department of Defense News Transcript*, 30 March 2003. Secretary of Defense Donald Rumsfeld said, "We know where they are. They're in the area around Tikrit and Baghdad and east, west, south and north somewhat."

[335] Kelly Kennedy, "Study: Wind blew deadly gas to U.S. troops in Gulf War," *USA Today*, 14 December 2012.

[336] Ibid. The Nasiriyah and Khamisiya munitions facilities were blown up by the U.S. Air Force on January 18, 1991 to prevent reporters from seeing weapons supplied by the U.S. The sarin gas released traveled high above a layer of cold air and into a swift wind stream that carried the gas as far as Saudi Arabia. The study found the gas can be blamed for symptoms of Gulf War illness which affected more than 250,000 war participants and countless civilians.

part of the United Nations inspection effort, all of the weapons that the United States had helped Saddam Hussein make in the 1980s.

What would happen to the president's deceptive 2003 cover story with the weapons destroyed in 1991? For obvious reasons, President Bush did not acknowledge his father's and the Reagan administration's delivery of weapons of mass destruction to Saddam Hussein. This was a real dilemma if there ever was one. The truth remains that Saddam Hussein had collaborated to create weapons of mass destruction with the United States—but not with al Qaeda.

Muslim Freedom Fighters as Allies

The Soviet invasion of Afghanistan began on December 24, 1979 and ended on February 15, 1989. Similar to the U.S. invasion of Iraq in 2003, the Soviet invasion was seen around the world as an unprovoked invasion of a sovereign country. The United Nations General Assembly passed United Nations Resolution 37/37 on November 29, 1982 demanding that Soviet Union forces withdraw from Afghanistan. The Soviet Union justified the invasion as coming to the aid of an ally and a necessary preemptive war against Islamic terrorists. President Reagan saw an opportunity to humiliate the Soviet Union. He instructed the Central Intelligence Agency to support the anti-Soviet resistance. The multi-billion dollar operation not only supported, but also helped create the joint Arab and Afghan resistance against the Soviet Union.

The Central Intelligence Agency and Pakistan's Inter-Services Intelligence launched the largest covert operation in history. The CIA funded and recruited almost 100,000 radical mujahedeen from over 40 Islamic countries as soldiers for America's proxy war. The rank and file of the mujahedeen was unaware that their jihad or holy war was actually being fought on behalf of the NWO. Weapons like the Stinger ground-to-air missiles were paid for by U.S. taxpayers. The Stinger and other weapons enabled the Arab and Afghan fighters to gain the upper hand against the Soviets in 1986. The multi-billion dollar effort—with $600 million allocated in 1987 alone—was funneled through Pakistani intelligence to sustain mujahedeen fighters.[337]

President Reagan failed to consider what might happen when the Soviets left or were defeated. As comedian George Carlin once said, "Well, if crime fighters fight crime and fire fighters fight fire, what do freedom fighters fight? They never mention that part to us, do they?"[338] President Reagan would not have appreciated the truth in this humor. After the Soviets were defeated in February 1989, Afghan Arab war veterans generally returned home and the native Afghan fighters became the Taliban.

---

[337] Richard Clarke, *Against All Enemies* (New York, NY: Free Press, 2004), 49-51.
[338] Comedian George Carlin was born 1937 and died on June 22, 2008.

When the Afghanistan War ended, Osama bin Laden did not go to his home country of Yemen but did return to Saudi Arabia as a war hero. He thanked Prince Bandar of Saudi Arabia and the Saudi intelligence chief, Prince Turki, for bringing the United States to help him. Prince Turki was the person who asked Osama bin Laden to lead an Arab resistance force for Saudi Arabia in Afghanistan. The direct quote from Osama bin Laden to Prince Bandar was, "Thank you. Thank you for bringing the Americans to help us to get rid of the secularist, atheist Soviets."[339]

When Iraq invaded Kuwait on August 2, 1990, Osama bin Laden asked Saudi King Fahd Bin-Abd-al-Aziz Al Saud to let him form a group to help liberate Kuwait.[340] The Saudi King, who serves the NWO, rejected bin Laden's offer. Bin Laden had recently returned from Afghanistan as a Saudi national hero and his influence was growing. The royal family feared bin Laden might use the opportunity to form an all-Arab liberation force not only to repel Saddam Hussein's forces from Kuwait, but to eliminate the Saudi royal family. King Fahd's decision to put the liberation of Kuwait and the defense of the Kingdom in the hands of "infidels" forever shattered Osama bin Laden's support for the Saudi royal family.[341]

1991 Iraq War

On August 2, 1990, Iraq invaded Kuwait with a green light from the U.S.[342] Saddam Hussein believed that the recently concluded war with Iran had also provided for Kuwait's defense. Iraq owed Kuwait fourteen billion dollars and at the end of the 1980-1988 Iraq and Iran War, Hussein expected debts that Iraq had accumulated to be forgiven. However, Kuwait refused to forgive Iraq's debts. Kuwait served the NWO by provoking an Iraqi invasion, thus driving down world oil prices and drilling oil from under Iraq. Kuwait was walking on thin ice, and Hussein just needed approval from the United States to set things straight.

A little over two years prior to the Gulf War in 1988, I was in the 107th Military Intelligence Battalion. I mention this because, even at that time, I was convinced that the Pentagon was orchestrating a Middle East war. My unit was rapidly undergoing a major makeover from jungle operations in Central America to desert warfare. America's weapons, equipment, and uniforms

---

[339] "Looking for Answers: Prince Bandar bin Sultan," *Frontline*, interview conducted in late September 2001.

[340] Richard Clarke, *Against All Enemies* (New York, New York: Free Press, 2004), 59 reported Osama bin Laden wanted to bring his al Qaeda fighters but al Qaeda did not exist.

[341] Ibid., 71. Allowing non-believers to establish military bases in Saudi Arabia is a direct violation of the Koran.

[342] "Excerpts from Iraqi Document on Meeting with U.S. Envoy," *The New York Times*, 23 September 1990.

went from jungle green to desert camouflage patterns. I did not know where we were going, but I suspected it would be someplace with lots of oil.

Given my desert makeover military experience, I was especially sensitive when I heard the news report given by State Department spokesperson Margaret Tutweiler on July 24, 1990. She sent a mixed message in her answer to a question by a reporter. She was asked, "Do you happen to know if the United States has any commitment to Kuwait, to defend Kuwait or to assist it against aggression?" Margaret Tutweiler replied, "We do not have any defense treaties with Kuwait, and there are no special defense or security commitments to Kuwait."[343] Saddam Hussein's intelligence agents were surely monitoring the pulse in Washington and immediately passed this on to their leader. This is almost a certainty because Iraq was already on the brink of war with Kuwait.

The very next day April Glaspie, the United States Ambassador to Iraq, was summoned to speak to Saddam Hussein.[344] In this meeting, he sought assurances that the United States would not intervene if Kuwait were attacked. In either a miscommunication of strategic proportions, or a trap for Hussein, Glaspie responded to his query with, "We have no opinion on the Arab-Arab conflicts, like your border disagreement with Kuwait."[345] The theory of a trap being laid for Hussein is reasonable because the United States wanted to level the playing field in the Middle East by setting in motion a series of events that would result in the destruction of significant Iraqi military capabilities. Prior to the Gulf War, Iraq had the largest military in the Middle East, and Iraq's powerful military was a serious threat to Israel.

After the meeting with Glaspie, Hussein did not need further U.S. assurances. Nonetheless, on July 31, 1990, Assistant Secretary of State for Near Eastern and South Asian Affairs John Kelly was testifying before a House foreign affairs subcommittee. Congressman Lee Hamilton asked Kelly, "If Iraq, for example, charged across the border into Kuwait and for whatever reason, what would be our position with regard to the use of U.S. forces?" Kelly replied, "I cannot get into the realm of what if answers." Congressman Hamilton asked the follow-up question, "In that circumstance, it is correct to say, however, that we do not have a treaty commitment which would obligate us to engage U.S. forces?" Kelly responded, "That is correct."[346]

---

[343] "The Long Road to War: To the Brink of War," *Frontline*, 17 March 2003.

[344] "Excerpts from Iraqi Document on Meeting With U.S. Envoy," *The New York Times*, 23 September 1990, 19.

[345] Ibid.

[346] "The Long Road to War: to the Brink of War," *Frontline*, 17 March 2003. Testimony in the Hearing before the Subcommittee on Europe and the Middle East of the House Committee on Foreign Affairs, "Developments in the Middle East," 31 July 1990.

The Gulf War started on January 17, 1991 and ended on February 28, 1991.[347] At the time, Iraq was the strongest military power among the Arab states. Over 177 million pounds of bombs were dropped on the people of Iraq. This bombing was one of the most concentrated aerial onslaughts in the history of the world. Depleted uranium weapons were used to incinerate people; their aftereffects continue to cause cancer. The country's infrastructure was destroyed, which, in turn, had a terrible effect on the population's health. Economic sanctions placed on the country multiplied the health problems. The United Nations estimated over 500,000 children were killed because of the sanctions; the death tolls were much higher when adults were counted.

When President George H. W. Bush decided to end military operations, Saddam Hussein was not expected to hold the reins of power for more than a few weeks. Secretary of State James Baker observed, "Did our Arab allies and everybody else think he would not survive a defeat of the type that we administered? Yes, they did not think he would survive."[348] To the surprise of the first President Bush, Saddam Hussein survived and, by surviving, he posed a threat to the Bush family, although he could do little in his country's weakened state to pose a threat to the United States. In April 1993, the United States learned that Hussein had sent his intelligence agents into Kuwait with the objective of assassinating former President George H. W. Bush. The unsuccessful assassination had been planned to take place during the allied Persian Gulf War victory celebrations earlier that month.[349]

2003-2011 Iraq War

With the previous refresher on the 1990-1991 Gulf War, the genesis of the second Iraq War in 2003 may be less startling. The 2003 invasion of Iraq began with NWO insiders knowing Iraq was not involved in the September 11, 2001 attacks.

---

[347] Edited by Douglas Harrecht, "Toting the Casualties of War," *Business Week Online*, 6 February 2003. The number of Iraqi deaths reported varies due to the fog of war, but the estimate is 158,000 Iraqi deaths, including 86,194 men (of which approximately 40,000 were soldiers), 39,612 women, and 32,195 children.

[348] "Gunning for Saddam: Interview James Baker," *Frontline*, mid October 2001. The quote is online at www.pbs.org/wgbh/pages/frontline/shows/gunning/interviews/baker.html.

[349] "History News Network: History Q & A," *History News Network*, 30 September 2002. The assassination was to take place between April 14 and April 16, 1993. The Kuwaiti authorities arrested 17 persons suspected in the plot to kill Present George H. W. Bush using explosives hidden in a Toyota Land cruiser. On June 26, 1993, the United States launched a cruise missile attack in Baghdad in retaliation for the assassination attempt on former President George H. W. Bush. The attack is believed to have killed between six and eight persons and injured approximately 12 others. On June 27, 1993, Madeleine Albright, U.S. Ambassador to the United Nations, addressed an emergency session of the Security Council to provide evidence for the attack. The full text is online at www.hnn.us/articles/1000.html.

President George W. Bush and his team were advised in the Central Intelligence Agency's October 2002 National Intelligence Estimate (NIE) that the United States "has no specific intelligence information that Saddam Hussein's regime has directed attacks against U.S. territory."[350] The report also noted that Iraq did not have a nuclear bomb or even the materials to make one. Americans tend to forget that Colin Powell and Condoleezza Rice both stated in early 2001 that Saddam Hussein had been disarmed and was no threat to the United States.[351] The bottom line is that there was no information that an attack by Iraq was planned and no evidence of weapons of mass destruction disclosed.[352] The NIE was very clear on the point that Iraq posed no clear and present nuclear bomb threat because Iraq was years away from developing nuclear bombs.

President Bush and his cabinet, packed with NWO insiders, absolutely knew that Iraq never posed a mushroom cloud threat or any other kind of weapons of mass destruction threat to the United States.[353] Yet the mushroom cloud rationale for invading Iraq was cunningly reinforced by other members of the Bush administration. On January 9, 2003, the president's spokesperson, Ari Fleischer, setting the stage for the president's State of the Union speech later that month, said, "We know for a fact that there are weapons there."[354] President Bush fanned America's fear with his statement that "the British government has learned that Saddam Hussein recently sought significant quantities of uranium from Africa."[355] We now know that this statement was based on a fraudulent document with forged signatures of officials not in office at the time.[356] The fraudulent forged documents about Saddam's uranium purchase were supplied by NWO agents in Italy's intelligence service.[357]

---

[350] Bob Woodward, *Plan of Attack* (New York, New York: Simon & Schuster 2004), 199.

[351] John Pilger, "Pilger Claims White House Knew Saddam was No Threat," *The Sydney Morning Herald*, 23 September 2003. Colin Powell in Cairo on February 24, 2001 said, "He (Saddam Hussein) has not developed any significant capability with respect to weapons of mass destruction. He is unable to project conventional power against his neighbors." Two months later, Condoleezza Rice said, "We are able to keep his arms from him. His military forces have not been rebuilt."

[352] Katherine Pfleger Shrader, "U.S. Weapons Inspector: Iraq Had No WMD," *Associated Press*, 16 September 2004.

[353] "Bush: Don't Wait for Mushroom Cloud," *CNN.com*, 8 October 2002.

[354] Ari Fleischer, "Press Briefing by Ari Fleischer," *Office of the Press Secretary*, 9 January 2003. The complete text is online at www.whitehouse.gov/news/releases/2003/01/20030109-8.html.

[355] President George W. Bush, "State of the Union," *The White House*, 28 January 2003. The complete text is online at www.whitehouse.gov/news/releases/2003/01/20030128-19.html.

[356] Dana Priest and Karen DeYoung, "CIA Questioned Documents Linking Iraq, Uranium Ore," *Washington Post*, 22 March 2003, A30.

[357] Bill Gertz, "FBI Probing Forged Papers on Niger Uranium," *The Washington Times*, 19 July 2003. Available online at www.washtimes.com/national/20030719-120154-5384r.htm.

Key NWO operatives Colin Powell and Tony Blair added fuel to this fire in February 2003. Colin Powell went before the United Nations and misled the world with a case for war based on fabricated information instead of facts.[358] Even what seemed to be concrete evidence, the Iraqi mobile labs, ended up being proven to be vehicles to inflate balloons.[359] Prime Minister Tony Blair, struggling to sell his people on the need for war, acknowledged the British government was caught plagiarizing a 12-year-old academic paper and presenting it as sensitive real-time intelligence.[360] Blair's intentionally frightening announcement that Iraq could launch weapons of mass destruction in 45 minutes was also fabricated.[361] On the eve of the invasion of Iraq, President Bush told the American people that "intelligence gathered by this and other governments[362] leaves no doubt that the Iraq regime continues to possess and conceal some of the most lethal weapons ever devised."[363]

Once the fog of war clears, the real NWO drivers for war are hard to hide.[364] Given the repeated threat of a clear and present mushroom cloud danger if the United States did not immediately invade Iraq, it is not surprising that three out of four Americans supported the decision for war.[365] Americans now know from leaked classified documents like the British Downing Street Memo[366]

---

[358] Colin L. Powell, "Remarks to the United Nations Security Council," *U.S. Department of State*, 5 February 2003. The complete text is online at www.state.gov/secretary/rm/2003/17300.htm.

[359] Peter Beaumont, Antony Barnett and Gaby Hinsliff, "Iraqi Mobile Labs Nothing to do with Germ Warfare, Report Finds," *Guardian Unlimited: The Observer*, 15 June 2003.

[360] Glenn Frankel, "Blair Acknowledges Flaws in Iraq Dossier," *Washington Post Foreign Service*, 8 February 2003, A15.

[361] Tom Happold and agencies, "Official Explodes Key WMD Claim," *Guardian Unlimited*, 29 May 2003.

[362] The American people deserve to know who fabricated the forged documents. Israel and the United States were also working hard to build a case to invade Iraq. The Israeli government has acknowledged providing the U.S. with incorrect intelligence. See Offer Shelah, "Israeli Intelligence Probe Asks: What Did We Know and When?," *The Forward Newspaper, The Situation*, 13 February 2004. Former CIA intelligence analyst Larry C. Johnson has written that Italy's SISME intelligence service had a hand in creating the forged documents. See "Dick Cheney's Covert Action," TomPaine.com, 19 October 2005. Available online at www.tompaine.com/articles/20051019/dick_cheneys_covert_action.php.

[363] President George W. Bush, "President Says Saddam Must Leave Iraq Within 48 Hours," *Office of the Press Secretary*, 17 March 2003. The complete text is online at www.whitehouse.gov/news/releases/2003/03/20030317-7.html.

[364] "Duelfer Report Further Disproves U.S. Claims on Iraq WMD," *Arms Control Association*, 15 October 2004.

[365] Richard Morin and Claudia Deane, "71% of Americans Support War, Poll Shows," *Washington Post*, 19 March 2003, A14. Also Gallup/USA Today poll on 21 March 2003 that showed 76 percent of Americans supported the decision to launch the war.

[366] David Manning, "The Secret Downing Street Memo," *The Sunday Times—Britain*, 1 May 2005. The memo was written by Matthew Rycroft on 23 July 2002. Available online at www.timesonline.co.uk/article/0,,2087-1593607,00.html.

that Iraq never had plans to attack the United States. The Bush administration knowingly sold as fact the lies that weapons of mass destruction existed and would be used.

Criticism of how the war was packaged for consumption by the American people is not an endorsement for Saddam Hussein. Hussein was a ruthless dictator who committed severe crimes against humanity. The critical point is that Hussein did not pose a threat to the United States. While he deserved to be in jail and tried for war crimes, the United States was not justified in starting a war by falsely claiming that Iraq posed a weapons of mass destruction threat to Americans.

You might be thinking that anyone who would gas his own population, as Hussein is accused of doing to the Kurds, is a threat to the United States. While this line of thinking is perhaps arguable, at least one key insider refutes this claim by President Bush and his administration. Stephen Pelletiere, the CIA's senior political analyst on Iraq during the Iran-Iraq War, claims that Saddam Hussein never gassed his own people.[367] It is important to note that there is no question that Hussein did use gas to kill people in combat operations against Iran. Pelletiere led the 1991 Army investigation that produced a classified version of the Halabja affair in which Hussein is accused of gassing residents of the city, many of them Kurds. The Halabja murders were specifically cited by President Bush to illustrate that Saddam Hussein gassed his own people.[368]

Pelletiere has criticized President Bush for deceiving the American people. Pelletiere explained President Bush lied to start a war, and Halabja was important because of the Darbandikhan dam. Pelletiere, who had access to the best information to determine Saddam's involvement at Halabja, wrote: "In the 1990's there was much discussion over the construction of a so-called Peace Pipeline that would bring the waters of the Tigris and Euphrates south to the parched Gulf states and, by extension, Israel."[369]

The classified investigation of the Halabja gassing found that civilians killed by Saddam Hussein were victims in a battle between Iraq and Iran for Halabja.[370] The classified investigation supported the argument that Iranian gas killed the Kurds because the bodies showed signs of death by a blood agent. Iran used a cyanide-based gas or blood agent during the battle in Halabja,

[367] Stephen C. Pelletiere, "A War Crime or an Act of War?," *The New York Times*, 31 January 2003.
[368] President George W. Bush, "State of the Union," *The White House*, 28 January 2003. President Bush said, "The dictator who is assembling the world's most dangerous weapons has already used them on whole villages -- leaving thousands of his own citizens dead, blind, or disfigured." The complete text is online at www.whitehouse.gov/news/releases/2003/01/20030128-19.html.
[369] Ibid.
[370] Ibid.

but Iraq did not possess a blood agent weapon at that time. Pelletiere further stressed that the United States' classified investigation did not uncover a single incident where Saddam Hussein used gas against his own people. The point in noting this is not to support Saddam Hussein in any way. Halabja is important because people were murdered and that the senior CIA analyst, Pelletiere, is on record as saying that the American people were lied to.

Americans were told in 2002 and 2003 that the reason for Iraq War was an imminent threat of a mushroom cloud from Saddam Hussein. Even over a decade later it is hard to see any benefit that Saddam Hussein could incur by starting a war with the United States. When the facts could not support that Iraq planned to attack the U.S., more emphasis was placed on the lie that Saddam Hussein had collaborated with the 9/11 terrorists. When the facts could not support this, the story was re-spun that Saddam Hussein possessed chemical or biological weapons of mass destruction. When this, in turn, proved untrue, the story was again re-spun with an even lower bar for war—that Saddam Hussein's crimes against the Iraqi people was the justification for invading the country. Since it was feared that one man's removal from power and imprisonment would be seen as a high price to pay for the deaths incurred, and the billions of dollars spent on the war, the rationale in late 2004 returned to an *intent* by Iraq for a weapons of mass destruction program. In anticipation of the truth that there were no weapons of mass destruction in Iraq, a secondary justification was presented that involved establishing that a democracy was necessary as a good example for other nations in the Middle East.

The bar for starting a war is now so low that any nation with the means to produce chemical weapons is on warning that a preemptive invasion by the United States is possible. Any nation with a golf course has the means to make, mix, and disperse chemical weapons. When you realize that over 30 nations have golf courses, does anyone believe the ability to have versus the intent to use is the appropriate standard for starting a war? One simple question that is worth asking yourself is, "Do you believe the United States would have started a war with Iraq if Iraq was not an oil-rich country?"

Walter Cronkite, "America's Most Trusted Person," spoke on the subject of the nature of the Iraq War on October 23, 2004. He said President Bush's unilateral preemptive policy had made the world a more dangerous place not only for the United States, but for nations around the world. He noted that countries in Africa and the Middle East were preparing to invade their neighbors using President Bush's preemptive strike policy as justification for their actions. He summarized, "The problem, quite clearly, is we have excited the Arab world, the Muslim world, to take up arms against us." He recommended gathering from retirement the most senior U.S. generals who opposed the war. Then he would ask this select group of outspoken opponents of the invasion to develop for immediate implementation a plan to withdraw all United States forces from Iraq within six months.[371]

While many people bought the top two lies for the Iraq War (i.e., responsible for the 9/11 attacks and weapons of mass destruction threat), the real reasons for the 2003 Iraq War are:

1. Continue the existing NWO power structure and its movement toward a one-world government.
2. Eliminate Saddam Hussein's program to frustrate the NWO one-world currency by offering an alternative to the U.S. dollar-based monetary system.
3. Secure control of Iraq's oil resources, not for U.S. citizens, but for NWO oil corporations.
4. Aid Israel by removing Iraq's leadership that wanted to retaliate for Israel's destruction of the Osiraq nuclear plant in 1981 and behind-the-scenes orchestration resulting in the 1991 U.S.-led Gulf War.[372]
5. Turn water into a weapon by occupying Iraq which controls the most extensive river system in the Middle East.[373]
6. Controlling Central Asia in the upcoming decades as key competitors China and Europe become increasingly dependent Central Asian resources.
7. Establish permanent military installations for U.S. forces to control both oil and water resources in Iraq.[374]
8. Revenge for the assassination attempt on the president's father, as well as a fear among the Bush family that Saddam Hussein would one day take revenge on a member of the Bush family.

---

[371] Walter Cronkite, comments in Santa Barbara at the Nuclear Age Peace Foundation, 23 October 2004. Also Thomas Schultz, "Cronkite: U.S. 'excited the Arab world' by waging war on Iraq," Nuclear Age Peace Foundation Press Release, 24 October 2004.

[372] From the NWO vantage point the U.S. is paying for the war that the NWO and Israel's leadership wanted with Iraq in blood and dollars. U.S. taxpayers fund most of the violence and U.S. soldiers pay the ultimate price with their lives and souls. Claims Israel benefited from the 2003 Iraq War include: eliminating Iraq as a threat, making the United States the primary focus of international anger, and positioning Iraq to help solve Israel's water shortage.

[373] Stephen C. Pelletiere, "A War Crime or an Act of War?," *The New York Times*, 31 January 2003. In this article the author describes how control of Iraq's Tigris, Euphrates, the Greater Zab and Lesser Zab rivers could alter the destiny of the Middle East for decades. The strategic value of Iraq's water is not a new development. In the 1990s, a "Peace Pipeline" was proposed to bring the waters of the Tigris and Euphrates south to the Gulf states and Israel.

[374] Christine Spolar, "14 'Enduring Bases' Set in Iraq," *Chicago Tribune*, 23 March 2004.

While individual members of the Bush administration would have prioritized the list differently, note that responding to a clear and present threat of a mushroom cloud from Iraq is not on the list of a key administration insider Richard Clarke.[375] Richard Clarke provides an insider perspective that the five real Bush Administration reasons for starting the 2003 Iraq War were: to clean up the mess left by the first Bush administration; to improve Israel's strategic position by eliminating a large, hostile army; to create an Arab democracy that could serve as a model to other Arab states; to permit the withdrawal of U.S. forces from Saudi Arabia; and to create another friendly source of oil for the United States.

The combination of no Iraqi plans for violence and no Iraqi weapons of mass destruction made the Iraq War an illegal war under U.S. and international law. This fact is realized by many people around the world including the former United Nations Secretary-General Kofi Annan. Kofi Annan said the U.S.-led invasion of Iraq was an illegal act that contravened the UN charter.[376] This may appear harsh to many Americans, but when a president misleads the country to start a war, he or she needs to be held accountable as a war criminal. Injustices must not be ignored or we will be a party to even greater injustices in the future.

The illegal and unnecessary deaths of thousands of Iraqis make George W. Bush a war criminal. For George W. Bush, the golden rule was: There is no golden rule, only profits to be made and perpetuation of the power of the NWO elite.[377] In a career-ending move, Richard Clarke, who served under three presidents, went on record saying that the actions by President George W. Bush had made the world a more dangerous place.[378] The body count of civilian bystanders in Iraq alone, not surprisingly a metric not officially maintained by the U.S. government, exceeded three times the number of 9/11 victims in the first year of war in Iraq.[379] Even if you were to

---

[375] Richard Clarke, *Against All Enemies* (New York, NY: Free Press, 2004), 265.

[376] "Iraq War Illegal, Says Annan," *BBC News*, 16 September, 2004.
Matthew Rycroft, "The Secret Downing Street Memo," *The Sunday Times*, 1 May 2005. This UK Eyes Only document was written on July 23, 2002. The Downing Street memo confirms that the Blair and Bush governments knew invading Iraq would be illegal and if the truth of the operation became known, the Blair and Bush leadership could be convicted of war crimes. Furthermore, the document confirms that the Bush administration was lying to the American people. The memo states that Iraq is not a threat, the decision to go to war was already made, and the intelligence would be "fixed" to sell the war to the American people. The Downing Street memo is available at www.timesonline.co.uk/article/0,,2087-1593607,00.html.

[377] George Bernard Shaw, *Man and Superman: Maxims for Revolutionists*, 1903 play. Shaw was an Irish dramatist and socialist (1856 - 1950). "The golden rule is that there are no golden rules."

[378] Richard Clarke, "Clarke's Take On Terror," *CBS*, 3/21/04. The online address is www.cbsnews.com/stories/2004/03/19/60minutes/main 607356.shtml.

[379] "700 Named in Iraq's Death Toll After a Year of Slaughter," *The Iraq Body Count Project*, 19 March 2004. The latest count of civilian deaths is available at www.iraqbodycount.net/.

believe Osama bin Laden was somehow responsible, how is America restoring justice by killing innocent people in other countries?

In summary, the NWO knew Iraq was years away from possessing a nuclear bomb. The mental image of a mushroom cloud was selected as the most saleable for promoting pre-emptive war. Thousands of innocent people have been killed not for freedom, but to advance the one-world plan.

7

WAR PROFITEERING

"In strict confidence . . . I should welcome almost any war, for I think this country needs one." President Theodore Roosevelt[380]

Wars threaten the United States. The concept of starting a "good war" because it will bring peace is misguided. Martin Luther King, Jr. eloquently made the same point when he said, "Wars are poor chisels for carving out peaceful tomorrows. We must pursue peaceful ends through peaceful means."[381] This chapter presents the ideas of Smedley Darlington Butler. This chapter ends with a warning that the NWO is turning the U.S. into Darth Vader.

Charles E. Wilson, a former President of General Electric and supervisor of war production efforts during World War II, worked to achieve an ongoing alliance between business and the military for "a permanent war economy."[382] His wish came true when the NWO Truman administration created a war economy that continues to this day.

When a country spends hundreds of billions of dollars on a military and no major threats exist, people will naturally think about cutting military spending. After the end of the Cold War, people in the war business (or defense industry, if you prefer this euphemistic label), started to get nervous: a future U.S. where defense spending could be reduced dramatically looked possible. Then after September 11, 2001 we were told the ridiculous story that 19 men killed thousands of innocent people, thereby establishing the necessary conditions for the next "justifiable" war. The story headline was that men armed only with box cutters were able to fly two airplanes into

---

[380] President Theodore Roosevelt (1858 - 1919), "Crucible of Empire," *Public Broadcasting Station*, 1999. President McKinley appointed Theodore Roosevelt in 1897 as the Assistant Secretary of the Navy. Roosevelt once said, "I should welcome almost any war, for I think this country needs one."

[381] Martin Luther King, Jr., "The Casualties of the War in Vietnam," speech in Los Angeles, California, 25 February 1967. In contrast to Martin Luther King, Jr.'s insights, the majority of the American people thought prior to the 2003 Iraq War that starting a war was the path to peace. Richard Morin and Claudia Deane, "71% of Americans Support War, Poll Shows," *The Washington Post*, 19 March 2003, 14.

[382] Chomsky, Noam, *American Power and the New Mandarins* (New York, New York: Pantheon, 1969).

two buildings in New York City and transform three World Trade Center buildings into dust. Americans were told to believe the destroyed Building 7, never hit by an airplane, collapsed demolition style for undetermined reasons. Within hours the new major threat, the war on terrorism, was born. This new enemy serves the NWO well as it is not well-defined.[383]

Smedley Darlington Butler (July 30, 1881-June 21, 1940), an amazing person few Americans have ever heard of, has given us a way to understand NWO violence. Butler was a United States Marine who served at levels from Second Lieutenant to Major General during his 33-year career.[384] He was widely respected in his time by both the political right and left, in part because he won the Congressional Medal of Honor—twice. The following photograph shows Smedley Butler as a Brigadier General.[385]

Butler is also famous for saving the country from a 1933 NWO plot to seize the United States government.[386] At the time the NWO was also planning to overthrow Hitler.[387] The NWO had financed and supported both Franklin Delano Roosevelt and Adolf Hitler. The plot to seize the

---

[383] If you replace the word terror with murder you can see how sustainable a terror war can be. A war to end murder will never end, and so it is true when terror is not understood to be a response to imperialism. Abstract nouns like murder and terror are hard to bring to a surrender-signing ceremony. The New World Order needs, and now has, an enemy that will exist for as long as they feel they need it.

[384] Joseph K. Leach, "Smedley Butler: Marine Corps Legend," accessed on 19 September 2004. The complete text is online at www.grunts.net/legends/butler.html. Butler retired from the Marines in 1931.

[385] Courtesy of the National Archives. This U.S. Naval History and Heritage Command photograph, number NH 64355, is undated. The photograph is available online at www.history.navy.mil/photos/images/h64000/h64355.jpg.

[386] Butler reported the NWO plot to the McCormack-Dickstein Committee, a precursor to the House Committee on Un-American Activities, on November 20, 1934.

[387] Smedley Butler with introduction by Adam Parfrey, *War Is a Racket* (Los Angeles, CA: Feral House, 1935, reprint edition April 2003), 16-17.

U.S. was bogus and really a maneuver to enable Roosevelt to become a dictator by using the coup attempt as the justification to suspend the Constitution. The NWO plot against Hitler was genuine and instigated because he had become powerful and was less willing to comply with their demands.

Butler was first approached by Bill Doyle and Gerald C. MacGuire who said that they represented nine bankers.[388] The NWO plotters included representatives of the DuPont, Mellon, Morgan, Pew, and Rockefeller hidden European banking interests. National City Bank was to provide the funding. The Remington Arms Company was to provide the weapons. Leadership personnel were to come from the Veterans of Foreign Wars, the American Liberty League, and the American Legion. Fortunately, Butler foiled the NWO plot.[389]

President Roosevelt started his presidency on March 4, 1933 and shortly thereafter became involved in NWO plots, including seeking war with Japan.[390] Historians often miss his NWO secret society relationships and fail to account for how he flawlessly served the NWO even after Butler exposed the coup. Roosevelt was a 32 degree Mason from a NWO family that became rich by selling opium. Roosevelt family members had for generations worked to advance a world government. One example involves his cousin, Clinton B. Roosevelt (November 3, 1804-August 8, 1898), who lived through the NWO Panic of 1837 and for the rest of his life supported one-world policies.[391] Roosevelt's family connections with the NWO appear throughout his rise in power. In 1913 he became the Assistant Secretary of the Navy with the help of elite insider Colonel House. Roosevelt's long-term relationships with these powerful people help explain how he became involved in a NWO plot in his first year as president.

Butler reported that Robert S. Clark, John W. Davis, and Grayson Mallet-Provost Murphy were tasked with organizing the false coup, designed to fail, in the hope of enabling Roosevelt to claim dictatorial emergency powers.[392] The NWO wanted FDR in power for a long time as he would do the dirty work of bringing the U.S. into a new World War.

---

[388] Jules Archer, *The Plot to Seize the White House* (New York, New York: Skyhorse Publishing, 2007), 11.

[389] *The Fascist Plot Officially Confirmed, 74th Congress, 1st Session, House of Representatives Report No. 153,* February 15, 1935. The 74th Congress used the term Fascist Plot to describe the New World Order Plot.

[390] Smedley Butler with introduction by Adam Parfrey, *War Is a Racket* (Los Angeles, CA: Feral House, 1935, reprint edition April 2003), 71.

[391] Clinton B. Roosevelt, *The Science of Government, Founded on Natural Law* (New York, New York: Dean & Trevett, 1841) and online at http://books.google.com/books?id=MVwBAAAAYAAJ&printsec=front cover&source=gbs_ge_summary_r&cad=0#v=onepage&q&f=false.

[392] All three men were senior NWO insiders. Robert S. Clark was one of the richest bankers in the country. John W. Davis was an attorney for J. P. Morgan. Grayson Mallet-Provost Murphy was a director of

The NWO U.S. government influence was so great with Roosevelt as president that Butler's testimony was censored in a secret session. A portion of Butler's testimony was published by the U.S. government.[393] In 1967, reporter John L. Spivak made public the unpublished official government record of Butler's testimony.[394] The testimony that the McCormack-Dickstein Committee tried to keep from the public identified the NWO involvement and true purpose of the plot. The fact that the NWO agents were identified in testimony by a witness recognized as highly credible, Smedley Butler, and still were not punished speaks volumes. The U.S. was in the control of an elite shadow government then, just as it is now. This is why the NWO plot Butler interrupted is often not covered in schools and, when taught, it is dismissed as a conspiracy of a few misguided Wall Street business people.

Unlike in the U.S., the NWO agents in Germany who planned to kill Hitler did not escape punishment and were executed in the Führer's "Night of Long Knives" which culminated in the deaths of at least 85 people.[395] The 1934 murders mark the beginning point of Hitler's break from serving the NWO. The Night of Long Knives is explained in the third Vigilant Christian book.

Butler's actions saved the United States from a potential civil war but did not prevent FDR from laying the path for World War II. Butler died in 1940. In the last nine years of his life, his views about war were transformed. Some of his thoughts are foundational for our understanding of war. His personal insights about bringing the flag of freedom to places far away are especially applicable for our time. His most famous observation about war was:

> "War is just a racket. It always has been. It is possibly the oldest, easily the most profitable, surely the most vicious. It is the only one international in scope. It is the only one in which the profits are reckoned in dollars and the losses in lives.

Guaranty Trust, a J. P. Morgan bank.

[393] The official testimony is *Investigation of Nazi Propaganda Activities and Investigation of Certain Other Propaganda Activities: Public Hearings Before the Special Committee on Un-American Activities, House of Representatives*, Seventy-third Congress, Second Session, at Washington, D.C., December 29, 1934. Hearings No. 73-D.C.-6, Part 1.

[394] John L. Spivak, *A Man in His Time* (New York, New York: Horizon Press, January 1, 1967). 12-17. The Great Depression produced a movement among World War I soldiers to demand their "war bonus" of approximately $1,000. Smedley supported the Bonus Marchers' cause. Due to his integrity and leadership, Smedley had the loyalty of 500,000 veterans in 1934. When companies like J. P. Morgan stood to lose money by the elimination of the gold standard, senior business leaders started a plot to overthrow President Franklin Delano Roosevelt. The plotters believed President Roosevelt's New Deal had to be stopped and they approached Smedley and asked him to lead the veterans in a coup.

[395] Ian Kershaw, *Hitler: 1889-1936 Hubris* (New York: New York, W. W. Norton & Company, 1999). The executions took place between June 30, 1934 and July 2, 1934.

"A racket is best described, I believe, as something that is not what it seems to the majority of people. Only a small "inside" group knows what it is about. It is conducted for the benefit of the very few at the expense of the masses. Out of war a few people make huge fortunes. [396]

"Like all the members of the military profession, I never had a thought of my own until I left the service. My mental faculties remained in suspended animation while I obeyed the orders of higher-ups. This is typical with everyone in the military service.

"I helped make Mexico, especially Tampico, safe for American oil interests in 1914. I helped make Haiti and Cuba a decent place for the National City Bank boys to collect revenues in. I helped in the raping of half a dozen Central American republics for the benefits of Wall Street. The record of racketeering is long. I helped purify Nicaragua for the international banking house of Brown Brothers in 1909-1912. I brought light to the Dominican Republic for American sugar interests in 1916. In China I helped to see to it that Standard Oil went its way unmolested.

"During those years, I had, as the boys in the back room would say, a swell racket. Looking back on it, I feel that I could have given Al Capone a few hints. The best he could do was to operate his racket in three districts. I operated on three continents.

"The trouble with America is that when the dollar only earns six percent over here, then it gets restless and goes overseas to get 100 percent. Then the flag follows the dollar and the soldiers follow the flag . . . Why don't those damn oil companies fly their own flags on their personal property—maybe a flag with a gas pump on it."[397]

Smedley Butler stands out among amazing Americans, not only because of his rare accomplishment in winning two Congressional Medals of Honor, but because he had the courage

---

[396] Ibid., 23.

[397] Smedley Butler with introduction by Adam Parfrey, *War Is a Racket* (Los Angeles, CA: Feral House, 1935, reprint edition April 2003), 1. Modern day war profiteering is perhaps best illustrated by Halliburton. Neil King, Jr. wrote about a 2004 example in his "Army Plan Lets Halliburton Keep Disputed Payments" article published in *The Wall Street Journal* on October 22, 2004. Halliburton's Kellogg Brown & Root (KBR) unit, which performs much of the company's Iraq work, has billed about $12 billion in Iraq. Approximately $3 billion remains in dispute. Army, Brig. Gen. Jerome Johnson, head of the Army's Field Support Command, called the move to hire the consultants the only way to resolve the dispute between Pentagon auditors and the Halliburton unit. Brig. Gen. Johnson wrote, "If supporting documentation just does not exist, we must have an equitable solution to declaring an acceptable cost level and moving forward . . . It would be totally inappropriate and unfair of us to disallow all costs when, in the fog of the contingency, KBR did not obtain sufficient supporting documentation."

to acknowledge his mistakes. By speaking the truth, he has helped future generations learn about the NWO, which he called the "inside" group orchestrating wars. He offered a new way of thinking about the defense of the nation.

A central theme Butler preached was the need to limit war profiteering. War profiteering consists of influencing, promoting, starting or supporting the continuation of war for personal economic benefit. To protect against the NWO war profiteering, Butler supported limiting the pay for all workers in defense industries, especially senior executives, to the same pay received by soldiers in the trenches. He felt that defense industry workers still had a better deal because they would not be killed or maimed in combat. While this would create a new set of problems, limiting the profit in war could be improved through more transparency on who benefits and open contract bidding.

The Bush family became rich and powerful as a result of serving the NWO in lucrative war deals. War profiteering in the Bush family started with George H. Walker and Samuel Prescott Bush, who were former President George W. Bush's great-grandfathers. George H. Walker was a St. Louis financier who specialized in corporate war contracts. Samuel Prescott Bush led a weapons business named the Buckeye Steel Castings Company. Samuel Prescott Bush's son, Prescott Bush, was a Connecticut senator and a director of weapons maker Dresser Industries, which is especially remembered for making the incendiary bombs that were dropped during World War II.[398] Prescott Bush is also famous in history for making millions through helping a key NWO front bank that supported Hitler's war machine. The company, Union Banking Corporation, was shut down under the *Trading with the Enemy Act* in 1942.[399]

George H. W. Bush is best known as a congressman, CIA director, Vice President, and America's forty-first President; he also has a personal history of war profiteering as senior advisor to the Carlyle Group and as a major investor in military defense-related companies. To illustrate how incestuous these relationships can be, former President George H. W. Bush was in Washington D.C. on September 11, 2001 attending a Carlyle directors meeting. The bin Laden family is a major investor in the NWO Carlyle Group. Osama bin Laden's brother was present at the Carlyle meeting and sitting next to former President Bush as they both watched the twin towers fall.[400] While Americans were still in shock at the horror of this mass murder, the Carlyle

[398] Kevin Phillips, "Bush Family Values: War, Wealth, Oil: Four generations have created an unsavory web of links that could prove an election-year Achilles' heel for the president," *The Los Angeles Times*, 8 February 2004.

[399] "Office of Alien Property Custodian, Vesting Order No. 248," *Signed by Leo T. Crowley*, 20 October 1942. Prescott Bush was a director of Union Banking Corporation from 1934 to 1943.

[400] "Exposed: The Carlyle Group," *Information Clearing House*, accessed on 19 September 2004 at www.informationclearinghouse.info/article3995.htm.

Group decided to take United Defense, a company that it controlled, public in order to reap the near-certain 9/11 market boost. The Army's fifth-largest contractor, United Defense Industries, went public on December 14, 2001.[401] In one day, Carlyle earned $237 million through the selling of shares in the company. The percentage of this profit that went to former President Bush has been kept secret so as to minimize the public outcry.[402]

Another American president, Dwight D. Eisenhower, both served the NWO and warned about their growing influence. In his farewell address he said, "We must guard against the acquisition of unwarranted influence, whether sought or unsought, by the military-industrial complex."[403] His statement has been criticized by some as so vague as to be meaningless. You do not have to look hard for specific examples. One specific example is former President George H. W. Bush. When his son, President George W. Bush started the 2003 Iraq War, both father and son profited.[404]

Smedley Butler proposed that a declaration of war could only be valid if approved by the people subject to conscription. Conscription or the draft, unlike today's volunteer military, requires service from the children of the rich and powerful, not just the children of non-elite citizens. He also wanted safeguards against accidentally starting a war, and to specifically prevent the NWO from sending U.S. soldiers into a situation where they would be massacred, thereby becoming the catalyst for a call to war. For these reasons, in peacetime, he wanted Navy operations limited to 200 miles from the U.S. coastline and military aircraft restricted to 500 miles from the U.S. coast. In addition, during peacetime, the Army would be prohibited from leaving the United States.

Butler's key conclusions are just as trenchant today. Four steps are needed to smash the war racket. We must identify the NWO agents promoting war, take the profit out of war, permit the youth of the land to decide if they are willing to die for the proposed conflict, and limit America's military forces to home defense purposes.[405]

---

[401] United Defense 2001 Press Release, "United Defense Industries Commences Initial Public Offering Today," *United Defense Public Relations*, 14 December 2001.

[402] Mark Fineman, "Arms Buildup Enriches Firm Staffed by Big Guns, Ex-President and Other Elites are Behind Weapon-Boosting Carlyle Group," *Los Angeles Times*, 10 January 2002.

[403] President Dwight D. Eisenhower, "Farewell Address," *Our Documents initiative*, 17 January 1961. The complete text is online at www.ourdocuments.gov.

[404] Mark Fineman, "Arms Buildup Enriches Firm Staffed by Big Guns, Ex-President and Other Elites are Behind Weapon-Boosting Carlyle Group," *Los Angeles Times*, 10 January 2002.

[405] Smedley Butler with introduction by Adam Parfrey, *War Is a Racket* (Los Angeles, CA: Feral House, 1935, reprint edition April 2003), 42.

Understanding WMD Proliferation

The NWO uses American tax dollars to speed the development of weapons of mass destruction in other countries, especially in China, Pakistan, Saudi Arabia, and North Korea.[406] In addition, NWO stolen U.S. nuclear plans helped make possible the emergence of the former Soviet Union as a nuclear power. The NWO theft is documented by the U.S. Army officer who was ordered in 1943 to ship nuclear bomb materials to the Soviet Union. The officer, Major George Racey Jordan, explained the treason in his book *From Major Jordan's Diaries*.[407] Jordan revealed that FDR's top advisor, Harry Hopkins, who was a senior NWO insider, directed the shipment of over $11 billion in lend-lease aid to the Soviet Union.

A post-war Congressional investigation concluded that Hopkins had given the Soviets the blueprints for the atomic bomb and nuclear materials. With Hopkins already dead, members of Congress were convinced it was in the best interest of the American people to let the treason go unprosecuted. The suppression of the truth, in this case Hopkins' work for the NWO, is never in the best interest of the American people. The truth, then and now, is that not prosecuting Executive Branch related crimes routinely serves the interest of the NWO.

Today, few people realize that the 20th century plans for all of the United States' most advanced nuclear bombs have been stolen and distributed to select countries that are needed to help in the establishment of ten global economic zones. *The United States House of Representatives Select Committee on U.S. National Security and Military/Commercial Concerns with the People's Republic of China* report in 1999 documents this fact.

For example, the Select Committee concluded that China has obtained the plans for every currently-deployed thermonuclear warhead in the U.S. ballistic missile arsenal, as well as futuristic weapons like the neutron bomb that have yet to be developed. China has aggressively marketed the stolen information around the world to North Korea, Saudi Arabia, Pakistan, and Iran.[408] This continues to happen with little notice paid by citizens because the NWO routinely controls people in the top U.S. government positions as well as the flow of information through media ownership.

---

[406] The United States House of Representatives Select Committee on U.S. National Security and Military/ Commercial Concerns with the People's Republic of China declassified report issued on 3 January 1999.

[407] Major George Racey Jordan, *From Major Jordan's Diaries* (The Boomailer, 1962).

[408] The United States House of Representatives Select Committee on U.S. National Security and Military/ Commercial Concerns with the People's Republic of China declassified report issued on 3 January 1999.

The Select Committee concluded that these thefts of nuclear secrets from America's national weapons laboratories enabled the People's Republic of China to design, develop, and successfully test modern strategic nuclear bombs sooner than would otherwise have been possible. China's thefts from the National Laboratories began at least as early as the late 1970s. Significant secrets are known to have been stolen, and almost certainly continue to the present. The 1999 Select Committee report proved to be accurate in 2004 when it was announced that four employees were fired after the disappearance of classified information from the Los Alamos labs.[409]

Overkill and Overspending

It is unfortunate that compassionate conservatism has nothing to do with prudent government spending. The war business rewards NWO insiders. America's representatives tremble in fear at the thought of opposing a military spending bill because such a stand is guaranteed to be used by political opponents when seeking reelection. We are bombarded with constant false messages that greater security is possible when more money is provided for the military, the intelligence community, and the development of weapons of mass destruction.

The United States and Russia both continue to carry a bigger nuclear stick than anyone could ever conceivably need as a deterrent or for any other reason.[410] Former Secretary of Defense Robert McNamara and author James Blight observed that between 1987 and 1998 the U.S. reduced its nuclear force from 13,655 strategic warheads to 7,256, and the Soviet Union (and then Russia) moved from 8,619 strategic warheads to 6,340.[411] Of the 7,256 U.S. nuclear warheads, 2,200 are on hair trigger alert. Missiles on land are ready for launch in two minutes, and missiles

---

[409] Mary Perea, "4 Workers Fired in Los Alamos Lab Scandal," *Associated Press*, 16 September 2004.

[410] Thomas B. Cochran, Matthew G. McKinzie, Robert S. Norris, William M. Arkin, Co-authors in the National Resources Defense Council Nuclear Program, *The U.S. Nuclear War Plan: A Time For Change*, (National Resources Defense Council, June 2001), 130. Also, Frances Fitzgerald, *Way Out There in the Blue: Reagan, Star Wars, and the End of the Cold War* (New York, New York: Touchstone, Simon and Schuster, April 2001), 85. Fitzgerald references McGeorge Bundy, *Danger and Survival: Choices About the Bomb in the First Fifty Years* (New York: Random House, 1988), 565. The United States and Russia maintain nuclear arsenals that are capable of destroying civilization on the planet. One U.S. nuclear submarine can carry 192 warheads and is capable by itself of destroying every large and medium-sized city in Russia and over one-third of Russia's citizenry.

[411] Robert S. McNamara and James G. Blight, *Wilson's Ghost: Reducing the Risk of Conflict, Killing, and Catastrophe in the 21st Century* (New York, New York: Public Affairs, 2001), 174.
Jon Brook Wolfsthal, Cristina-Astrid Chuen, Emily Ewell Daughtry, Editors, *Nuclear Status Report: Nuclear Weapons, Fissile Material, And Export Controls in the Former Soviet Union, Number 6*, (Carnegie Endowment for International Peace and the Monterey Institute of International Studies, June 2001), 2. Also, Thomas B. Cochran, Matthew G. McKinzie, Robert S. Norris, William M. Arkin, Co-authors in the National Resources Defense Council Nuclear Program, *The U.S. Nuclear War Plan: A Time for Change*, (National Resources Defense Council, June 2001), 18.

on two submarines in the Atlantic and two submarines in the Pacific can be launched in 15 minutes.[412]

Nuclear bombs are in at least 14 countries with many more countries having the potential to make them.[413] More than 3,700 metric tons of highly enriched uranium and plutonium are dispersed in at least 60 countries.[414] No matter how much military spending is increased, unless the NWO is opposed, the 21st century will likely be the bloodiest in history. Estimates of 225 million civilians killed by acts of terror in the 21st century could reach much higher, as the NWO goal is to have a maximum world population of 500 million.[415]

The NWO influence on the U.S. has resulted in over five trillion dollars being spent on nuclear bombs since 1945. During this time more than 70,000 nuclear bombs have been developed.[416] Multiple presidents have been shocked at the cost and size of the U.S. arsenal. When President George W. Bush received his initial security briefing on the U.S. nuclear arsenal, he replied, "I had no idea we had so many weapons . . . what do we need them for?"[417] The common rationale supplied during the Cold War is that this massive arsenal was needed to defeat communism. This response was ridiculous then, but continues to be communicated. As each year passes, more people will likely realize that communism fell apart, not because of the number of missiles we developed, but because communism destroys the essential entrepreneurial spirit.

Consider the money that could have been kept in taxpayers' pockets or directed to support programs to benefit America's citizens. The total Pentagon spending between 1940 and 1998 exceeded $19 trillion. The magnitude of this amount can be appreciated when compared to the second highest government expenditure for the same period, which was $7.9 trillion for Social Security payments.[418] What would schools, transportation systems, health care options, and

---

[412] Bruce G. Blair, "America Doesn't Need All These Warheads," *International Herald Tribune*, 14 June 2000, 6.

[413] In 2005, the nuclear club included the United States, the Russian Federation, Great Britain, France, China, Israel, India, Pakistan, and North Korea. While nuclear bombs deployed by the United States outside its borders are classified, the United States is likely to have nuclear weapons in Great Britain, Turkey, Germany, Belgium, Italy and the Netherlands. Iran's nuclear program is expected to increase the number of countries to 15.

[414] David Albright, Frans Berkhout, and William Walker, "Global Fissile Material Inventories," *The Institute for Science and International Security*, June 2004.

[415] Robert S. McNamara and James G. Blight, *Wilson's Ghost: Reducing The Risk Of Conflict, Killing, And Catastrophe In The 21st Century* (New York, New York: Public Affairs, 2001), 26 for the estimate of 225 million.

[416] Stephen I. Schwartz, *Atomic Audit, The Costs and Consequences of U.S. Nuclear Weapons Since 1940* (Washington, D.C.: Brookings Institution Press, 1998).

[417] John Barry and Evan Thomas, "Dropping the Bomb," *Newsweek*, 25 June 2001.

[418] Ken Silverstein, *Private Warriors* (New York, NY: Verso, October 2000), Page viii.

employment opportunities be like if a portion of the trillions of dollars spent on nuclear bombs had been spent to improve the United States? Some may argue that defense spending is only a small percentage of the total U.S. Gross Domestic Product (GDP). However, when billions and trillions are at risk of being wasted and, furthermore, create nuclear overkill that lowers U.S. security, the percent of U.S. GDP becomes irrelevant. When it comes to defense spending, what is relevant is asking if the dollars spent have made people safer.

History teaches us that the true cost of war is routinely underestimated; almost always wars are projected to cost only a fraction of their true price tag. To illustrate, the Civil War was estimated by Lincoln's Secretary of the Treasury to cost $240 million, or seven percent of the U.S. GDP, however, the actual cost for the North was $3.2 billion. The official projection was 13 times too low.[419] Why are overly optimistic war costs routinely put before Congress and the American public? Because the reality is that most people would not support going to war if they understood the true cost of war. As Senator Hiram Johnson said during World War I, "The first casualty when war comes is truth."[420]

Imagine what the public reaction would have been to the Vietnam War if citizens knew the Pentagon's war estimates throughout the 1960s were in error on the low side by 90%.[421] The Pentagon's error is compounded when the actual costs, including inflation and other post-war factors, are considered. Of course, the real cost is in lost lives and human suffering, but realizing that financial costs are not honestly projected or disclosed is important.

The Afghanistan and Iraq expense is ongoing and far higher than what was sold to the American people. Donald Rumsfeld knowingly lied when he said, "Well, the Office of Management and Budget has come up with a number that's something *under $50 billion* for the cost. How much of that would be the U.S. burden, and how much would be other countries, is an open question."[422] Lawrence Lindsey, President George W. Bush's chief economic adviser, was fired prior to Rumsfeld's statement because he calculated the cost of invading Iraq at $100 billion to

---

[419] Carl Kaysen and others, "War With Iraq: Costs, Consequences and Alternatives," *The American Academy of Arts and Sciences*, December 2002, 59 and online at www.amacad.org/publications/monographs/War_with_ Iraq.pdf).

[420] Senator Hiram Johnson (1866-1945), a progressive Republican Senator in California, his statement to the United States Senate in 1917. "The first casualty when war comes is truth."

[421] Arthur Okun, *The Political Economy of Prosperity* (Washington, D.C.: Brookings, 1970), Chapter 3.

[422] P.J. Crowley and Sonal Shah, "The WMD Sequel: Iraq, Afghanistan and Deficit Reduction," Center for American Progress, 30 March 2004. The U.S. is spending over $4.7 billion a month fighting in Iraq and Afghanistan.

$200 billion.[423] America has already far surpassed even Lindsey's calculation. By the beginning of 2013, the cost of the wars in Afghanistan and Iraq exceeded $2 trillion.[424]

Overkill and overspending can be better understood when contrasted with opportunities to help the world. Sadly, the NWO has used countries to buy unneeded weapons and fight wars which continue worldwide hunger and the cycle of poverty. What would the world look like today if the over five trillion dollars that the United States wasted on additional nuclear bombs after 1945 was invested in programs to break the cycle of poverty at home and around the world?

All Americans should try to imagine what the U.S. would look like if over half of all spending by Congress did not go to the war business. Just a small fraction of this spending could mean the difference in a number of important programs of social uplift. Over 48 million Americans lack health insurance, and nearly one in five U.S. children live in poverty.[425] The price of dominating the world with weapons is increased preventable suffering, endless wars, and the spiritual death of the country. The price of NWO wars is high, and military overspending is guaranteed to eventually bankrupt the entire country.

Does it make sense to have a U.S. military budget that exceeds that of the rest of the world combined? When a nation allows itself to be used by the NWO to dominate the earth and spends more on weapons than all nations combined, the price paid by its citizens is very high. Martin Luther King, Jr. saw this clearly when he said, "A nation that continues year after year to spend more money on military defense than on programs of social uplift is approaching spiritual death."[426]

Almost every American knows someone who makes their living from the war business. Smedley Butler's observations earlier in this chapter are important to remember. If you are

---

[423] James Fallows, "Bush's Lost Year," *The Atlantic Monthly*, October 2004, 70. A guaranteed way to be forced out of the Bush administration was to offer a realistic estimate for the cost of a war. Lawrence Lindsey, President George W. Bush's chief economic adviser, learned this when he was fired in December 2002 for calculating the cost of invading Iraq at $100 billion to $200 billion. This was a direct contradiction of the statements by Donald Rumsfeld and Paul Wolfowitz that the U.S. costs would be offset by Iraq's oil revenues and contributions from allies.

[424] Daniel Trotta, "Iraq War costs U.S. more than $2 trillion: study," *Reuters*, 14 March 2013. Cost of wars are calculated by adding funds allocated to Congress for the wars in Iraq and Afghanistan. Total costs of the wars allocated by Congress to date as of September 30, 2012 were $1.38 trillion (with $807 billion to Iraq and $571 billion to Afghanistan).

[425] David Morgan, "One in four Americans without health coverage: study," *Reuters*, 19 April 2012. The study by the Commonwealth Fund found that 26 percent of non-elderly adults went without insurance -- a percentage that researchers said equals about 48 million people.
According to the U.S. Census Bureau, 17.6% or nearly one in five children live in poverty.

[426] Martin Luther King, Jr., statement at Riverside Church, 4 April 1967.

earning an income from the war business, you are likely blinded by your conflict of interest and may not realize this until after the conflict of interest ends. America's number one export is weapons.[427]. Weapon sales are not going unnoticed. Creating international hatred for the U.S. is part of the NWO one-world plan to destroy the U.S. The benefit of dominating the world with weapons is not increased security for Americans but the advancement of the NWO's one-world plans, which are paving the way for the Antichrist.

International Arms Sales and Mercenary Corporations

When he was running for the presidency, candidate George W. Bush said, "We should not keep weapons that our military planners do not need. These unneeded weapons are the expensive relics of dead conflicts. And they do nothing to make us more secure. In addition, the United States should remove as many weapons as possible from high-alert, hair-trigger status—another unnecessary vestige of Cold War confrontation."[428]

Once in office, President George W. Bush had a change of heart. He promoted efforts to become the world leader of international arms sales and simultaneously cut programs that would have eliminated nuclear bombs at home and abroad. He also initiated efforts to obtain Congressional approval for a new class of "mini-nukes."[429] The campaign promises in May 2000 that sounded so wonderful were, in retrospect, just "lines" to get people to vote for him. He did not even bother to address this topic when he campaigned for reelection in 2004. NWO insider Barack Obama followed the same pattern with campaign promises to end the Iraq War and actions, once elected, that accelerated war spending.

At first glance, being the leading seller and distributor of weapons would appear financially profitable.[430] But the NWO has the U.S. not only sell the most weapons but also buy the most

---

[427] Wade Boese, "Global Arms Market Still U.S. Domain," *Arms Control Today* (October 2004, Volume 34, Number 8), 39. In 2004 the U.S. sold 57% of the weapons in the world.
Jasmin Melvin, "U.S. Leads World in Foreign Weapons Sales: Report," *Reuters*, 6 September 2009 and online at www.reuters.com/article/2009/09/06/us-arms-usa-idUSTRE5851XH20090906.In 2008, the U.S. market position increased to 68.4% or two-thirds of all weapons sold. In 2013 the U.S. continued as the dominant seller and distributor of weapons.

[428] George W. Bush, as a candidate for President, statement on 23 May 2000 regarding national security issues and the prospect of a brighter future.

[429] Congress passed the Omnibus Appropriations Bill on November 20, 2004. This bill denied funding for new nuclear "bunker buster" weapons that President Bush promoted. The Bush administration request for funds to build a facility for plutonium pits for new nuclear bombs was approved but reduced from $29.8 million to $7 million.

[430] *Holy Bible: New American Standard Bible* (Grand Rapids, Michigan: Zondervan, 2002), 812. Matthew 26:52: "Put your sword back into its place; for all those who take up the sword shall perish by the sword." If the Bible is a source of guidance for you, does this mean that unless the United States changes

weapons. The Stockholm International Peace Research Institute or SIPRI reported that in 2010 the U.S. bought 42.8% of all weapons sold globally.[431]

In general, the official NWO policy is to use the U.S. to promote weapons sales as aggressively as possible in most places around the world. As the U.S. economy become unable to sustain massive weapons "gifts" to other countries, the NWO will use China to increasingly fill the void.[432] A chaotic and insecure world is the ideal state for keeping people distracted from seeing the NWO threat. Raymond Mabus, a former ambassador to Saudi Arabia, summed up how the U.S. views weapons sales when he said, "It is our job to do everything possible, and legal, to make sure they buy American."[433] Unlike economic aid, when military aid is given, Congress is not required to vote. A study by Lora Lumpe of the Federation of American Scientists found that the U.S. shipped some seven billion dollars' worth of free military equipment abroad between 1990 and 1996.[434] Secret U.S. wars have escalated since 1996, and the amount of military equipment delivered now is likely much higher.

U.S. foreign aid is substantial, but not after military aid is subtracted. When the military aid is added, the U.S. routinely tops the giving charts. When military aid is excluded, U.S. foreign aid as a percentage of gross national product (GNP) often ranks last among the world's wealthiest countries at about 0.1 percent.[435]

Major General Smedley Butler offered a perspective on selling weapons that is worth remembering. He said, "Do you really think that if you start handing your Democratic friend ammunition, you won't get into it, too? You can't help it."[436] Promoting weapons, one of the United States' top exports, keeps America's defense factories warm at the moment, but will one day come back to haunt the country.[437] Butler concluded that if you sell weapons to the winners,

---

the policy of being the number one sword wielder, the United States will someday perish by nuclear bombs?

[431] World military spending in 2010 was estimated at 1.630 trillion and the Stockholm International Peace Research Institute report is online at www.sipri.org/research/armaments/milex/factsheet2010.

[432] Shaun Waterman, "China overtakes U.K. as fifth-largest arms exporter; U.S. still No. 1," *The Washington Times*, 18 March 2013.

[433] Ken Silverstein, *Private Warriors* (New York, NY: Verso, October 2000), 30. Raymond Mabus, a former ambassador to Saudi Arabia, interview with the Boston Globe in 1996.

[434] Ibid., 31.

[435] Multiple sources estimate the 2003 to 2011 foreign aid percentage of GNP is about .1 percent see "Terrorism Questions & Answers: Foreign Aid," *Council on Foreign Relations*, August 2002. Available online at www.cfrterrorism.org/policy/foreignaid.html#Q4.

[436] Smedley Butler with introduction by Adam Parfrey, *War Is a Racket* (Los Angeles, CA: Feral House, 1935, reprint edition April 2003), 51.

[437] William Greider, *Fortress America: The American Military and the Consequences of Peace* (Public Affairs, New York, December 1999), 183.

the winners will hate you because you took advantage of them in their time of need.[438] If you are selling weapons to the losers, you need to get in the fight because losers don't exist after they lose or are so bankrupt that they cannot pay for the weapons you sold them. The NWO, by using countries as fronts, directs the anger at specific nations and away from them. This anger is essential to win support for world government and to destroy countries.

The NWO is increasingly using mercenary corporations. Companies that sell mercenary combat forces are far from new. If there is anything good about the war in Iraq, it is that Americans are becoming aware of mercenary corporations as they hear the odd and unfamiliar names of the companies operating in Iraq. Unfortunately the name of the company is revealed when an employee is taken hostage or killed. It is also noteworthy that people tend to care less about mercenaries than they do about soldiers who are killed. Often the dead mercenary does not even show up in the news. The bottom line is that the capture or murder of mercenaries carries almost no political risk.

Politicians like mercenaries because even if they are American citizens and are killed, they don't get added in with the U.S. body count. For the military, the situation is a mixed bag. Companies like Military Professional Resources, Inc. (MPRI) can send out twenty former U.S. colonels to a hot spot in the matter of a day. MPRI, founded in 1987 by retired Army General Vernon Lewis, is one of the largest mercenary training firms. As currently configured, significant command voids would be created if the U.S. Army had to group twenty former field officers for an assignment in just a few days' time.[439] The military has to give up some control when using mercenaries, but it is viewed as worth it by many senior commanders who are only a few years away from lucrative retirement years made possible through mercenary corporations.

A summary of one private mercenary corporation will help illustrate the privatization of the U.S. military. Vinnell, a company started in 1931, came on the defense scene in 1946 as a government contractor. In 1975 Vinnell won a contract to train Saudi Arabia's National Guard. In 1992 the company was acquired by BDM. A joint venture with Saudi Arabia, called Vinnell Arabia, was started in 1995. BDM at the time was owned by the Carlyle Group. Former senior U.S. officials who have had leadership positions with Vinnell include former Secretary of State James Baker, former White House budget Chief Richard Darman, and former Secretary of Defense Frank Carlucci. In 1997, Vinnell was acquired by TRW, which was then acquired in 2002 by Northrop Grumman Corporation.[440] In 2003, Vinnell was awarded a $48 million contract to

---

[438] Ibid., 51.

[439] Ibid., 166-167.

[440] These private mercenary corporations tend to change their corporate ownership often; it is analogous to a soldier changing his or her camouflage.

train the nucleus of a new Iraqi Army. The $48 million figure is significant, as Congress receives notification only if a contract is worth more than $50 million.

Booz-Allen Hamilton, one of the biggest consulting firms in the U.S., is another NWO front firm. It oversees the Saudi Marine Corps and also runs the Saudi Armed Forces Staff College. They teach senior-level military skills and tactical training. Another firm, DynCorp, is active in Latin America, Africa, and now Iraq. The company has over 17,000 employees, over 550 operating facilities around the world, and annual revenues of $1.3 billion. DynCorp, like many of the private mercenary corporations, has its corporate office in Virginia.[441] The Virginia headquarters is convenient as it is widely understood that the larger mercenary corporations often receive their operating instructions directly from the CIA headquarters in Langley, Virginia.[442]

In 2011 the United Arab Emirates hired Erik Prince, the billionaire founder of mercenaries-of-death-for-the-highest-bidder firm Blackwater Worldwide to create an 800-member battalion of foreign "only" troops for the United Arab Emirates. The reason for the $529 million contract with Erik Prince is that in 2011 former Egyptian dictator Hosni Mubarak could not get his military to slaughter unarmed peaceful citizens. Erik Prince gives the United Arab Emirates dictator Sheik Mohamed bin Zayed al-Nahyan the option of slaughtering peaceful people demanding civil rights.

The Death of the Proxmire Law

The revolving door that exists between the people who serve the United States and the defense contractors who sell these same people weapons undermines America's democracy. Senior members of the military and Pentagon sometimes have an incentive to help war businesses because they are remembered when they retire with significant salaries and bonuses in the war industry. The limited efforts in the 1990s to monitor these revolving doors illustrate just how widespread these practices have become.

In the 1990s, a law sponsored by former Wisconsin Senator William Proxmire provided information on the conflict of interest between the military and defense contractors. The Proxmire Law required former Pentagon employees to file a disclosure report upon taking a position in the defense industry paying more than $25,000 a year. The Proxmire Law was repealed in 1996 even though the law never prevented anyone from taking a position with a

---

[441] Ken Silverstein, *Private Warriors* (New York, New York: Verso, October 2000), 180-182.

[442] Langley, Virginia is the headquarters for the Central Intelligence Agency. The headquarters compound was named the George H.W. Bush Center for Central Intelligence in 1998.

defense contractor.[443] All Proxmire Law records were shredded by the Pentagon except for the years 1992 to 1995. In that time, 2,482 officers above the rank of lieutenant colonel went to work in the weapons and war business.[444]

One of the best reports on the revolving door is in the book *Private Warriors*. Author Ken Silverstein observes, "The Defense Security Cooperation Agency (DSCA), the Pentagon bureau that oversees the government's Foreign Military Sales program, is a prime example of the revolving door." Nine out of ten of the last DSCA leaders went on to work in the arms industry after leaving the DSCA. With the growth of private mercenary corporations, the conflict of interest issues are increasing.

Becoming the NWO's Darth Vader

The NWO has used the U.S. to participate in great evil. Contrary to what many people may wish to believe, Vietnam and the Native Americans are not America's only "massacres," and Americans are not exempt from torturing people or sponsoring massacres. Massacres or the killing of civilians, including women and children, are becoming increasingly accepted. A media story about U.S. bombs falling in a far-off place to counter terrorism may not even result in the listener thinking about what this means to the innocent people who happen to be near the explosion.

Americans see movies like *Black Hawk Down* and leave the theater thinking about the two UH-60 Blackhawk helicopters that were shot down and the daring fighting the movie portrayed.[445] Others leave the theater stunned by the poverty of the people in Somalia or the loss of the 18 Americans who were killed in Mogadishu. Few people leaving the theater would likely be thinking about the five hundred local people massacred and the thousand more who were injured during the fiasco. Even today, the fact that hundreds of innocent women and children were killed in the crossfire is unknown to most Americans.

How many Americans see the events in Somalia on October 3, 1993 as a massacre? Americans should consider how we would react if a foreign power flew in with helicopters to arrest a local leader. To give a historical perspective for how an American might feel, we can go back to March 5, 1770, when British soldiers killed five colonists. Schools teach high school students about

---

[443] Ken Silverstein, *Private Warriors* (New York, New York: Verso, October 2000), 192. The Pentagon requested the law be eliminated and Congress repealed the Proxmire Law in February 1996.

[444] Ibid., 191-193.

[445] Mark Bowden, *Black Hawk Down: A Story of Modern War* (New York, New York: Penguin Books, February 2000). About 120 U.S. soldiers attempted to capture two top lieutenants of Somalian warlord Mohamed Farrah Aidid. To learn more, visit www.blackhawkdown.com.

this event, known as the Boston Massacre, to illustrate the evils of being occupied by a foreign power.

How will the Black Hawk event be viewed in Somalia as the story is told from one generation to the next? How does the son or daughter of one of the many local people who was killed fighting "foreign invaders" feel about the United States? How will the people of Somalia, a country that is 99% Muslim, view non-Muslims? What will they say to their children? Has this and other NWO orchestrated intervention in Africa planted the seeds of future violence?

The answers to the preceding questions are not promising for Americans wishing to travel or do volunteer work in Somalia any time in the next twenty years. Michael Vlahos, a political scientist and former Cold War policy analyst, observes, "We, the United States, may become the Darth Vader wearing the black helmet. We've created an industrial system that works for us and some allies but is imperial and seems oppressive to many others. We increasingly will find ourselves in the same position as empires of the past, the Persians and Romans, Spain under Phillip II, the British in the late nineteenth century."[446] Vlahos' observations are valuable, although he failed to observe that the system does not work for U.S. citizens in the long run either.

The Darth Vader reference to the science fiction movie *Star Wars* is a powerful one. Specifically, Darth Vader starts off as a good person or "force" and becomes corrupt. He eventually becomes a lead agent of evil in the empire. Although this analogy may initially sound crazy, when you consider America's far and away number one leadership in weapons of death around the world, disdain for international justice, massive arsenal of nuclear bombs, military bases in over 130 countries, torture programs, assassination lists, and policies of preemptive wars, the comparison is not so crazy.[447]

---

[446] William Greider, *Fortress America: The American Military and the Consequences of Peace* (New York, New York: Public Affairs, December 1999), 147.

[447] Kelley Beaucar Vlahos, "Analysts Ponder U.S. Basing in Iraq," *Fox News*, 1 November 2004. Available online at www.foxnews.com/story/0,2933,137210,00.html.
On 07/15/2004, the United States House of Representatives passed H.AMDT.706 - H.R.4818: to prohibit Economic Support Funding assistance to the government of any country that is a party to the International Criminal Court and has not signed an Article 98 agreement to surrender U.S. nationals to the ICC by a vote of 241-166.

8

MIND CONTROL

During a war, news should be given out for instruction rather than information.[448]
Joseph Goebbels

CIA mind control experiments from the late 1940s to the late 1960s were exposed in 1974.[449] The first projects were started by Nazi war criminals who were secretly brought to the U.S. and is explained in Chapter 3.[450] The rocket program dimension of this secret program named Operation Paperclip is explained in Chapter 9.

Bluebird, Artichoke, MKULTRA and MKDELTA

The U.S. mind control project was given the code name "Bluebird" in 1947.[451] In 1951, the code name became Artichoke, and in 1953 the program name was changed to MKULTRA. CIA Director Richard Helms confirmed the MKULTRA program existed, and claimed it ended in 1973. He did not tell Congress and the American people that a new program, MKDELTA continued to operate.

The mind control program focused on how to reduce intelligence, make people more docile, decrease the global population, and deceive people that the NWO is only a conspiracy theory. In light of the negative knee-jerk reaction many people have when the existence of the NWO is presented,

---

[448] Joseph Goebbels (October 29, 1897-1 May 1945) was the Nazi minister in charge of "public enlightenment and propaganda" from 1933 to 1945.

[449] Carol Rutz, *A Nation Betrayed: Secret Cold War Experiments Performed on our Children and Other Innocent People* (Grand Lake, Michigan: Fidelity Publishing, 2001). Alan W. Scheflin and Edward M. Opton Jr. also provide concrete examples of CIA mind control experiments in their 1978 *The Mind Manipulators* book.

[450] Operation Paperclip was the Office of Strategic Services (OSS) program that gave new identities to Nazi leaders.

[451] Dr. Colin A. Ross, *Bluebird: Deliberate Creation of Multiple Personality by Psychiatrists* (Richardson, Texas: Manitou Communications, Inc., 2000).

the mind control efforts appear to be generally successful. For these reasons, claims that the public is being exposed to a mass medication cocktail as part of a mind control objective deserve serious consideration.[452] Illegal drugs are also believed to be part of the mind control suite of ingredients and may be a key reason the CIA is actively involved in importing narcotics into the country.[453] Radiation is another believed component where electromagnetic wireless radiation or a medical X-ray triggers a cancer introduced via vaccines, food, blood transfusions, or sexual activity.[454]

Some of the details of MKULTRA have never been disclosed because in 1973 Richard Helms ordered all the files destroyed.[455] Fortunately, thousands of documents were not destroyed.[456] In 1974, MKULTRA secrets were published by reporter Seymour Hersh.[457] One document, a CIA inspector general report from 1963, revealed the MKULTRA project was putting "the rights and interests of all Americans in jeopardy" and violated the CIA charter.[458] MKULTRA was temporarily suspended, which prompted Helms to say "for over a decade Clandestine Services has had the mission of maintaining a capability for influencing human behavior.[459] The official

---

[452] Anahad O'Conner, Air Pollution Linked to Heart and Brain Risks, *The New York Times*, 15 February 2012. Common air pollutants include carbon monoxide, nitrogen dioxide, sulfur dioxide which are dangerous to humans. Three 2012 medical studies found people exposed to higher levels of air pollution experience cognitive deterioration.

[453] Alfred W. McCoy and Cathleen B. Read, *The Politics of Heroin: CIA Complicity in the Global Drug Trade* (New York, NY: Harper and Row, Publishers, Inc., 1972).

[454] Edward T. Haslam, *Dr. Mary's Monkey: How the Unsolved Murder of a Doctor, a Secret Laboratory in New Orleans and Cancer-Causing Monkey Viruses are Linked to Lee Harvey Oswald, the JFK Assassination and Emerging Global Epidemics* (Walterville, OR: TrineDay, 2007). He provides a summary of his work in the video online at www.youtube.com/watch?v=s-8RPHdu8tA. Haslam research provides a window into the JFK assassination as Lee Harvey Oswald worked with people at the secret New Orleans laboratory.

[455] Richard McGarrah Helms was born on March 30, 1913 and died on October 22, 2002.
Stephen Lendman, "MK-ULTRA: The CIA's Mind Control Program," *Steve Lendman*, 16 February 2010 and online at http://sjlendman.blogspot.com/2010/02/mk-ultra-cias-mind-control-program.html.

[456] Alfred W. McCoy, *A Question of Torture: CIA Interrogation, from the Cold War to the War on Terror* (New York, NY: Metropolitan Books, 2006), 28.
A clerical error sent some of the documents to the wrong office, so when CIA workers were destroying the files, key documents were missed and later released under a Freedom of Information Act request by investigative journalist John Marks.

[457] Seymour Hersh, "Huge CIA Operation Reported in US Against Antiwar Forces, Other Dissidents in Nixon Years," *The New York Times*, 22 December 1974.

[458] "Report of Inspection of MKULTRA," CIA, 26 July 1963. Portions of the CIA Inspector General report are online at www.teachpeace.com/mkultra.htm.
Alfred W. McCoy, *A Question of Torture: CIA Interrogation, from the Cold War to the War on Terror* (New York, NY: Metropolitan Books, 2006), 50.

[459] "Report of Inspection of MKULTRA," CIA, 26 July 1963. Portions of the CIA Inspector General report are online at www.teachpeace.com/mkultra.htm.

suspension was soon lifted and Helms was granted permission to continue the agency's "positive operational capability to use drugs."

An interesting insight into the character of CIA Director Helms came in 1977 when he was convicted of lying to the United States Congress. Helms was caught making bold false statements to the Senate Select Committee on Intelligence, ranging from the CIA's involvement in assassinations to programs intended to destabilize entire countries. He paid a $2,000 fine but avoided jail when his two-year prison sentence was suspended.[460]

The MKULTRA findings were used to create the infamous 1963 *Kubark Counterintelligence Interrogation* torture manual.[461] Intelligence insiders know Kubark is a cryptonym for the CIA. The torture manual is the foundation for the CIA's 1983 *Human Resource Exploitation Training Manual* and the Honduran Battalion 316 torture manual.[462] The 1963 and 1983 torture manuals were first obtained in 1997 when the *Baltimore Sun* requested the information under the Freedom of Information Act.[463]

The publication by Seymour Hersh of the illegal MKULTRA mind control experiments on American citizens, especially on children, shocked the American people.[464] Years later, the U.S. government confirmed that between 1944 and 1974, several thousand human radiation experiments were conducted involving both non-consenting adults and children.[465] Carol Rutz subsequently documented experiments that included feeding radioactive cereal to children in the

---

[460] Thomas Powers, *The Man Who Kept the Secrets: Richard Helms and the CIA* (New York: Knopf, 1979).

[461] The once Secret No Foreign Dissemination torture manual is online www.gwu.edu/~nsarchiv/NSAEBB/NSAEBB122/index.htm#kubark.

[462] The formerly Secret 1983 torture manual is online at Ibid. The classified torture manual is online www.gwu.edu/~nsarchiv/NSAEBB/NSAEBB122/index.htm#kubark and www.gwu.edu/~nsarchiv/NSAEBB/NSAEBB122/CIA%20Human%20Res%20Exploit%20H0-L17.pdf.

[463] The Freedom of Information Act was enacted by President Lyndon B. Johnson on July 4, 1966 as 5 U.S.C. § 552 and went into effect in 1967.

[464] Seymour Hersh, "Huge CIA Operation Reported in US Against Antiwar Forces, Other Dissidents in Nixon Years," *The New York Times*, 22 December 1974.

[465] William Jefferson Blythe III is better known as President Bill Clinton. Clinton entered the NWO elite as a Rhodes Scholarship recipient. He appointed the Advisory Committee on Human Radiation Experiments on January 15, 1994 to keep the hidden hand of the NWO hidden. Secret and illegal testing on the general public, including children, was documented in the Advisory Committee report. The illegal human experimentation was determined to have been well intended and found to have "contributed significantly to advances in medicine and thus to the health of the public." The Advisory Committee on Human Radiation Experiments report is online at www.hss.energy.gov/HealthSafety/ohre/roadmap/achre/index.html.

1940s and 1950s.[466] The documentary *Declassified: Human Experimentation* is recommended in order to learn more.[467]

Congressional investigations were initiated in 1975 and led by Senator Frank Church.[468] His committee was known as the Church Committee and was supplemented by the Nedzi Committee which was replaced by the Pike Committee.[469] The Pike Committee was the first serious Congressional investigation of CIA activities. The House voted to suppress the Pike Committee report claiming the report would damage national security.[470] Congressman Pike objected to attempts to both censor and rewrite the report.

On February 16, 1976, a leaked version of the report was published by *The Village Voice* with the title "The Report on the CIA that President Ford Doesn't Want You to Read."[471]

Vice-President Nelson Rockefeller was assigned in order to cover-up the damage done by the Pike Committee. Rockefeller's service to the NWO had a significant impact on the United States in the administrations of Franklin Roosevelt, Harry Truman, Dwight Eisenhower, and Gerald Ford.[472] His leadership after the Pike Committee also effectively ended additional investigations of domestic intelligence activities that exposed the NWO's hidden hand. Even with Rockefeller's attempt to manage the damage, the public had solid confirmation that illegal mind control experiments were conducted and that the head of the CIA had lied to the American people. The

---

[466] Carol Rutz, *A Nation Betrayed: Secret Cold War Experiments Performed on our Children and Other Innocent People* (Grand Lake, Michigan: Fidelity Publishing, 2001).

[467] The documentary *Declassified Human Experimentation* (History Channel, 1 January 2008) explains U.S. government experiments on civilians. The documentary is online at www.youtube.com/watch?feature=player_embedded&v=-m7ex21XQjw.

[468] Ibid. The book, *Mind Controllers* by Dr. Armen Victorian, was published by Lewis International Inc. in 2000 and has additional information.

[469] Gordon Thomas, *Secrets and Lies: A History of CIA Mind Control and Germ Warfare* (Saybrook, Connecticut: Konecky, William S. Associates, Inc., 2007).

[470] The vote was 246 to 124 and took place on January 29, 1976.

[471] Gerald K. Haines, "The Pike Committee Investigations and the CIA: Looking for a Rogue Elephant," *CIA*, 14 April 2007 and online at www.cia.gov/library/center-for-the-study-of-intelligence/csi-publications/csi-studies/studies/winter98_99/art07.html. Haines is an employee of the CIA and his article was updated on 27 June 2008. *The Village Voice* version of the Pike Report was published in Britain in 1977 and includes an introduction by former CIA officer Philip Agee. Also see the August 3, 1977 report by Congress online at www.teachpeace.com/ProjectMKULTRA_Report.pdf.

[472] Nelson Rockefeller (July 8, 1908-January 26, 1979) was the 41st Vice President of the United States (1974-1977). An example of his statements to advance world government include: "And so the nation-state, standing alone, threatens in many ways to seem as anachronistic as the Greek city-state eventually became in ancient times." The quote is from a lecture at Harvard University in 1962 on the future of federalism.

disclosures also revealed that the mind control experiments were not conducted for the benefit of citizens or U.S. national security. Claims that student classrooms were used for secret testing on children all of a sudden were transformed from conspiracy nonsense into reality.

The Rockefeller "management" of the illegal tests for the NWO may be why classroom radon and many other known dangers remain uncorrected.[473] Unfortunately, with few exceptions, these experiments being conducted on our children, in attempts to help minimize their resistance to the New World Order's agenda, go undetected. As a result, the secret experiments for chemical, biological, and psychological mind control continue today.

Electromagnetic Control

A more modern version of MKULTRA likely still operates.[474] This new program uses commonly known and classified technologies ranging from electromagnetic radiation manipulation to the highly classified High Frequency Active Auroral Research Program discussed in the next chapter.

Reports of electromagnetic behavior control and weapons were once thought futuristic and dismissed as conspiracy nonsense.[475] The dismissal of electromagnetic mind control and weapons is no longer an issue as the public is increasingly learning about electromagnetic technologies ranging from products to eliminate cockroaches to E-bombs.[476] The Goodlife Pest Repeller Ultimate product uses electromagnetic energy to "irritate the nervous system of pests."[477] The E-bomb releases radio waves that can kill humans. The Active Denial System (ADS) is another publicly known directed energy weapon. In 2002 in Iraq, ADS was expected to be the first deployed use of high-power microwave weapons.[478] While ADS was presented as only burning a thin layer of skin, doctors in Iraq suspect a version of this system explains why Iraqis have been microwaved to death.

---

[473] Ben Hall, "Nashville Schools Test for Radon After 20-Year Delay," *News Channel 5*, 21 March 2011 and online at www.newschannel5.com/story/14292493/metro-schools-test-for-radon-after-20-year-delay. Other examples include schools serve harmful foods and expose students to dangerous electromagnetic fields.

[474] MKULTRA was also called Monarch or the Monarch Butterfly program.

[475] Opall, Barbara. "U.S. Explores Russian Mind-Control Technology," *Defense News*, 11-17 Jan 1993, 29.

[476] Brian Hoyle, "EMF Used as Weapons, 70 years of Awareness," *EMF Journal*, 28 February 2009 and online at http://emfjournal.com/2009/02/28/emf-used-as-weapons-70-years-of-awareness/. Very low frequency electromagnetic radiation is capable of inducing the brain to release chemicals to decrease alertness and release histamine.

[477] Goodlife corporation product advertising for their Pest Repeller Ultimate product on March 11, 2012 and online at www.pestrepellerultimate.com/a/rodent_2.htm.

[478] George Edmonson, "Super-Secret Microwave Weapons May Be Used in Iraq," *Cox News Service*, 14 August 2002 and online at www.seattlepi.com/news/article/Super-secret-microwave-weapons-may-be-used-in-Iraq-1093533.php.

On what may be a related note, after doctors in Iraq complained of people burned to death in ways never before seen, Pentagon officials made publicly false statements that the ADS was never deployed to Iraq.[479] According to the Pentagon, the ADS was only deployed in Afghanistan.[480] A version of the ADS is deployed at select U.S. prisons as a pain gun and is called the Assault Intervention Device.[481]

Nazi, CIA, and Fluoride Mind Control

In 2009 I was walking on the public grounds between Israel's Supreme Court and the Knesset, which is also known as Israel's Parliament. A group of Israelis were handing out literature opposing their government's attempt to institute mind control by adding fluoride to public drinking water. The Israelis claimed fluoride was being added to the water to make people more docile and reduce opposition to government actions to discriminate against and kill Palestinians.

My experience in Israel prompted me to inquire if the CIA had tested fluoride as a mind control drug. I found the answer is yes and is documented in a CIA memo that former CIA Director Richard Helms failed to destroy.[482] The surviving fluoride document is "Behavior Control Materials and Advanced Research," dated March 16, 1966.[483]

---

[479] Richard Lardner, "Pentagon Nixes Ray Gun Weapon in Iraq," *USA Today*, 29 August 2007 and online at www.usatoday.com/news/washington/2007-08-29-1998518105_x.htm.

[480] Dan Cairns, "US Army Heat-Ray Gun in Afghanistan," *BBC*, 15 July 2010 and online at www.bbc.co.uk/newsbeat/10646540.

[481] Bill Christensen, "Assault Intervention Device - A Pain Ray Gun," Technovelgy.com, 22 September 2010 and online at www.technovelgy.com/ct/Science-Fiction-News.asp?NewsNum=3024.
The Assault Intervention Device is a uses a directed beam of electromagnetic radiation waves to create pain and has the potential to make people sterile along with causing cancer.

[482] Trowbridge H. Ford, "Richard Helms: The Most Dangerous CIA Director," *Veterans Today*, 23 August 2011 and online at www.veteranstoday.com/2011/08/23/richard-helms-the-most-dangerous-cia-director/.
In 1935 Helms worked for United Press in Germany and interviewed Adolf Hitler. Helms joined the Office of Strategic Services and worked with mind control scientist Stanley Lovell. In 1960 he was directly involved in secret operations with Lee Harvey Oswald and the Gary Powers U2 shoot down. He oversaw the NWO and CIA program called Operation CHAOS to spy on Americans. He was both convicted of lying to the American people and sentenced in 1977 to a two-year prison sentence. His sentence was suspended and he was given special honors by presidents Ronald Reagan and George W. Bush. Reagan presented this NWO agent the Medal of Freedom and Bush permitted him to be buried with military honors at Arlington National Cemetery.

[483] Christopher Bryson, *The Fluoride Deception* (New York: Seven Stories Press, 2004), 92. The memo from the CIA Technical Services Division, reported on the disabling effects of "dinitrofluoride derivatives of acetic acid" and confirmed clinical tests were being conducted.

In the years after World War II, NWO mind control experiments were increasingly disclosed. The 1964 *Dr. Strangelove* satire is an example of public conditioning to dismiss people reporting fluoride information as lunatics. The film by Stanley Kubrick presented off-the-wall notions that a single U.S. Air Force officer could exploit fail-safe systems to commence nuclear war. The officer, General Jack Ripper, also declares that water is being fluoridated as part of a "conspiracy to sap and pollute" our bodies.[484] We now know that the claims in the film have turned out to be real, including that the fail-safe system that allowed General Ripper to commence nuclear war was the actual top-secret fail-safe system at the time.[485] We also know Kubrick worked secretly for people advancing the NWO. The "crazy" idea that water fluoridation serves a hidden purpose is not easily dismissed.[486] *The New York Times* published an article in 2004 explaining why *Dr. Strangelove* was far closer to a documentary than had been thought for decades.[487]

Journalist John Marks obtained additional mind control documents under the Freedom of Information Act, and by 1977 some 6,000 CIA MKULTRA related documents were confirmed to exist.[488] The Director of the CIA in 1977, Admiral Stansfield M. Turner, revealed that 5,000 CIA mind control program documents were not shared with the Senate intelligence committee

---

[484] In the film General Jack D. Ripper, played by Sterling Hayden, is presented as crazy and his fluoridation of water statement put anyone claiming sodium fluoride was a health concern into the conspiracy nut category which did help the public be deceived to dismiss it was really being tested and deployed by the NWO.

[485] Stanley Kubrick (July 26, 1928-March 7, 1999) was a Jewish-American director making films to condition the public and participated in top-secret government projects.

[486] Fred Kaplan, "Truth Stranger Than Strangelove," *The New York Times*, 10 October 2004 and online at www.nytimes.com/2004/10/10/movies/10kapl.html?_r=1&pagewanted=all&position=.
Similar to *Dr. Strangelove* being more truth than fiction, William Karel made a fictional 2002 film, *Dark Side of the Moon* which was narrated by Andrew Solomon and co-produced by Point du Jour Production with ARTE France. The film is packed with elite members of secret societies advancing the NWO. Buzz Aldrin, Christiane Kubrick, Lawrence Eagleburger, Alexander Haig, Henry Kissinger, Donald Rumsfeld, Richard Helms, Vernon Walters, and Nixon's secretary Eve Kendall read scripts with hard-to-believe statements about the first moon landing. A central theme is Kubrick made videos and pictures in the event that no live pictures could be transmitted from the moon.

[487] Ibid. Kaplan's article notes that after watching Dr. Strangelove, Daniel Ellsberg (born April 7, 1931) exclaimed, "That was a documentary!" Daniel Ellsberg's statement is noteworthy. He was the person who informed Robert McNamara of the Gulf of Tonkin incident. Ellsberg was employed by the NWO's RAND Corporation when he released the classified Pentagon Papers. Portions of the Pentagon Papers were published by *The New York Times* and on June 13, 2011, the National Archives published the complete version which is online at www.archives.gov/research/pentagon-papers. The Pentagon Papers served to shift the focus from the CIA and NWO placing the blame on the U.S. military. Had the CIA role been honestly investigated, the hidden hand of the NWO would have been exposed as the entity responsible for the Vietnam War.

[488] Nicholas M. Horrock, "C.I.A. Data Show 14-Year Project On Controlling Human Behavior," *New York Times*, 21 July 1977 and online at www.wanttoknow.info/770721nytimes.ciahumanbehaviorcontrol.

in 1975.[489] Declassified mind control documents are shocking, and confirm that the CIA was successful in making people do things they would not do normally; in addition, those experimented upon have no memory of their actions ranging from sex to secret agent work.[490]

The CIA studies are not surprising given that Nazi mind control scientists were recruited in Operation Paperclip, and I. G. Farben, the German chemical conglomerate, produced a wide range of chemicals including sodium fluoride. You won't have to search long to find "experts" claiming Nazi and CIA human fluoride mind control programs are a myth, but they never explain why Richard Helms illegally destroyed the secret mind control documents.[491]

Scientists have known for many years that fluoride is a toxic waste and is in nerve gas and rat poison. Fluoride is a Schedule 2 Poison under the Poisons Act of 1972.[492] The next time you brush your teeth with fluoride toothpaste, read the warning label instructing you not to swallow fluoride and "if accidentally swallowed, get medical help or contact a Poison Control Center right away." Fluoride, a by-product of aluminum manufacturing, is also suspected to be linked to cognitive disorders, including Alzheimer's Disease.[493]

Dr. Emanuel H. Bronner tried to warn the public with a letter to the editor published in 1952.[494] He wrote:

> "There is a sinister network of subversive agents, Godless intellectual parasites, working in our country today whose ramifications grow more extensive, more successful and more alarming each new year and whose true objective is to demoralize, paralyze

---

[489] Ibid.

[490] CIA document numbers 190684, 17395, 17748, 190691, 190527 and 140393 available online at www.wanttoknow.info/mind_control/cia_mind_control_experiments_sex_abuse.

[491] Thomas Powers, *The man who kept the secrets: Richard Helms and the CIA* (New York: Knopf, 1979). Joseph Borkin, *The Crime and Punishment of I. G. Farben: The Unholy Alliance Between Hitler and the Great Chemical Combine* (Pocket, 1997). Borkin was an attorney who during World War II helped prosecute I. G. Farben cartels. As the chief of the Patent and Cartel section of the Antitrust Division of the Department of Justice, Borkin's knowledge of how the Nazi's used fluoride was extensive. In 1943 he co-authored a book, *Germany's Master Plan*, which explained Hitler's plan for a New World Order.

[492] Dr. Barry Durrant-Peatfield, "The Effects of Fluoride on the Thyroid Gland," *Rense.com*, 9 September 2004 and online at www.rense.com/general57/FLUR.HTM.

[493] Arthur S. Kraus and William F. Forbes, "Aluminum, Fluoride and the Prevention of Alzheimer's Disease," *Canadian Journal of Public Health*, March-April 1992 and see http://findarticles.com/p/articles/mi_m0887/is_n7-8_v11/ai_12560842/.

[494] Emanual H. Bronner (February 1, 1908-March 7, 1997), Letter to the editor - "Just One Turn On One Value And!!!," *Catholic Mirror*, Springfield, Massachusetts, January 1952. Dr. Bronner emigrated to the U.S. in 1929 and is the creator of Dr. Bronner's castile soap.

and destroy our great Republic—from within if they can, according to their plan—for their own possession . . . Fluoridation of our community water systems can well become their most subtle weapon for our sure physical and mental deterioration. As a research chemist of established standing, I built within the past 22 years 3 American chemical plants and licensed 6 of my 53 patents. Based on my years of practical experience in the health food and chemical field, let me warn: fluoridation of drinking water is criminal insanity, sure national suicide. DON'T DO IT!!

"Even in very small quantities, sodium fluoride is a deadly poison to which no effective antidote has been found. Every exterminator knows that it is the most effective rat-killer. Sodium Fluoride is entirely different from organic calcium-fluoro-phosphate needed by our bodies and provided by nature, in God's great providence and love, to build and strengthen our bones and our teeth. This organic calcium-fluoro-phosphate, derived from proper foods, is an edible organic salt, insoluble in water and assimilable by the human body; whereas the non-organic sodium fluoride used in fluoridating water is instant poison to the body and fully water soluble. The body refuses to assimilate it."[495]

Dr. Bronner also rejected the often made case that fluoride promotes healthy teeth. He wrote:

Careful, bona fide laboratory experimentation by conscientious, patriotic research chemists, and actual medical experience, have both revealed that instead of preserving or promoting dental health, fluoridated drinking water destroys teeth before adulthood and after, by the destructive mottling and other pathological conditions it actually causes in them, and also creates many other very grave pathological conditions in the internal organisms of bodies consuming it. How then can it be called a health plan? What's behind it?[496]

While Dr. Bronner was ridiculed for his position, today there are over 28,000 members in the Fluoride Action Network.[497] At some point in the future, people will likely realize what is already known in Europe, that fluoridated water is harmful.[498] In the U.S., the major centers that evaluate fluoridated water are occupied by NWO agents and people with financial conflicts of

---

[495] Ibid.

[496] Ibid.

[497] The Fluoride Action Network is working to end fluoridation of public drinking water. Additional information on the Fluoride Action Network is online at www.fluoridealert.org/.

[498] Continental Europe does not allow water fluoridation. For more information, read the 2003 report "Water fluoridation contravenes UK law, EU directives and the European Convention on Human Rights and Biomedicine" online at www.greenparty.org.uk/files/reports/2003/F%20illegality.htm.

interest. One fluoride research example made news in 2005 when Harvard professor Chester Douglass was accused of burying research that fluoridated tap water caused bone cancer.[499] Douglass, the editor in chief for the industry-funded Colgate Oral Care Report, found himself in the spotlight for suppressing research that had the potential to halt all water fluoridation in the U.S.[500] To illustrate that a harmful product can be used for decades before people are informed, it was only in 2012 that most people learned that the secret formula in Coke and Pepsi contained a cancer causing ingredient.[501]

Many soft drinks and juices are made with fluoridated water. Cities and towns that do not have fluoride in their water supply often find that private foundations, serving as NWO fronts, will offer to pay for fluoridation.[502] The NWO routinely pays experts to make false safety claims, the Food and Drug Administration's fluoride endorsement is a case in point. To help protect the public, secret society members should not be allowed to work in the Food and Drug Administration or in any government position. Exposing the NWO and firing its agents will help restore the Food and Drug Administration to serve a serious public protection function.

In light of past NWO and CIA mind control efforts, Bisphenol A, Aspartame, Chemtrails, electromagnetic radiation, and combinations including music may serve a secret purpose.

Bisphenol A

Bisphenol A (BPA) is a chemical with hormone-like properties that may alter sexual orientation.[503] A major BPA study found people who ate canned soup compared with people who ate fresh soup experienced a 1,221 percent jump in BPA levels.[504] While BPA is in thousands of products in the U.S., including baby bottles, it is illegal for BPA to be in European-sold baby

---

[499] Juliet Eilperin, "Professor at Harvard Is Being Investigated," *The Washington Post*, 13 July 2005 and online at www.washingtonpost.com/wp-dyn/content/article/2005/07/12/AR2005071201277.html.

[500] The February 14, 2006 *Fox 25 Boston* report on Chester Douglass is online at http://video.google.com/videoplay?docid=-6559260786488769155#.

[501] Candice Choi, "Coke, Pepsi Make Changes to Avoid Cancer Warning," *Associated Press*, 8 March 2012 and online at http://abcnews.go.com/Health/wireStory/coke-pepsi-make-avoid-cancer-warning-15878247#.T1sBq_Un8WY.

[502] The American Dental Association (ADA) is actively involved in helping communities obtain funding for water fluoridation. The ADA position is online at www.ada.org/2467.aspx.

[503] Abby A. Li, Michael J. Baum, Laura J. McIntosh, Mark Day, Feng Liu, L. and Earl Gray Jr., "Building a Scientific Framework for Studying Hormonal Effects on Behavior and on the Development of the Sexually Dimorphic Nervous System," *NeuroToxicology*, May 2008, Volume 29 and Issue 3, 504-519.

[504] "Soaring BPA Levels Found in People Who Eat Canned Foods," *MyHealthNewsDaily*, 23 November 2011 and online at www.foxnews.com/health/2011/11/23/soaring-bpa-levels-found-in-people-who-eat-canned-foods/.

bottles.[505] BPA in baby bottles can leak, especially when milk in the bottle is warmed in a microwave oven. The potential adverse health impact on pregnant women from eating canned foods laced with BPA and on babies drinking from BPA is why many countries declare it a toxic substance.[506] Canada is an example of one country where BPA is officially declared a toxic substance.[507] Given what is known about BPA and the many safe alternative, it is alarming that widespread use in the United States is common.[508]

Aspartame

Aspartame, also known as NutraSweet, is an artificial sweetener in thousands of foods, and as a result is part of the daily diet of many people. Aspartame's approval is one of the most contested in FDA history.[509] People rarely realize that Aspartame is synthesized by fermenting protein in genetically modified E-Coli bacteria.[510] The horrendous toxicity of Aspartame has been well documented, but powerful members of secret societies advancing the NWO are assigned to make sure it remains part of the daily diet for many people.[511] One of the better known examples of Aspartame front men is former Secretary of Defense Donald Rumsfeld, who was the Chief Executive Officer of G. D. Searle & Co., the corporation that made Aspartame.[512]

---

[505] "EU Bans Bisphenol A Chemical From Babies' Bottles," *BBC*, 25 November 2010 and online www.bbc.co.uk/news/world-europe-11843820.

[506] "Concern Over Canned Foods: Our Tests Find Wide Range of Bisphenol A in Soups, Juice, and More," *Consumer Reports*, December 2009 and online at www.consumerreports.org/cro/magazine-archive/december-2009/food/bpa/overview/bisphenol-a-ov.htm.

[507] Martin Mittelstaedt, "Canada First to Declare Bisphenol A Toxic," *The Globe and Mail*, 13 October 2010 and online at www.theglobeandmail.com/news/national/canada-first-to-declare-bisphenol-a-toxic/article1755272/.

[508] David Derbyshire, "Gender Bending Chemical in Food Tins May Cut Male Fertility," *Mail Online*, 5 August 2010 and online at www.dailymail.co.uk/news/article-1300402/Gender-bending-chemical-food-tins-cut-male-fertility.html.

[509] The Aspartame human health concerns were presented on December 29, 1996 by *60 Minutes* in the news segment "How Sweet is It." Several educational videos are online at videos at www.teachpeace.com/aspartame.htm.

[510] Dr. James Bowen, "Aspartame Murders Infants - Violates Federal Genocide Law," Rense.com, 6 May 2000 and online at www.rense.com/general/asp.htm. Dr. James Bowen wrote: "At every point in the fertility process APM [Aspartame] destroys, beginning with the gleam in Mom and Pop's eyes: it ruins female sexual response and induces male sexual dysfunction. Beyond this, Aspartame disrupts fetal development by aborting it or inducing defects. When a child is born, Aspartame may have damaged the DNA of the baby, cursing future generations."

[511] Dr. Betty Martini, "EU Calls for Investigation of Aspartame and Stevia," *Rense.com*, 12 April 2003 and online at www.rense.com/general37/ste.htm. She also published "Study Proves Aspartame Lung and Liver Cancer," *Rense.com*, 19 October 2010.

[512] Aspartame is made by G. D. Searle & Co. Rumsfeld was the CEO from 1977 to 1985. Aspartame's initial U.S. Food and Drug Administration approval was in 1974. Rumsfeld led G. D. Searle & Co. during a

Aspartame, while shown to produce brain cancers in animals, was approved after a new FDA Commissioner was appointed and overruled two separate panels that recommended the FDA not approve it.[513] Scientific bias was proven by the investigative television show *60 Minutes*. Mike Wallace reported that all 74 industry funded Aspartame studies concluded the food additive was safe while the 83 independent studies reported potential health hazards.[514] Aspartame may also contribute to plummeting sperm counts throughout the developed world.[515]

Chemtrails

Chemtrails are chemicals that are sprayed over populated areas and have the potential to distribute mind control drugs.[516] In 2007, television station KSLA 12 reported on Chemtrails in the Shreveport, Louisiana area. The KSLA investigative team hired environmental testing professionals who confirmed the presence of barium on the ground and in water. As part of the investigation, Mark Ryan, the Director of the Poison Control Center, was interviewed by KSLA 12. Ryan confirmed that long term barium exposure causes problems including high blood pressure and weakened immune systems.[517]

For people who claim Chemtrails are not real, in 2001, the 107th Congress proved Chemtrails are real with House Resolution 2977, which is also known as the *Space Preservation Act*.[518] The

---

period of time Aspartame was seriously challenged by medical professionals and consumer health advocates.

[513] The FDA Commissioner was Dr. Arthur Hayes Jr. He was appointed in 1981. After overruling the scientific safety objections, he went to work for Burson Marsteller which was the public relations firm for G. D. Searle & Co. Hayes died on February 11, 2010 from leukemia.

[514] Mike Wallace, "How Sweet is It," *60 Minutes*, 29 December 1996. Dr. Ralph Walton was interviewed and alleged the Aspartame industry influences research findings. Dr. Walton said "I think it's inappropriate for researchers to have a vested interest in the outcome of their research."

[515] F. William Engdale, *Seeds of Destruction: The Hidden Agenda of Genetic Manipulation* (Global Research, 2007), 59, 63 and 229. Heather Turgeon, "Low Sperm Count: Why Male Fertility is Falling," *The Daily Beast*, 4 January 2011 and online at www.thedailybeast.com/articles/2011/01/04/low-sperm-count-why-male-fertility-is-falling.html. Evidence increasingly shows that the NWO seeks to achieve a massive population reduction via chemicals that decrease male fertility. More information is needed on Aspartame although a study in China showed men with the highest BPA levels had the lowest sperm counts. Researchers from Harvard have found a relationship between BPA and sperm counts.

[516] William Thomas, *Chemtrails Confirmed* (Carson City, NV: Bridger House Publishers, Inc., 2004).

[517] Mark Ryan's statement is online at www.youtube.com/watch?v=okB-489l6MI&feature=player_embedded. For reasons unknown the KSLA 12 original report is not available from KSLA 12 and a follow-up report posted on November 11, 2007 and updated on December 21, 2007 titled, "Local Bioweapons Expert: No Sinister Intent in Secret Testing of Americans" attempted to dismiss the original report. The follow-up report is online at www.ksla.com/story/7345087/local-bioweapons-expert-no-sinister-intent-in-secret-testing-of-americans.

[518] House Resolution 2977 is online at www.teachpeace.com/spacepreservationact.htm.

thought of populated areas being sprayed with biological or chemical agents by the U.S. Air Force and CIA seems impossible to believe except when we remember that in 1977 the U.S. Senate confirmed it had happened in 239 populated areas between 1949 and 1969.[519]

Chemtrail program insiders are thought to spray the chemicals believing the classified project will cool the planet to counter global warming.[520] The downside of stratospheric geoengineering is far more insidious and includes:

- droughts in large parts of the world and millions of starving people
- changes in soil pH levels making only modified and patented seeds useful[521]
- health problems for some people consuming water with Chemtrail chemicals
- rapid warming when Chemtrails are stopped
- ocean CO_2 acidification

Chemtrails may be integrated with directed energy systems.[522] Chemtrails and directed energy systems are also suspected to be part of an NWO plan to communicate subliminal messages.[523] This dimension of the NWO agenda, believed to be called project Blue Beam, is explained in *Vigilant Christian III: The Occult Religion of the 9/11 Attackers*.[524] While the public deserves to know what is being sprayed and why, the unfortunate reality is that until a whistleblower comes forward, the truth of what is going on will remain top secret.

---

[519] "Project MKULTRA, The CIA's Program of Research in Behavior Modification: Joint Hearing Before the Select Committee on Intelligence and the Subcommittee on Health and Scientific Research of the Committee on Human Resources," *United States Senate: Ninety-Fifth Congress*, 3 August 1977 and online at www.teachpeace.com/ProjectMKULTRA_Report.pdf.

[520] Jerry E. Smith, *Weather Warfare: The Military's Plan to Draft Mother Nature* (Kempton, Illinois: Adventures Unlimited Press, 2006), 221-265. Other claims to deceive Chemtrail participants are suspected to be increasing plant productivity, reversing rising sea levels, reducing ice melting, and making monitoring aircraft or missiles more accurate.

[521] Michael Murphy, "Gates Foundation Invests in Monsanto: Could Aluminum Resistant Seeds and Geo-Engineering be the Motive?," *Northland New Zealand Chemtrails Watch*, 30 August 2010.
Monsanto has patented seeds that prosper in high soil Ph environments and are aluminum resistant. Why is it important that a seed is aluminum resistant? The Monsanto patent #7582809 was granted on September 1, 2009.

[522] Ibid., 306-307 for possible HAARP integration.

[523] Dr. Nick Begich, *Controlling the Human Mind: The Technologies of Political Control or Tools for Peak Performance* (Anchorage, Alaska: Earthpluse Press Inc., 2006).

[524] The alleged Blue Beam technology is to use Satellites to serve as powerful movie projectors. The NWO may use this technology to deceive people to believe the Antichrist is the Messiah.

Wireless Schools

The electromagnet radiation from the wireless routers used in schools can be much higher than what many other wireless routers produce. Mary Garofalo, a reporter for the Canadian *16:9* television show, interviewed parents claiming children in wireless classrooms are unknowingly part of electromagnetic experiments with a wireless router producing exposures comparable to standing near a cell phone tower.[525] When Garofalo and her team tested the level of electromagnetic radiation exposure in schools, they found the levels far exceeded generally accepted safe levels.[526] She interviewed parents concerned about the increasing wireless school trend. Parents and children attribute anxiety, brain fog, dizziness, headaches, fatigue, sleep disorders, memory loss, and depression resulting from time in Wi-Fi schools.[527] The *16:9* investigative team checked the Canadian government's claims that Wi-Fi schools are safe and found the government statements were false. The scientific studies the Canadian government provided as proof that wireless schools are safe were shown to have not made this claim.[528]

For parents who want an alternative to having their children be NWO classroom experiments, there is an alternative—even faster fiber optic cables. To eliminate electromagnetic radiation dangers, in April 2009, the town of Herouville Saint-Clair in France replaced wireless in schools and public buildings with electromagnetic radiation safe fiber optic cables.[529]

People have different abilities to tolerate electromagnetic radiation exposures, but everyone is at risk of serious health problems. Minimizing electromagnetic radiation dangers requires ongoing vigilance. More people are using more devices that are generating more electromagnetic radiation. As people access more data from more places, more powerful antennas are installed. For example, gas and electric meters are sometimes replaced with "Smart Meters" that can broadcast resource use to the utility company. These Smart Meters are often adjacent to where people sleep and can broadcast electromagnetic radiation that is far more powerful than cell phones.[530]

---

[525] Mary Garofalo, *16:9 The Bigger Picture: WiFi in School Dangers* (GlobalTV.com and broadcast December 20, 2010). Online at www.globalnews.ca/16x9/video/wifi+1/video.html?v=1934227800&p=1&s=dd#october17/video.

[526] Ibid. Also see www.teachpeace.com/emfguidelines.htm.

[527] Ibid.

[528] Ibid. Canada's government provided a total of 16 scientific studies and not even a single scientific study communicated the levels of school children electromagnetic radiation exposures was deemed safe.

[529] Ibid.

[530] Smart Meters also serve a NWO intelligence collection function building on the PROMIS program that is explained in *Vigilant Christian IV- 9/11: The Secret War.* For more information about Smart Meters, see www.teachpeace.com/newsletternov2011.htm.

Moving away from an electromagnetic radiation danger is effective but not always achievable. Fortunately, shielding is helpful in many situations. Low frequency magnetic fields can be effectively shielded with high permeability alloys and less exotic metals. Electromagnetic radiation shielding and avoidance is especially recommended for young children. With electromagnetic radiation exposure being a part of modern life, the following seven prudent steps deserve consideration.

1. Children under the age of 16 should minimize cell phone use and ideally not use cell phones.[531]
2. People using cell phones should use it in the speaker mode or with a headset so as to benefit from the electromagnetic radiation reduction that even a gap of 12 inches offers.[532]
3. Discontinue using microwaves ovens.
4. Turn off home wireless networks.
5. Refuse Smart Meters.[533]
6. Do not use electric blankets.
7. Contact local schools to replace wireless schools with fiber optic cables.

Since we spend a significant portion of each day at home, reduce your electromagnetic radiation exposure through testing. Testing for electromagnetic radiation is the only way to really know where your hot spots are and successfully eliminate them. You may be surprised as often the microwave oven, wireless home phone, electric warming blankets, and fluorescent lights emit electromagnetic radiation levels far beyond internationally recognized safe standards.

We live in a dynamic world. In the past, electromagnetic emissions were a small fraction of current emissions. Low emissions have helped establish a false understanding that electromagnetic radiation dangers are only applicable to power lines and cell phone towers. Devices will increasingly be capable of processing more information and as a result, electromagnetic radiation dangers will continue to rise.

---

[531] A 2012 report of the International Agency for Research on Cancer of the World Health Organization considers that RF exposure (such as from mobile phones) is "possibly carcinogenic for humans." In February 2013, the Belgian Public Health Minister, Laurette Onkelinx announced that mobile phones sale to young children will be banned in shops and on the Internet. She said "If a risk exists, protection is necessary."

[532] Ibid. Belgium mandated the sale of headsets with all mobile phones.

[533] Spencer Ackerman, "CIA Chief: We'll Spy on You Through Your Dishwasher," *Wired*, 15 March 2012 and online at www.wired.com/dangerroom/2012/03/petraeus-tv-remote/.

Mind Control Music

Mind control music bearing visible NWO symbols integrated into their performances are evident in shows by Lady Gaga, Madonna, and many other performers. Lady Gaga's *Born This Way* and Madonna's *Express Yourself* are examples of songs that seek to modify and control human behavior. On the surface the songs are positive messages of tolerance, but on a deeper level the truth is twisted. MKULTRA or Monarch mind control program songs are often so similar that even the performers occasionally complain.[534]

The presence of NWO symbols and messages in music has led to multiple analysts explaining the NWO purpose of music on YouTube. While some of the YouTube information is disinformation, the information in the first Vigilant Christian book will enable you to appreciate that some analysts are accurate in their explanation of occult lyrics. People who think Lady Gaga is innocent fun or wish to learn more about the music their children are listening to are encouraged to enter the name of the performer followed with "occult symbolism" in Google or another search engine.

Combinations

Often there may be a combination of mind control approaches at work, making understanding their effects very difficult. Combinations of select vaccines, BPA, fluoride, Aspartame, Chemtrails, electromagnetic radiation, music, genetically modified food, and other ingredients working together may be part of the poisonous mass medication cocktail to alter human fertility and behavior. Science does show otherwise harmless items can become harmful when combined. For example, two radio frequency beams may have harmless radio frequency properties, but when a person is placed in their intersection point the person can be harmed.[535] Micro Air Vehicles are extremely small drones and can deliver behavior altering drugs and kill targets.[536] A Micro Air Vehicle configured with an electromagnetic gun, also known as a heart attack gun, kills in a way that is undetected.[537] Embedded computer chips and other components of the NWO mind

---

[534] Jocelyn Vena, "Lady Gaga's 'Born This Way' Sounds Very Familiar' To Madonna," *MTV*, 13 January 2012 and online at www.mtv.com/news/articles/1677260/madonna-lady-gaga-born-this-way.jhtml. The code names MKULTRA and Monarch refer to mind control programs. Monarch is often used to describe the NWO's music mind control programs. Monarch is associated with the Monarch butterfly and a tool a ruling monarch uses on the masses.

[535] The intersection point can modify the pressure of gases and liquids in a human.

[536] John Horgan, "Unmanned Flight," *National Geographic*, March 2013 issue. The Micro Air Vehicle program is based at Wright-Patterson Air Force Base in Dayton, Ohio. The program is operated by the U.S. Air Force's Air Vehicles Directorate.

[537] Michael Zennie, "Death from a swarm of tiny drones: U.S. Air Force releases terrifying video of tiny flybots that can hover, stalk and even kill targets," *MailOnline*, 19 February 2013. For more information

control program also have the potential to integrate and magnify current programs.[538] The potential for embedded computer chips to facilitate absolute control via the one-world monetary system is explained in *Vigilant Christian V: Perfect Money Planning*.

Precautionary Principle Conclusion

The unfortunately long history of NWO mind control experiments using intelligence services as fronts means there is every reason to believe mind control methods are now widely deployed. The widespread and unnecessary distribution of known harmful drugs in products, especially in the infant and young children markets, is a possible sign of NWO programs to modify behavior and control the masses. As illustrated by the Georgia Guidestones, the NWO seeks to reduce and control the global population. For this reason it is not surprising that mind control technologies often seek to achieve one or both of these goals.

With exposures to toxic chemicals and radiation increasing, the precautionary principle provides helpful guidance. The precautionary principle states that if something is suspected of being harmful, people should be warned in the absence of scientific consensus. With the precautionary principle the burden of proof is on the scientists claiming something is safe, not on a person claiming a human health hazard is present. Applying the precautionary principle would immediately prohibit Bisphenol A, Aspartame, fluoridated water, wireless networks in schools, and Chemtrails, and require all genetically modified foods to be labeled or deemed illegal.

---

about Micro Air Vehicles and NWO assassinations to silence the truth, read Chapter 7 in *Vigilant Christian IV: 9/11 - The Secret War.*

[538] Lev Grossman, "Meet the Chipsons," *Time*, 3 March 2002 and online at www.time.com/time/magazine/article/0,9171,1101020311-214099,00.html.

9

Space and Skybusting

"Every gun that is made, every warship launched, every rocket fired, signifies in the final sense a theft from those who hunger and are not fed, those who are cold and are not clothed." President Dwight D. Eisenhower [539]

This chapter explains New World Order space and skybusting technology that threatens the United States and the rest of the world as well. NWO space programs put offensive weapons into space using the U.S. government as a front. U.S. Air Force weapons systems are capable of radiating the ionosphere with energy that can turn airplanes, missiles, buildings, and people into dust; such are the capabilities of NWO skybusting technology. While the complete inventory of NWO weapons is a closely guarded secret, the known programs are designed to threaten the survival of everyone and can become the ultimate hammer to enforce a one-world government.

Skybusting Geo-Engineering and HAARP Destruction

Skybusting started in 1946 when the General Electric Corporation discovered that dropping dry ice into a cold chamber created ice crystals identical to those found in clouds. This discovery led to experiments in which dry ice was dropped from planes to create snow. A few years later researchers discovered that silver iodide dispersed at high altitudes would produce rain.

During the Vietnam War when peacemakers were singing "make love, not war" the 54th Weather Reconnaissance Squadron began a highly classified operation to "make mud, not war."[540] The U.S. military successfully seeded clouds with silver iodide, which extended the monsoon period in Vietnam by 30 to 45 days. This classified military program, called Operation Popeye, proved the U.S. had the technology to produce rain that would interrupt enemy supplies delivered

---

[539] Dwight D. Eisenhower statement on April 16, 1953.
[540] Donovan Webster and Karen Rowan, "The Biggest Weather-Control Flubs in History," *Discover: The Magazine of Science, Technology, and the Future,* June 2008 issue and online at http://discovermagazine. com/2008/jun/06-biggest-weather-weather-change-flubs-in-history#.UT92MVfeJ_M.

on mud roads and paths. The program was continued from 1967 to 1972 under the code name Operation Motorpool.[541] Anyone who claims that the U.S. cannot modify the weather is either ignorant of what has been possible for over 60 years or is being paid to sell lies.

The first ionospheric heaters were built at Platteville, Colorado in the 1960s. In 1966 Penn State electrical engineers built a 500 kilowatt ionospheric heater with an effective radiated power of 14 megawatts.[542] The super powerful transmitter and antenna array were moved to Alaska in 1983.

In the 1990s geo-engineering and weather modification advanced to a new level with the military's High Frequency Active Auroral Research Program or HAARP. This high energy vaporizing technology is increasingly understood to be a source of hurricanes and other forms of unusual extreme weather. HAARP operators can direct a beam of radio frequency energy with great precision, which is a key reason Hurricane Erin is believed by scientist Judy Wood to be the energy source for particle beams that, combined with explosives, turned three World Trade Center buildings into dust on September 11, 2001. While the evidence that explosives were used on 9/11 is substantial, we should be open to the possibility that classified weapons were also used. The following drawing shows Hurricane Erin on September 11, 2001.[543]

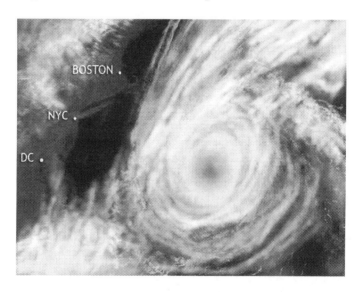

---

[541] Ibid.

[542] Jeane Manning and Dr. Nick Begich, *Angels Don't Play This HAARP: Advances in Tesla Technology* (Anchorage, Alaska: Earthpulse Press, 1995), 41.

[543] Teach Peace Foundation drawing of Hurricane Erin based on the actual U.S. National Hurricane Center photograph. The September 11, 2001 *CNN* article, "Weakening Hurricane Erin spawns strong waves along East Coast provides additional information."

Erin developed on September 1 and began to dissipate on September 5. Erin gradually increased from September 6 and on September 9 became a hurricane with peak winds of 120 mph.[544] While New York City remained sunny on 9/11, Erin's path moved closer to the city and attained its largest size on September 11.[545] While Erin was projected by the National Hurricane Center as a stronger force than Hurricane Katrina, the public was not widely alerted before, on, or after 9/11.[546] Hurricane Erin weakened starting on September 11 and turned to the northeast. Erin became extratropical on September 15 and lost its identity near Greenland on September 17. Hurricane Erin as a possible source of power to shoot a directed free-energy weapon to turn three World Trade Center buildings to dust is explained in the third and fourth Vigilant Christian books.[547]

Directed free-energy technology was first announced in 1934 by inventor Nikola Tesla, who named his charged particle beam projector "Teleforce." Though it is initially hard to believe, Wood's evidence that directed free-energy was used during the 9/11 attacks is overwhelming.[548]

Tesla said teleforce "was based upon an entirely new principle of physics that no one has ever dreamed about." He reported that teleforce involves four new inventions. The first is a method and apparatus for producing rays and manifestations of energy in free air. The second is a method to produce great electrical force. The third is a method for amplifying the electrical force. The fourth is a method for producing an electrical repelling force.[549] Tesla saw his weapon as a means of defense with which a country could destroy an attacking enemy's aircraft fleet even 250 miles away.

The NWO "Skybuster and Ground Dustifier" technology vaporizes solid materials in the air or on the ground. Just as the NWO used the resources of the U.S. to create the Manhattan Project to build an atomic bomb, the NWO used the U.S. HAARP program to create directed free-energy weapons. While this government program is classified and generally unknown by

---

[544] The Twin Towers were built to withstand hurricane winds up to 140 mph.

[545] Judy Wood, B.S., M.S., Ph.D., *Where Did the Towers Go?* (The New Investigation, 2010), 396.

[546] Ibid.

[547] Hurricane Erin as part of the 9/11 ritual is explained in *Vigilant Christian III: The Occult Religion of the 9/11 Attackers.*

[548] Nikola Tesla (10 July 1856-7 January 1943) was a scientist nominated for the Nobel Prize in Physics.

[549] "Tesla, at 78, Bares New 'Death-Beam'," *The New York Times*, 11 July 1934 and online at http://select. nytimes.com/gst/abstract.html?res= FB0817FD3E5B107A93C3A8178CD85F408385F9.
Jeane Manning and Dr. Nick Begich, *Angels Don't Play This HAARP: Advances in Tesla Technology* (Anchorage, Alaska: Earthpulse Press, 1995), 25.

most Americans, disclosures since 1994, including the History Channel HAARP documentary, explain how the technology can focus energy and even start earthquakes.[550]

Dr. Rosalie Bertell's *Planet Earth: The Latest Weapon of War* and other more recent books on HAARP provide supporting information that these modern weapons can vaporize buildings, manipulate global weather, knock out electronic communications, and even change people's moods and mental states. HAARP stations are in at least 19 locations, including Alaska, Greenland, and Norway. According to Bertell, the stations work together to boil the upper atmosphere, thereby disrupting communications, manipulating brain waves, causing earthquakes, and connecting with other systems to produce particle beam weapons.

Following the trail of money our government spends may reveal the truth. To create the atomic bomb, the Manhattan Project spent over $24 billion in current dollars. A Skybuster and Ground Dustifier weapon would be expensive; it would also need to be kept secret. Could this be why on the day before September 11, 2001, Donald Rumsfeld tried to eliminate the money trail that could possibly be traced back to a HAARP program? Rumsfeld's Pentagon press conference announcement that, "According to some estimates we [the U.S. government] cannot track $2.3 trillion in transactions" is suspicious.

Why is knowing about HAARP important to preventing an American Hiroshima or a triggering event that could cause World War III? It is important because if you do not know about the technology that exists and how it is used, you can be deceived about who the real enemy is and talked into believing that war with the wrong people is the answer. Proof of this is the fact that those who cannot explain HAARP are often the same people who can be deceived into believing that a man in Afghanistan gave 19 people box cutters to attack America.

Space Programs and Operation Paperclip

The process of the NWO putting weapons in space has its roots in the final days of World War II. The following drawing shows the NWO All-Seeing Eye, the 1935 to 1945 national flag of Germany, and the U.S. flag held together with a paperclip.[551]

---

[550] "Chemtrails and HAARP Weather Warfare," *History Channel*, March 2009 and online at www.youtube. com/watch?v=bVei0uPwp1w.

[551] Teach Peace Foundation 2013 drawing of the New World Order All-Seeing Eye symbol attached with a paperclip to the Nazi and U.S. flag. The code name "Paperclip" is claimed to have been selected because a new identity was attached to personnel files with a paperclip.

In a secret program called Operation Paperclip, NWO agents in the CIA brought Nazi scientists to the United States.[552] The head of Hitler's team that built the V-1 and V-2 rockets, Wernher von Braun, was made the first director of NASA's Marshall Space Flight Center in Huntsville.[553] Major General Walter Dornberger was Hitler's military liaison to von Braun's rocket team.[554] He also came to the U.S. as part of Operation Paperclip. Dornberger is the person who created the idea of "missile defense" as an offensive program with nuclear powered satellites that could destroy targets on earth.[555]

Operation Paperclip is described in detail in Linda Hunt's book, *Secret Agenda*.[556] In it Hunt describes how 1,500 top Nazi scientists were smuggled into the U.S. through Boston, Massachusetts and West Palm Beach, Florida. One hundred scientists, along with 100 V-2 rockets, were brought to Huntsville, Alabama.

In Germany, the Nazis had a concentration camp called Dora where 40,000 Jews, French resistance fighters, homosexuals, communists, and other prisoners of war (including a black American GI) were brought to build the V-1 and V-2 inside a mountain tunnel called Mittelwerk. By the time the slaves were liberated by the allies, over 25,000 had perished at the hands of the

---

[552] *Arsenal of Hypocrisy, The Space Program and the Military Industrial Complex,* AOH Productions Inc., 2003.

[553] Ibid.

[554] Ibid.

[555] Ibid.

[556] Linda Hunt, *Secret Agenda: The United States Government, Nazi Scientists, and Project Paperclip, 1945 to 1990* (New York, New York: St. Martin's Press, 1991).

Nazi rocketeers. Several times Dornberger and von Braun met with Hitler requesting more money and slaves so they could step up their rocket production effort. They showed Hitler films of the V-2 rocket launches in an effort to prove that they were making significant progress. As the war neared its end and Germany began to lose, Hitler became more anxious to use the rockets to terrorize the cities of London, Paris, and Brussels.

After the war, according to author Jack Manno in his book *Arming the Heavens: The Hidden Military Agenda for Space, 1945-1995*, Dornberger was brought to the U.S. and was appointed as a vice-president at Bell Aviation Corporation, and went on to serve on the first military oversight committee that ensured that NASA was controlled by the Pentagon.[557]

Another former Nazi, Kurt Debus, who was the chief of V-2 launch operations in Hitler's Germany, later became Chief of Operations for NASA at Cape Canaveral. When tourists visit the Kennedy Space Center they often pass by a portrait of the former German SS member in the entrance honoring Debus's service as the center's first director.

Nick Cook spent 10 years researching secret military programs in the U.S., and in his book, *The Hunt for Zero Point*, he states that he believes that over $20 billion a year is spent on these programs outside the purview of Congress.[558] Cook traces the roots of the secret U.S. programs back to the Nazi scientists who were brought to this country after WW II. He states:

> We know the size and scope of Operation Paperclip, which was huge. And we know that the U.S. operates a very deeply secret defense architecture for secret weapons programs . . . it is highly compartmentalized . . . and one of the things that's intrigued me over the years is, how did they develop it? What model did they base it on? It is remarkably similar to the system that was operated by the Germans—specifically the SS—for their top-secret weapons programs. What I do mean is that if you follow the trail of Nazi scientists and engineers who were recruited by America at the end of the Second World War, the unfortunate corollary is that by taking on the science, you take on—unwittingly—some of the ideology . . . What do you lose along the way?

---

[557] Jack Manno, *Arming the Heavens: The Hidden Military Agenda for Space, 1945-1995* (New York, New York: Dodd Mead, 1984).
[558] Nick Cook, *The Hunt for Zero Point: Inside the Classified World of Antigravity Technology* (New York, New York: Broadway Books, 2002).

The Trojan Horse of Missile Defense

The idea of missile defense became well known to Americans on March 23, 1983, when President Ronald Reagan announced his vision of a world safe from nuclear threats.[559] Many nations depend on nuclear missiles for deterring attack. If Nation A develops weapons capable of knocking out Nation B's deterrent, Nation B will be insecure. If attacked, Nation B will still have a deterrent since it is unlikely Nation A could knock out all of Nation B's nuclear missiles. The potential of being attacked by a larger force makes Nation B and other nations develop more weapons and go to a hair trigger launch status to better insure they could use their nuclear weapons if being attacked. Unfortunately, this kind of missile defense ultimately increases the chances of a nuclear strike due to a false warning, thereby making everyone less safe.

President Reagan's Strategic Defense Initiative or SDI was later called Star Wars because of the popularity of the *Star Wars* movies. President Reagan made a public appeal because he needed approval from Congress for what would be a multi-billion dollar funding request. In March 1985, the Reagan administration launched SDI and asked Congress to appropriate $26 billion to support the program for a five-year period.[560] In the years since Reagan first secured billions for space weapons, taxpayer funding for these programs has continued to increase.

Space Weapon Secrecy

The NWO seeks to control space as a means to establish and enforce their world government. While U.S. Air Force planning documents do directly declare that weapons will be put in space, presidents only discuss scientific and peaceful space exploration because a public space weapons announcement could enable other nations to take the issue to an international court to oppose U.S. efforts. The issues of who owns space and negative worldwide public opinion could stall current efforts to build and deploy space-based weapons. Billions of dollars of current space-related commerce could come to a standstill if a court prohibited satellite orbits, since virtually all satellites could be deemed to be weapons and, therefore, prohibited from orbits over protesting countries. Distinguishing non-commercial satellites with hidden weapons systems from commercial satellites would be impossible without a verification program to inspect them before they were put into orbit. An international court would certainly raise questions and could rule that space-based weapons that orbit other countries are acts of war.

---

[559] "Reagan Announces SDI," *PBS*, 23 March 1983. The video can be viewed at www.pbs.org/wgbh/amex/reagan/sfeature/sdi.html.

[560] Frances Fitzgerald, *Way out There in the Blue: Reagan, Star Wars, and the End of the Cold War* (New York, New York: Touchstone, Simon and Schuster, April 2001).

Many other issues to space-based weapons arise when the classified program is officially confirmed by a government. A U.S. space weapons announcement would likely result in a protest from the Russian Federation on the grounds that Article IV of the October 10, 1967 Outer Space Treaty was being violated. Article IV prohibits the placement of an offensive capability in orbit around the Earth.[561]

If the public became informed about the risks that are presented when nuclear powered satellites are launched into space there would be an outcry. Just imagine a Chernobyl or Fukushima nuclear reactor launched in a rocket and blowing up, raining the entire periodic chart of radioactive elements across thousands of miles. There are now at least 34 nuclear reactor cores in satellites currently orbiting the earth.[562] In 2013, the U.S. government acknowledged restarting plutonium production to power space vehicles.[563] Nuclear powered satellites, part of the HAARP concert of weapons, are capable of destroying targets from space.

Global Security Decreases as the Safety Window Shrinks

Under the old mutually-assured destruction or MAD scenario, a safety window of several minutes to an hour existed before it would become necessary to launch a counter-strike in the event of nuclear attack. Space-based weapons, especially high-powered lasers, may be able to hit earth-based targets much faster than earth-based missiles, which can reduce the safety window and lead to a mistake.[564] The National Missile Defense system differs from a missile hitting a missile because it uses directed energy to create a shield that destroys missiles.[565] In the

---

[561] "Treaty on Principles Governing the Activities of States in the Exploration and Use of Outerspace, Including the Moon and Other Celestial Bodies," *Outer Space Treaty*, 10 October 1967. The Arms Control Today makes the treaty available online at www.armscontrol.org/documents/outerspace.asp. The treaty was signed at Washington, London, and Moscow on 27 January 1967. Ratification advised by the U.S. Senate on 25 April 1967 and ratified by the U.S. President on 24 May 1967. U.S. ratification deposited at Washington, London, and Moscow on 10 October 1967. Proclaimed by the U.S. President on 10 October 1967. Entered into force on 10 October 1967.

[562] *Arsenal of Hypocrisy, the Space Program and the Military Industrial Complex*, AOH Productions Inc., 2003. The 34 nuclear reactor cores were launched by the United States and the former Soviet Union going back to the 1960s.

[563] Irene Klotz, "U.S. restarts plutonium production for space probes," *Reuters*, 18 March 2013.

[564] Space-based weapons can reduce the "time on target" element although a submarine could conceivable launch a short range missile a few miles from the U.S. coastline and hit a nearby city in a time span of a few minutes. A surprise attack by a bomb in a delivery vehicle other than a missile, a moving truck for example, could be without warning.

[565] Highly classified directed energy weapons are beginning to be revealed. The use of this type of weapon system on September 11, 2001 is explained in the fourth Vigilant Christian book and in greater detail by Judy Wood. She is the author of the 2010 book *Where Did the Towers Go?*

directed-energy missile defense world that safety window is cut down to only a few minutes, or even seconds.[566] This has many countries, including U.S. allies, worried.

The Cuban missile crisis of 1962, or even the 1995 Norwegian weather rocket incident, show us that the chain of mutually-assured destruction would have occurred in seconds instead of several minutes. Put another way, if National Missile Defense existed decades ago, you would likely not be reading this book. Consider how fast events unfolded in the 1995 Norwegian weather rocket incident. The Norwegians launched a weather rocket after informing the Russians of the launch. Unfortunately, the Norwegian notification never made it to the Russian missile command. Thus the Russian military thought that a U.S. Trident submarine had launched a first strike attack and President Boris Yeltsin activated his nuclear briefcase.[567] Fortunately for the world, the flight of the missile was monitored for several minutes and a Russian technician determined that the missile was moving away from Moscow.[568] Had the extra minutes vanished, and President Yeltsin ordered a counter-attack, the Norwegian weather rocket could have triggered an escalation that would have destroyed the world.

In 2001, U.S. Representative Edward J. Markey, a Democrat from Massachusetts, stressed the brief window of time for nuclear destruction through toasters. Markey sent toasters to all 535 members of Congress. He and a group of other concerned citizens wanted to remind policy makers that "in the time it takes to make toast, we could all be toast."[569]

Cooperative Programs Unravel

Will non-proliferation programs that require cooperation with nations stall or terminate? During the Clinton administration, the Nuclear Cities Initiative, Defense Threat Reduction Agency, and other cooperative threat reduction programs helped increase global security. As a result of the Nunn-Lugar-Domenici Cooperative Threat Reduction program, the Ukraine, Belarus, and Kazakhstan were denuclearized. This cooperative program funded the deactivation

---

[566] Critical to the first layer of protection in the National Missile Defense program is the ability to knock out an incoming missile when it leaves the ground and begins its boost phase. Boost-phase missile defense interceptors require near-instantaneous authorization to respond to a missile launch and must be located in space; otherwise the brief boost phase will be missed.

[567] Joseph Cirincione, Editor, *Repairing the Regime: Preventing the Spread of Weapons of Mass Destruction*, (New York, New York: Routledge, April 2000), 58. Mr. Cirincione also notes that another version of this story is the Russian military provoked this incident to force Norway to halt the future launches that the Russian military believed were actually electronic reconnaissance missions.

[568] Peter J. Boyer, "When Missiles Collide," *The New Yorker*, 11 September 2000.

[569] Jim Geraghty, "Markey's N-alert: We could be toast," *The Boston Globe*, 7 September 2001, A15.

of 4,838 nuclear warheads and the elimination of 387 nuclear ballistic missiles, 343 ballistic missile silos, 136 nuclear submarine launch tubes, and 49 long-range nuclear bombers.[570]

Unfortunately, the Anti-Ballistic Missile Treaty and subsequent arms control efforts that played a major role in the reduction of weapons of mass destruction are either already terminated or are in the process of being terminated.

The Anti-Ballistic Missile Treaty of 1972, terminated by the United States in 2002, limited the U.S. and the former Soviet Union to two anti-ballistic missile deployment areas. The treaty served to prevent a nationwide anti-ballistic missile defense capability.[571] The idea was that each country would leave unchallenged the penetration capability of the other's retaliatory missile forces.[572] For Russia, the Anti-Ballistic Missile Treaty signed by Leonid Brezhnev and Richard M. Nixon was the foundation for all other arms control agreements.

Now that the Anti-Ballistic Missile Treaty has been canceled, the Intermediate-Range Nuclear Forces (INF) Treaty may also unravel, enabling other countries to reintroduce shorter range missiles that could easily defeat the National Defense System through flying under the shield.[573] The secret U.S. energy shield is believed to be why Russian Federation President Vladimir Putin said on February 10, 2007 that the INF Treaty no longer served Russia's interest.[574]

Following the Anti-Ballistic Missile Treaty termination, will the non-nuclear nations take the next step and begin abandoning the Nuclear Non-Proliferation Treaty? Sadly, I am convinced that the answer is yes. The Nuclear Non-Proliferation Treaty is supported by 187 countries and has served to motivate the vast majority of countries not to develop nuclear bombs based on a pledge from the nuclear nations that they will continue efforts and eventually become nuclear-weapons-free.[575] International agreements have proven to prevent and slow the proliferation

---

[570] Joseph Cirincione, Editor, *Repairing the Regime: Preventing the Spread of Weapons of Mass Destruction* (New York, New York: Routledge), April 2000, 4.

[571] Amy Goldstein and Alan Sipress, "ABM Withdrawal Likely, But Not Set, Bush Says," *Washington Post*, 24 August 2001, A01.

[572] To read the Anti-Ballistic Missile Treaty go to www.armscontrol.org/documents/abmtreaty.asp.

[573] To read the Intermediate-Range Nuclear Forces Treaty go to www.armscontrol.org/documents/inf.asp. The treaty is formally titled *The Treaty Between the United States of America and the Union of Soviet Socialist Republics on the Elimination of Their Intermediate-Range and Shorter-Range Missiles.*

[574] Baker Spring, "Russian Withdrawal from INF Treaty Will Put the Ball in Europe's Court," *The Heritage Foundation*, 22 February 2007 and online at www.heritage.org/research/reports/2007/02/russian-withdrawal-from-inf-treaty-will-put-the-ball-in-europes-court. Putin spoke at the 43rd Munich Conference on Security Policy on February 10, 2007.

[575] To read the Nuclear Non-Proliferation Treaty go to www.armscontrol.org/documents/npt.asp. A total of 187 parties had signed the treaty as of March 2002.

of weapons of mass destruction. The already too high price we must pay in dollars is further increased as decades of non-proliferation agreements unravel.

Non-proliferation efforts have proven to be more effective and less expensive than weapons systems. However, weapons proliferation makes a lot of sense to NWO insiders and people who value war profiteering opportunities. With respect to the Comprehensive Test Ban Treaty, Anti-Ballistic Missile Treaty, and National Missile Defense, the U.S. is appearing as a rogue nation to the rest of the world.[576] This is by design, as the NWO wants the U.S. to assume a Darth Vader role.

The ultimate issue is not whether directed free-energy weapons or other approaches can successfully destroy missiles. The more important point is, how does NWO development and control of these systems as part of a one-world government threaten life, liberty, and the pursuit of happiness?

Space Control

What is needed for the NWO to control space? Presidents serving the NWO promote a "space vision" as camouflage to conceal developing weapons in space.[577] Barack Obama signed a major NASA act becoming a law on October 11, 2010 that serves to secretly transform space missions into a U.S. Space Force.[578] The 2010 development was no surprise because the November 2003 U.S. Air Force *Transformation Flight Plan* provided insights calling for a U.S. Space Force.[579]

The U.S. Air Force *Space Command Strategic Master Plan FY06 and Beyond* directly calls for the U.S. to dominate space with approximately $500 billion to be spent on space weapons systems.[580] In the report, General Lance W. Lord says, "This plan is the command's roadmap

---

[576] "Stop The World, I Want To Get Off: Has George Bush Ever Met A Treaty That He Liked?," *The Economist*, 28 July 2001, 35. Bush administration actions: March 28th—Abandons the 1997 Kyoto Protocol; May 1st—Threatens to abrogate the 1972 Anti-Ballistic Missile Treaty; July 21st—Threatens to withdraw from a United Nations conference to impose limits on illegal trafficking of small arms; and July 25th—Rejects proposed enforcement measures for the 1972 Biological Weapons Convention.

[577] Tariq Malik, "President Obama Signs New Vision for U.S. Space Exploration Into Law," *Space.com*, 11 October 2010. The article is online at www.space.com/9305-president-obama-signs-vision-space-exploration-law.html.
Miles O'Brien and CNN senior White House correspondent John King, "Bush Unveils Vision for Moon and Beyond: President Seeks $1 billion More in NASA Funding," *CNN.com*, 15 January 2004.

[578] Ibid.

[579] *The U.S. Air Force Transformation Flight Plan*, produced by HQ USAF/XPXC Future Concepts and Transformation Division, November 2003.

[580] *Strategic Master Plan FY06 and Beyond*, Air Force Space Command, HQ AFSPC/XPXP, 1 October 2003 available online from the Center For Defense Information at www.cdi.org/news/space-security/afspc-strategic-master-plan-06-beyond.pdf.

to ensure our military remains dominant in space, in the air, on the ground and on the sea."[581] The *Space Command Strategic Master Plan FY06 and Beyond* is packed with so much detailed offensive space program information, it is amazing the document is not classified. Another U.S. Space Command resource that describes the space weapons is the *Vision for 2020.*[582]

While the Central Intelligence Agency and National Security Agency are generally more known to the American public, the National Reconnaissance Office (NRO), located in Chantilly, Virginia, is America's largest spy agency. The NRO was created in 1960 and its existence was classified until 1992. In 2001 the NRO received over $6 billion a year in funding.[583] To help put the $6 billion in perspective, most nations spend less than $6 billion on their entire defense budget. The NRO's intelligence, defense, and space capabilities combined with the existing U.S. Air Force Space Command is the NWO launching pad to dominate space.

Abolish Space Weapons

This generation has the opportunity to make the world a safer place through the maintenance of a weapons-free zone in space. This is only possible when the NWO agenda for global domination is exposed. Exposing the NWO can stop their sabotage of global disarmament programs. Worldwide security decreases as the NWO, using the U.S. Air Force, increasingly becomes the "master of space." The ideological similarities between the NWO master of space objectives and Hitler's "Germany over all" objectives are not accidental.[584] The language of NWO dominance is littered throughout the Air Force's space plans. Military personnel often fail to see the Hitler-like "over all" dominance in official documents.

In 1961 President Dwight D. Eisenhower warned the American public, "In the councils of government, we must guard against the acquisition of unwarranted influence, whether sought or unsought, by the military industrial complex. The potential for the disastrous rise of misplaced power exists and will persist. We must never let the weight of this combination endanger our liberties or democratic processes. We should take nothing for granted. Only an alert and knowledgeable citizenry can compel the proper meshing of the huge industrial and military machine of defense with our peaceful methods and goals, so that security and liberty may prosper together."[585]

---

[581] Ibid., Foreword, i.

[582] *Vision for 2020*, U.S. Space Command, February 1997. Available online at the Federation of American Scientists site at http://fas.org/spp/military/docops/usspac/visbook.pdf.

[583] Walter Pincus, "Satellite Agency Has Tradition of Secrecy," *Washington Post*, 25 August 2001, A10.

[584] *Arsenal of Hypocrisy, The Space Program And The Military Industrial Complex*, AOH Productions Inc., 2003.

[585] President Dwight D. Eisenhower, "Farewell Address," *Our Documents initiative*, 17 January 1961. The online address is www.ourdocuments.gov.1 961. President Eisenhower can be heard making this

10

Global Hiroshima?

"Maintain humanity under 500,000,000 in perpetual balance with nature." Georgia
Guidestones

Aaron Russo reported that in 2000, Nick Rockefeller informed him of a plan to decrease the global population.[586] Are we witnessing this plan in action with the global effect of nuclear pollution and other means to increase birth defects, infant mortality, and death rates? While the reasons are debated by scientists, the global decline in fertility and birth rates signal a plan to decrease the global population may be underway.

Georgia Guidestones

The Georgia Guidestones communicate the misguided New World Order agenda in the form of commandments envisioned for a post American world.[587] The above quote is the first commandment, which if adhered to would mean that over 6 billion people would need to

---

warning in the documentary, *Arsenal of Hypocrisy, The Space Program and the Military Industrial Complex*, AOH Productions Inc., 2003.

[586] Aaron Russo was an American who worked passionately to expose how evil is organized. He was a film producer known for producing *America: Freedom to Fascism, Trading Places*, and *Mad as Hell*. He was a friend of Nick Rockefeller who in 2000 attempted to recruit Russo into the New World Order. Russo refused and began publically speaking that a man connected to one of the Rockefeller patriarchs (either John D. Rockefeller or William Rockefeller), named Nick Rockerfeller, warned him about 9/11 some eleven months in advance. Russo was diagnosed with bladder cancer in 2001 and died on August 24, 2007. Alex Jones, "Nick Rockefeller Revealed Elite Agenda to Aaron Russo During Friendship," *Jones Report*, 21 February 2007 and online at www.jonesreport.com/articles/210207_rockefeller_friendship. html. For more information see the 2006 Alex Jones documentary, *Reflections and Warnings: An Interview with Aaron Russo*.

[587] *The Georgia Guidestones*, published by Elberton Granite Finishing Co., Inc. and printed by *The Sun*, Hartwell, Georgia, March 1981. The book is online at www.wired.com/images/multimedia/ magazine/1705/Wired_May_2009_Georgia_Guidestones.pdf and Randall Sullivan wrote an excellent article on the subject for *Wired Magazine* on 20 April 2009 titled, "American Stonehenge: Monumental

be exterminated, possibly through Hiroshima-like events, a range of environmental factors increasing infertility rates, and World War III. Chapter 8 presented information that the population reduction may be occurring through a mass medication cocktail that could include Bisphenol A, Aspartame, fluoride, Chemtrails, electromagnetic radiation exposures, and genetically modified foods.

The Georgia Guidestones consist of ten commandments engraved on a stone monument located in Elbert County, Georgia in close proximity to what the Cherokee Indians called "Al-yeh-li A lo-Hee," which means the center of the world.[588] The stones are oriented with each line of the axis toward specific areas of the moon's annual rotation around the Earth. The capstone has a hole that uses the noon sunlight to identify the day of the year. Another hole in the center support is designed to locate the North Star. A third hole, known as the "mail slot," is positioned for the sun to pass through it on an equinox or solstice.[589]

Instructions for the Post-Apocalypse." (See www.wired.com/science/discoveries/magazine/17-05/ff_guidestones? currentPage=all).

[588] Clay Ouzts, "Georgia Guidestones," *The New Georgia Encyclopedia*, 16 March 2009 online at www.georgiaencyclopedia.org/nge/Article.jsp?id=h-3163.

[589] Equinox occurs about March 21st and September 22nd. Equinox is the time when the sun crosses the plane of the earth's equator, making night and day of approximately equal length all over the earth. The solstice also occurs twice a year. Solstice is when the sun is at its greatest distance from the equator. In the Northern Hemisphere the longest day of the year is about June 21 and the shortest day of the year is about December 21.

If the story of the Georgia Guidestones was limited to its astrologic alignment, it would be simply an interesting tourist attraction. Unfortunately this is one of the most bizarre and occult monuments in the United States because it calls for the elimination of billions of people. The monument, increasingly known as the Ten Commandments of the Antichrist or Dajjal, has horrific messages.[590] The Georgia Guidestones validate prophecies in holy books that the Antichrist will seek to resemble Christ but with a deceptive message that is actually opposite.

The six astrologically aligned "X" pattern granite stones evoke a Stonehenge-like familiarity. The ten "guides" etched in the granite are written in eight different languages. Moving clockwise around the monument from due north, the languages are English, Spanish, Swahili, Hindi, Hebrew, Arabic, Chinese, and Russian. The "mystery" of the stones was intended to provide its creators with plausible maneuvering room to both avoid answering questions and give NWO supporters the ability to deceive. To illustrate this point, the "master builder" of the project, Joe H. Fendley, is portrayed as someone who just "happened" to get involved. The following is from his company's 1981 *The Georgia Guidestones* book.

> "What started out as a usual Friday afternoon mid-summer has ended in the production erection of one of the world's most unusual monuments produced under the most unusual conditions.

> "Joe Fendley, president of Elbert Granite Finishing Company, Inc. in Elberton, Georgia, was spending Friday afternoon in June 1979 as he spends most Friday afternoons . . . studying his weekly reports and generally closing up shop for a weekend . . . and then it all started.

> "A neatly dressed man walked into Fendley's Tate Street office and said he wanted to buy a monument. Since everyone else in the office was busy, Fendley decided to talk to the stranger himself and explained that his company does not sell directly to the public, but only on a wholesale basis.

---

[590] The term Antichrist, also known as the Dajjal in Islam, refers to one who fulfills Biblical prophecies for Christians and Hadith prophecies for Muslims. The word Antichrist is in John's epistles five times. A different name is used 33 times in Revelation. In Revelation he is called 'the Beast from the Abyss.' Other names for the Antichrist in the Bible include lawless one, son of perdition, man of sin, and the destroyer. The actual name of the Antichrist is provided in Revelation 9:11. "And they had a king over them, which is the angel of the bottomless pit, whose name in the Hebrew tongue is Abaddon, but in the Greek tongue hath his name Apollyon." The name of Satan's powerful tool is Apollo. This is likely why in the ancient Greek and Roman religion and modern Greco-Roman Neopaganism Apollo is worshiped. This Apollo is understood to be a god bringing deadly plague and performing great signs at the Oracle in Delphi. Both Christianity and Islam teach the Antichrist is defeated by Jesus.

"Not to be discouraged, the middle-aged man, who identified himself only as Mr. Robert C. Christian, said he wanted to know the cost of building a monument to the conservation of mankind and began telling Fendley what type of monument he wanted. With this he outlined the size in metric measurements."

The story that was put out for public consumption was that the mysterious Mr. Christian said that he represented a secret group that had been working on the monument design for more than 20 years. The official story and true purpose of the stones can begin to be seen when you realize that Fendley, the self-acknowledged master builder of the stones, was a York Rite and Scottish Rite 32 degree Mason in 1981.[591] The deceptive story continued with Fendley introducing Mr. Christian to banker Wyatt C. Martin, who promised to keep the project anonymous, taking the true identity of Mr. Christian to the grave.[592] The third key party involved in the transaction, Wayne Mullinex, provided the land for the monument.

The mysterious story becomes less mysterious when you realize Fendley, Martin, and Mullinex were Masons in the Elberton Philomathea Masonic Lodge #25. Freemasonry is the largest and oldest secret society working to bring about a one-world government. The key facts, omitted from the official story and *The Georgia Guidestones* book, dispel the secrecy as well as the nonsense that the stones are to help humanity. As Woodrow Wilson observed, "Everybody knows that corruption thrives in secret places, and avoids public places, and we believe it is a fair presumption that secrecy means impropriety."[593]

The negative eugenic messages on the polished granite may also prompt thoughts of Hitler and Nazi Germany (e.g., "maintain humanity under 500,000,000" and portraying people as "a cancer on the earth").

---

[591] *The Georgia Guidestones*, published by Elberton Granite Finishing Co., Inc. and printed by *The Sun*, Hartwell, Georgia, March 1981, page 31. The sun and the pyramid are powerful occult symbols in Freemasonry. *The Georgia Guidestones* book is interestingly made by *The Sun* printing company in Hartwell, Georgia and the granite is from Pyramid Quarry.

[592] Ibid, 38. The pseudonym R. C. Christian was likely chosen to conceal the anti-Christian purpose of the monument. Mr. Christian is quoted by Fendley and Martin as saying, "My name is not Christian; I only use that name because I am a follower of the teachings of Jesus Christ" even though in John 18:20 Jesus taught transparency and did nothing in secret. "Mr. Christian" is clearly insulting all the Abrahamic faiths with the Guidestones top commandment mandating that over 6 billion people alive today should not exist.

[593] Woodrow Wilson, *The New Freedom*, Tutis Digital Publishing Private Limited, 2008, page 46. Tutis Digital Publishing Private Limited is a division of Corah Hub Online Services Private Limited which is a subsidiary of Vishal Information Technologies Limited in Mumbai, India. The online version of the book at www.gutenberg.org/etext/14811 is not copyrighted in the United States.

The ten Georgia Guidestones messages are designed to appear benevolent, but each has a dark hidden meaning.

1. Maintain humanity under 500,000,000 in perpetual balance with nature.
2. Guide reproduction wisely—improving fitness and diversity.
3. Unite humanity with a living new language.
4. Rule passion—faith—tradition—and all things with tempered reason.
5. Protect people and nations with fair laws and just courts.
6. Let all nations rule internally resolving external disputes in a world court.
7. Avoid petty laws and useless officials.
8. Balance personal rights with social duties.
9. Prize truth—beauty—love—seeking harmony with the infinite.
10. Be not a cancer on the earth.

At times many forget that organized evil exists in our world, and that real people do from time-to-time commit mass murder. When you understand this, you understand that the NWO is the reemergence of the Nazi agenda. Money fortunately leaves a trail. This money trail enables us to see the truth that at the very top of the NWO are the same families that financed Hitler and even Lenin. Information about the Hitler and Lenin NWO connection is in *Vigilant Christian III: The Occult Religion of the 9/11 Attackers.*

NWO enslavement is far worse than seeing loved ones struggle to find jobs, or the knowledge that children are born increasingly enslaved with massive amounts of debt. If you find the Georgia Guidestones overwhelming, prayers that your worries be replaced with trust in God can help. You may also find the information in Chapter 12 especially helpful.

This dark occult monument for a post-Apocalypse America shows that the goals of the NWO require more than an American Hiroshima. Population reduction of billions of people requires a Global Hiroshima. While a nuclear false-flag attack could be used in the United States to mislead people to drive a dagger into the Constitution, on the global scale the NWO actually needs non-nuclear alternatives so that after the mass murders they can live on the planet. A global nuclear war presents the problem of nuclear winter.

To make a global population reduction possible, many things are needed, including: secrecy, control of central banks, control of the biggest media corporations, control of major drug corporations, people in place to influence passage of government laws, leadership infiltrations in the World Health Organization, and a means to manage people who know the truth. Unfortunately, much of everything needed is already waiting in the wings.

Operation Roundup

Operation Roundup was called Rex 84 during the Reagan administration. Roundup is more than a weed killer that for over 25 years has been sold by the Monsanto corporation. Operation Roundup is a plan to arrest and exterminate people who speak the truth about the New World Order. Activating this plan is unnecessary as long as U.S. citizens remain asleep as their liberties are stripped away.

Roundup is what leaders seeking totalitarian rule routinely initiate when the hidden hand of power becomes visible to the majority of the people. Social media products serve to create lists of people, and their relationship to people who are aware the NWO is real. Facebook was funded by people directly linked to the CIA and NWO. A key purpose of monitoring Facebook, library records, voting records, Internet sites visited, and email is to identify and prioritize people for Operation Roundup.

The diabolical plan both identifies people who are awake and draws people that would come to realize the NWO is real into the trap during the early phase of Operation Roundup. This evil trap should not be surprising, as history confirms that most if not all dictators or groups seeking to seize power develop lists of people they want to eliminate. For example, Hitler had his list of people that were to be eliminated within the first phase of his lockdown on power. Hitler's 1934 Night of Long Knives is one example, and book four in this series explains this dimension of this event. Christians and non-Christians, all children of God, should work together because the NWO will seek to eliminate everyone opposed to living under their slavery, regardless of their faith.

People in Germany once thought sending people to death camps could never happen in their country. Could people ever be rounded up and sent to concentration camps here? The answer is not only yes, but Executive Orders giving the ice-thin perception that concentration camps would be legal already exist.

Executive Orders associated with the Federal Emergency Management Agency that can suspend the Constitution and the Bill of Rights already exist. Over the last few decades the NWO has broadened the Federal Emergency Management Agency powers with additional Executive Orders. The Executive Orders build on earlier legislation that restricts personal freedoms, such as the 1950 Defense Production Act and the National Security Act of 1947. We should also not forget that a classified version of the Patriot Act exists.[594] In 2010, the U.S. military was given a training manual with detailed instructions on how to imprison U.S. citizens deemed political dissidents.[595] All it takes to enforce Executive Orders to turn the U.S. into an extreme fascist state is the stroke of the president's pen.[596]

Denver Airport NWO Clues

The Denver Airport is an occult New World Order cathedral complete with the dedication plaque. The following is a photograph of the NWO dedication plaque.[597]

---

[594] Senator Ron Wyden revealed there is an even more draconian classified version of the Patriot Act.

[595] The Department of Defense Field Manual is FM 3-39.40. The "Internment and Resettlement Operations" training manual is online at http://info.publicintelligence.net/USArmy-InternmentResettlement.pdf.

[596] Some of the Executive Orders giving the government control are 10990 (transportation), 10955 (media), 10997 (electrical power, gas, petroleum, fuels and minerals), 10998 (all transportation vehicles including personal cars), 10999 (food resources and farms), 11000 (forced civilian work brigades under government supervision), 11001 (health, education and welfare functions), 11002 (Postmaster General to operate a national registration of all persons), 11003 (take over all airports and aircraft), 11004 (allows the Housing and Finance Authority to relocate communities and designate areas to be abandoned), 11005 (take over railroads, inland waterways and public storage facilities), 11051 (puts all Executive Orders into effect in times of increased international tensions and economic or financial crisis), 11310 (grants authority to the Department of Justice to enforce the plans set out in Executive Orders), 11049 (assigns emergency preparedness function to federal departments and agencies), and 11921 (allows the Federal Emergency Preparedness Agency to develop plans to establish control over the mechanisms of production and distribution, of energy sources, wages, salaries, credit and the flow of money in U.S. financial institution).

[597] Teach Peace Foundation photograph. Additional New World Order Denver Airport symbols are online at www.vigilantchristian.org/denverairport.html.

To understand the NWO symbols in the Denver Airport requires understanding that the NWO religion is the religion of the ancient Egyptian pharaohs. The twisted NWO beliefs are discussed in detail in *Vigilant Christian III: The Occult Religion of the 9/11 Attackers*[598] Symbols are often displayed by putting messages in the public thoroughfare in a way that escapes public understanding to hoodwink people into supporting the one-world agenda. A desire to hoodwink people and increase dark deception energy was behind Freemason President Franklin Roosevelt placing the All Seeing Eye on the back of the U.S. dollar bill.

The Denver International Airport apocalyptic glowing red eyes horse, Masonic capstone, nightmarish murals, gargoyles, embedded floor symbols, and the swastika shaped runways are seen daily by thousands of people, yet few understand what they are looking at. Starting with the pale horse, or the horse of the Apocalypse in Revelation 6:7-8, we learn, "When He opened the fourth seal, I heard the voice of the fourth living creature saying, 'Come and see.' So I looked, and behold, a pale horse. And the name of him who sat on it was Death, and Hades followed with him. And power was given to them over a fourth of the earth, to kill with sword, with hunger, with death, and by the beasts of the earth." The pale horse of the Apocalypse that welcomes people to Denver Airport is shown in the following picture.[599]

---

[598] The NWO continues beliefs sometimes described as the Egyptian mystery religion but most clearly described as Luciferianism. The direct NWO connection to the belief system of the Pharaohs is why many one-world secret society fronts such as the Freemasons routinely use of Egyptian occult symbols.

[599] Teach Peace Foundation 2010 Denver International Airport photograph. The color photograph is available at www.vigilantchristian.org/denverairport.html and the eyes of the Denver International Airport pale horse are red lights.

In the Bible this pale horse is the fourth horse of death. The horse of death with demonic red glowing eyes will deliver death with famine, weapons, and disease. The Denver Airport's pale horse is 32 feet high with veins on the brink of exploding. The statue fell on its creator and killed him, earning the nicknames Bluecifer, Satan's Steed, and Blue Devil. No matter how you look at it, this is certainly not appropriate for children, or a comforting symbol for people concerned about air travel safety.

People often find claims that the Denver Airport is an occult cathedral absurd until they read the Freemasonry capstone. Carved in stone, the March 19, 1994 dedication capstone was laid by the Prince Hall Grand Lodge F & A. M. of Colorado and Jurisdiction. The grandmaster of this lodge is Claude W. Gray, Sr. A second lodge, the Grand Lodge of A.F. & A.M. of Colorado, is listed with Benjamin H. Bell, Jr. as Grand Master. In the middle of the dedication names is the Masonic square and compass symbol. Under the symbol and date is "New World Airport Commission." Buried below the dedication is a capsule that is to be opened in 2094. In 2010, outside the window behind the Denver Airport Freemasonry capstone was a 26 foot high statue of Anubis, the Egyptian god of death.[600]

---

[600] Teach Peace Foundation 2010 Denver International Airport photograph. The Egyptian god of the dead, Anubis, was reported by Denver local news (see the video at www.youtube.com/watch?v=mulrh R15ucY).

The following 1994 and 1995 nightmarish murals by Leo Tanguma were added to interior airport walls. Tanguma was assisted by Cheryl Detwiler, Bill Meredith, John Ochsner, and Leticia Tanguma. The Denver International Airport website claims the murals communicate children of the world dreaming of peace.[601] Even with only a basic knowledge of occult symbolism it is clear that the two murals tell the American and Global Hiroshima story. When all four murals are combined, we see the story of the one-world government and rise of the Antichrist, who is represented by a boy in a Bavarian costume. The assigned names are false, so I have provided accurate names and the sequence for reading the murals.

The following picture, the first mural in the series, is officially titled "Peace and Harmony with Nature" but should be titled "Global Hiroshima."[602]

---

[601] See the Denver Airport explanation that the murals are children of the world dreaming of peace at http://flydenver.com/publicart. The plaque at the airport reads: "The Children of the World Dream of Peace" is a powerful mural expressing the artist's desire to abolish violence in society. One part of the diptych exhibits the tragedy and devastation of war and its impact on humanity. The mural then moves to images of smiling children from around the world celebrating peace prevailing over war."

[602] Teach Peace Foundation 2010 Denver International Airport photograph.

The Global Hiroshima mural shows green gas choking a city, forests burning out of control, animals becoming extinct, plants dying, children crying, and the death of three girls in open-caskets. The three girls represent the death of many Africans, the death of many Native Americans, and the death of Jews and Christians. The girl in the open-casket on the right is wearing a "Juden" star and has a rose and a Bible under her hand representing a key NWO objective, to eliminate Jews and Christians. A leopard is shown sacrificed on an altar, and both a leopard and a similar looking young woman seem to reappear in the fourth mural. One child holds the Mayan tablet communicating the end of an era.

The following picture shows the second mural, which is connected to the third mural by a rainbow and is read from right to left.[603]

---

[603] Ibid. More photos of the NWO murals are online at www.vigilantchristian.org/denverairport.html.

The second mural shows a ghostly demon soldier awaking to slaughter humanity. This mural should be called "World War III." The all-powerful demon soldier wears a gas mask. He holds a machine gun in his left hand and a scimitar or large curved sword in his right hand. This soldier of death is trying to kill a dove with the scimitar, a Masonic symbol and traditional Muslim sword. The NWO soldier uses the Muslim sword to destroy three buildings and kill the dove of peace. The three buildings may represent the Twin Towers and Building 7 destroyed on September 11, 2001.

Mothers in a never-ending line hold their dead children in their arms. A dead child holds her teddy bear. A rainbow at the top of the picture transforms into deadly gas, and a new holocaust strikes the earth. The World War III mural shows people dying from bio-weapons, and the mural links a letter written by Hama Herchenberg with the gassing of Jews. The letter written by Herchenberg is in the bottom right of the mural. She was 14 years old when she was murdered at Auschwitz. Her letter has the following message.

I was once a little child who longed for other worlds. But I am no more a child for I have known fear. I have learned to hate . . . How tragic, then, is youth which lives with enemies, with gallows ropes. Yet, I still believe I only sleep today, that I'll wake up, a child again, and start to laugh and play.

Since most of the Jews at Auschwitz and other prisoners were killed by Zkylon B gas, the mural signals that the NWO plan includes bio-weapons, although guns and other weapons are also used.

The following photograph shows the third mural which communicates that militarism is dead.[604]

The appropriate title for this mural is "Trading Liberty for False Security." The machine gun is broken and two doves sit on the weapon. A new world leader is using a hammer to turn the scimitar into something useful. The nations of the world following a World War III Global Hiroshima event agree to disarm and form a one-world government. All the weapons are delivered to a German world leader wearing Bavarian clothing. A boy representing the U.S. in a boy scout uniform gives all his weapons to the German one-world leader. In this mural, the victor of World War II is surrendering U.S. national sovereignty after World War III.

The following photograph of the fourth mural should be called the "Christ Rejected."[605]

---

[604] Ibid.

[605] Ibid.

The NWO is established, and nowhere in the picture is anyone with Jewish or Christian symbols to be found. In this mural the global population now adhere to the NWO Georgia Guidestones commandment to keep humanity under 500 million people. The people in the mural appear to be at an altar, and instead of celebrating the Eucharist, they are mesmerized by a genetically modified plant on the altar.

The people in the mural appear to react joyfully to the elimination of billions of people. The NWO plan to mix animals with humans to create a new species is revealed as the baby tigers have human faces. All animals and people in the mural focus their attention on a new god represented by a genetically modified plant. The genetically modified plant is important because total control is achieved by a one world currency, driving down fertility with genetically modified food, and through withholding food from people who refuse to worship a New Age god. The people in the mural celebrate a New Age religion that promotes the individual becoming god. A rejected Christ is shown as a small dove trapped in the New Age plant. Whales signify the oceans are no longer polluted by leaping out of the water to celebrate with humanity the arrival of the NWO.

Understanding many of the other Denver Airport symbols, including the gargoyles, embedded floor symbols, the swastika shaped runway, or even the shape of the airport roof is more difficult. However, we know that gargoyles are a symbol for evil and are sometimes used to frighten people.

A legend from around 631 to 641 AD provides some insights on gargoyles. The legend is that St. Romanus delivered the people in what is today Rouen, France from a monster called Gargouille. St. Romanus was a former chancellor of Merovingian King Clotaire II. The gargoyle of this legend was a dragon with bat-like wings and the ability to breathe fire from its mouth. St. Romanus defeated the beast and tried to burn the whole creature, but the head and neck would not burn. The reason was that the fire breath had tempered this part of its body. In lieu of burning, the head was mounted on the exterior walls of a newly built church to scare off evil spirits. On the outside of a church, gargoyles were believed to keep evil out, but when put inside a building, as is the case at the Denver Airport, the NWO belief is that gargoyles keep evil in the building.

On a related note to keeping evil *in* the Denver Airport, unlike most airports that have fences designed to keep people out, the Denver Airport's barb wire on its fences face inside. This airport is different from other U.S. airports in that it has a large underground facility. The runways are also unique as the swastika shape is believed by the NWO to attract and focus dark spiritual energy, which also explains the shape of the airport roof.

The natural question is why the NWO would want to attract and focus a dark energy. The full answer requires reading *Vigilant Christian III: The Occult Religion of the 9/11 Attackers*. A brief explanation is that the NWO believes dark energy helps them keep the public in the dark and thereby minimize one-world government resistance.

The symbols embedded in the floor appear to be carefully crafted calls for acts of evil. Each embedded message has an innocent meaning and a dark meaning. For example, across from the mural I described as "World War III," the letters Au and Ag are in the floor and depicted in a cart. The innocent meaning is that the letters are simply the periodic table symbols for gold and silver.[606] The likely darker meaning is that when the Antichrist controls the world and a one-world currency is needed to buy food, gold and silver forms of currency will be made illegal and carted away.

The reason the pale horse of death and other occult symbols are at the Denver Airport is that this facility was created to be the NWO's primary processing facility should eliminating a domestic NWO resistance in America be deemed necessary. There are over 100 other lesser processing sites around the country established as part of Operation Roundup.

---

[606] Disinformation on the symbols confuses people. For example, the Au and Ag are sometime incorrectly understood to be the symbols for Australia Antigen which has the symbol HBsAg.

The Denver Airport has many more occult symbols, including a sun and black disk in the Great Hall. I recommend looking for the Denver Airport logo. You can see the number 666, the number of the Antichrist, in the center of the logo.[607]

The Denver Airport logo and additional information on the symbols and prophecies are explained in *Vigilant Christian III: The Occult Religion of the 9/11 Attackers*.

Omnicide Threat

Omnicide is human extinction as a result of human action. Omnicide can happen quickly with global nuclear war or slowly as the world is polluted. Authors Praful Bidwai and Achin Vanaik help put in context the importance of safeguarding against the use of nuclear bombs, "The nuclear bomb is the most anti-democratic, anti-national, anti-human, outright evil thing that man has ever made. If you are religious, then remember that this bomb is Man's challenge to God. It's worded quite simply: We have the power to destroy everything that You have created. If you're not religious, then look at it this way. This world of ours is four billion, six hundred million years old. It could end in an afternoon."[608]

The U.S. nuclear arsenal is ridiculously large arsenal with over 7,000 warheads. The thousands of warheads only increase the risk of mass deaths, hurt international goodwill, and waste tax dollars. As additional background on the insane number of nuclear warheads, consider the destructive power of one U.S. W87 strategic 250 Kt nuclear warhead. This weapon of mass destruction has an explosive force equal to 250,000 tons of dynamite.[609] Nuclear scientists

---

[607] Teach Peace Foundation 2013 drawing of the Denver International Airport logo. In this drawing the logo is turned 180 degrees. There is a black 6, a white 6, and a final black 6 in the center.

[608] Praful Bidwai and Achin Vanaik, *New Nukes: India, Pakistan and Global Nuclear Disarmament* (Interlink Books, New York, 2000), preface xxix.
On a related note, on July 16, 1945, the first atomic bomb was detonated at a site in New Mexico named "Trinity."

[609] For more information on the explosive power of nuclear bombs, visit the Federation of American Scientist Web site at www.fas.org/nuke.

concluded over 30 years ago that multiple nuclear explosions would threaten life on the planet due to the nuclear winter effect.[610] No one knows for sure the exact point at which a nuclear winter would occur. Many scientists believe the risk of a nuclear winter exists if 100 standard U.S. nuclear bombs are detonated.[611]

Rosalie Bertell is a Catholic nun with a doctorate in biometry, which is the use of mathematics to understand and predict biological processes. She served as a consultant for the U.S. Nuclear Regulatory Commission and is a founder of the International Commission for Health Professionals in Geneva. Her book, *No Immediate Danger*, documents how nuclear power is leading to the death of everything.[612] Dr. Bertell explains that the words "no immediate danger" are routinely used to falsely imply "no danger" from nuclear power plant radiation releases, when in fact there is a long term danger which scientists have concluded is omnicide. Nuclear power is sold to the public as opening a future of prosperity when it is leading to the death of the human species.

In 1943 Hermann Müller received a Nobel Prize for his work on the genetic effects of radiation. In 1964 Müeller published "Radiation and Heredity," respected then and now by medical/biological nuclear experts.[613] It explains that human produced ionizing radiation leads to omnicide. Müller's work shows how human-made radioactive elements reduce the survival ability of the human species through DNA damage, which damages several generations through exposures. The ultimate price of nuclear bombs and nuclear power is paid by our progeny.

World Health Organization Corruption

The World Health Organization (WHO) is firmly in the control of the NWO. Occasionally the media will report a scandal, but routinely it is framed as only personal greed and pharmaceutical industry corruption. One of the many examples is the 2010 report. Professor Juhani Eskola, a Finnish member of the World Health Organization board, recommended the Swine Flu vaccine. Over 6.2 million euros to fund Dr. Eskola's research center came from GlaxoSmithKline,[614]

---

[610] Carl Sagan, "The Nuclear Winter," *Council for a Livable World*, speech given in Boston, MA, 1983.

[611] Robock, Alan. "New Models Confirm Nuclear Winter," *Bulletin of the Atomic Scientist*, September 1989, 32-35.

[612] Rosalie Bertell, *No Immediate Danger* (Summertown, Tennessee: The Book Publishing Company, 1985). Also recommended is the Nuclear Disaster Case Study online at www.teachpeace.com/teachpeacemoment10.htm.

[613] Hermann Müller, "Radiation and Heredity," *American Journal of Public Health*, Volume 54, Number 1, 1964, 42-50.

[614] Dr. Mercola, "WHO Advisor Secretly Pads Pockets with Big Pharma Money," 7 January 2010, online at http://articles.mercola.com/sites/articles/archive/2010/01/07/WHO-Advisor-Secretly-Pads-Pockets-With-Big-Pharma-Money.aspx and documents acquired through the Danish Freedom of Information Act, Eskola's Finnish institute, THL.

which produces the H1N1 vaccine Pandemrix. Eskola recommended Pandemrix to the Finnish government, which purchased the vaccine for its national pandemic reserve stockpile.

Eskola's conflict of interest raises serious questions that apply to other WHO Strategic Advisory Group of Experts (SAGE) members. SAGE is the elite group that recommends the vaccine products and quantities WHO member countries purchase. Outrage by European consumer protection groups resulted in investigations finding that in addition to Eskola, at least four other members of SAGE were proven to have taken bribes or have serious conflicts of interest.[615] The revelations of the conflicts of interest fueled concerns that the Swine Flu threat was overestimated to generate billions in pharmaceutical industry profits and lead the way to legislation forcing acceptance of vaccines.[616]

The story of how the U.S. government, European health agencies, and WHO have been infiltrated by the NWO is not commonly known. Most often, the collusion of government agencies and pharmaceutical giants is summarized as only institutional arrogance, power, and greed. The thimerosal-tainted vaccinations scandal illustrates the potential for a far greater NWO vaccination population-reduction opportunity.[617]

---

[615] Five of the 15 people on the emergency committee received money from pharmaceutical corporations.

[616] Emily Mullin, "Swine Flu Could Raise Constitutional Issues," *Scripps Howard News Service*, 3 November 2009 online at www.naplesnews.com/news/2009 /nov/03/swine-flu-could-raise-constitutional-issues/.
Bloomberg Businessweek, "Report Says Swine Flu Cost Britain $1.8 billion," *Associated Press*, 1 July 2010 and online at www.businessweek.com/ap/financialnews/D9GM7QIG1.htm.
Sophie Borland, "Swine Flu Advisers' Ties to Drug Firms: Five WHO Experts Linked with Vaccine Producers," *Mail Online*, 13 August 2010, online at www.dailymail.co.uk/health/article-1302505/WHO-swine-flu-advisers-ties-drug-firms-Experts-linked-vaccineproducers.html#ixzz1OmOizXD7.

[617] Robert F. Kennedy Jr., "Deadly Immunity," *Salon.com* co-published with *Rolling Stone Magazine*, 16 June 2005. Dr. Boyd Haley heads the chemistry department at the University of Kentucky and a global expert on mercury toxicity. He said: "You couldn't even construct a study that shows thimerosal is safe . . . It's just too darn toxic. If you inject thimerosal into an animal, its brain will sicken. If you apply it to living tissue, the cells die. If you put it in a petri dish, the culture dies. Knowing these things, it would be shocking if one could inject it into an infant without causing damage."
The 2010 Swine Flu World Health Organization SAGE bribes led to an increased interest in the NWO and WHO connection. Kennedy's 2005 article contained information making the NWO elite uncomfortable. On January 16, 2011, Kennedy's article was removed from Salon's website see www.salon.com/about/inside_salon/2011/01/16/dangerous_immunity for the explanation citing a misattributed quote, a "dropped word," two sentences transposed in a quote, a statement that a meeting agenda addressed a topic it did not, and one incorrect percentage calculations. To dismiss this amazing 4,660 word article years after it was published instead of simply correcting the minor mistakes speaks volumes about the NWO media influence.

Vaccination Security Threat

Vaccines have been employed to improve health and save lives. People should not ignore the benefits of science and dismiss vaccines that have been proven to be beneficial. However, I bring up the vaccination security threat so that people will be aware that epidemiology experts are raising serious concerns over global vaccination programs.

The fact that many vaccines are often life savers provides an opportunity for the NWO to exploit vaccines for their own dark agenda. The information contained in this section is meant to prompt your thinking about a possible national security threat far greater than anything the world will ever see from NWO bogeymen. Robert F. Kennedy Jr.'s "Deadly Immunity," an article published in 2005, provides insights on how and why the Centers for Disease Control and Prevention (CDC) meets secretly with the WHO.[618] Kennedy reported a CDC epidemiologist, Tom Verstraeten, analyzed the agency's medical records and found a mercury-based preservative appeared to be responsible for the dramatic increase in autism and a host of other neurological disorders among children. Instead of protecting the public, the CDC paid the Institute of Medicine to conduct a study to "rule out" the thimerosal link to autism and all other brain disorders.[619]

A review of the problems with the Swine Flu, or H1N1, vaccine highlights the security threat and the NWO opportunity to do great harm. Epidemiology professionals voicing concerns about the vaccination's safety are feared and even hated because their work can frustrate the multi-billion drug business.[620] Donald Rumsfeld provides an example of how the drug business is both corrupt and infiltrated into the government at high levels. Rumsfeld, the former chairman of the Tamiflu patent holder Gilead Sciences, benefited financially when on November 1, 2005 his boss President George W. Bush pronounced a pandemic flu warning. When Bush asked Congress to approve over $1 billion in order to produce Tamiflu, Gilead's market value increased by 50%.[621]

---

[618] Ibid.

[619] Ibid. The Institute of Medicine is an advisory organization that is part of the National Academy of Sciences. The Institute of Medicine produced the CDC requested report in May 2004 but according to Kennedy "may have satisfied the CDC, but convinced no one."

[620] The November 2009 *The Atlantic* issue describes one incident on page 48. Worldwide acknowledged epidemiology expert Dr. Tom Jefferson's "outspokenness has made him something of a pariah." As background we learn from *The Atlantic* article that not only does Dr. Jefferson know the flu-vaccine literature perhaps better than anyone on the planet, he has a track record of courageous behavior including working as a medical officer during the 1992 siege of Sarajevo.
Lone Simonsen, a professor of global health at George Washington University in Washington, D.C., is another internationally recognized epidemiology leader questioning vaccine effectiveness.

[621] "Bush Seeks $1.2B for U.S. Flu Vaccines," *Associated Press*, 1 November 2005, online at http://archive.newsmax.com/archives/articles/2005/11/1/103418.shtml and USA Today, "Bush Outlines $7.1 Billion

Could the NWO really be working to achieve a global Hitlerian final solution?[622] History repeatedly confirms the answer is yes, and at a minimum it is a reasonable theory to help understand what is actually happening, and the real threat to global security. The vaccination security threat information uncovered by Edward Haslam's research proves that in the 1960s a secret U.S. laboratory in New Orleans was working on cancer-causing monkey vaccine viruses that are linked to global epidemics.[623] The secret New Orleans laboratory research also sheds light on the work that CIA officer Lee Harvey Oswald performed prior to his becoming famous as the patsy who assassinated President John F. Kennedy.[624]

In 2009 the United Kingdom's Health Protection Agency warned that the Swine Flu vaccine is linked to the deadly nerve disease known as Guillain-Barre Syndrome. A government leaked letter revealed the risk of contracting Guillain-Barre Syndrome was eight times greater for people already exposed to an infamous 1976 Swine Flu vaccine.[625] A dangerous ingredient, squalene, is a naturally occurring oil found in the human brain and other places. When it is administered as a vaccine, medical professionals routinely object, and there is not a single vaccine containing squalene that is approved for use in the U.S.[626]

Medical experts have found that when squalene is injected, the body creates antibodies to attack the oil. The result of the attack on the oil is a range of human illnesses which are collectively called "Gulf War Syndrome." Many medical experts believe squalene is responsible for the wide variety of symptoms, although some Gulf War veterans have become sick from other causes, including: proximity to Iraqi biological and chemical weapon sites when they were destroyed by the U.S. in 1991, exposure to depleted uranium, and exposure to burning oil

---

Strategy to Fight Flu," 1 November 2005, online at www.usatoday.com/news/washington/2005-11-01-bush-flu_x.htm.

[622] Yoshihiro Kawaoka, "Gene from 1918 Virus Proves Key to Virulent Influenza," *University of Wisconsin-Madison*, 6 October 2004, online at www.news.wisc.edu/releases/10241.html and *BBC News*, "Killer flu recreated in the lab," October 2004, online at http://news.bbc.co.uk/2/hi/health/3719990.stm.

[623] Edward T. Haslam, *Dr. Mary's Monkey: How the Unsolved Murder of a Doctor, a Secret Laboratory in New Orleans and Cancer-Causing Monkey Viruses are Linked to Lee Harvey Oswald, the JFK Assassination and Emerging Global Epidemics* (Walterville, OR: TrineDay, 2007).

[624] Judyth Vary Baker, *Me and Lee: How I came to know, love and lose Lee Harvey Oswald* (Walterville, OR: Trine Day LLC, 2010).

[625] Alex Newman, "Risks of the Swine Flu Vaccine," *New American*, 3 September 2009, www.thenewamerican.com/index.php/usnews/health-care/1813.

[626] Meryl Nass, M.D., is one professional who objects to squaline injections and notes that Novartis and GlaxoSmithKline will make use of squaline as a "novel feature of the H1N1 vaccines."

fields.[627] The debilitating set of phenomena has resulted in at least 175,000 of the 700,000 U.S. military personnel who served during the first war in Iraq becoming seriously ill.[628]

A Tulane Medical School study published in *Experimental Molecular Pathology* found, "The substantial majority (95%) of overtly ill deployed Gulf War Syndrome patients had antibodies to squalene. All (100%) Gulf War Syndrome patients immunized for service in Desert Shield/Desert Storm who did not deploy, but had the same signs and symptoms as those who did deploy, had antibodies to squalene."[629]

The Tulane Medical School study reinforced a 2004 University of Florida in Gainesville finding. Adjuvants are mixes of oil and water that stimulate the immune system to boost the body's response to antigens. The Gainesville researchers reported that adjuvants are a concern for multiple reasons, including that mice injected with adjuvant oils developed conditions of the type that occur when the body's immune system produces an excessive protective reaction.[630]

Another study published in the *American Journal of Pathology* highlighted problems with the use of squalene. One finding is that injecting squalene into rats results in what humans know as rheumatoid arthritis, or "chronic, immune-mediated joint-specific inflammation."

Bloomberg reported on July 13, 2009, that the Centers for Disease Control announced it agreed to pay London-based Glaxo and Switzerland-based Novartis more than $415 million for adjuvants.[631] Peper Long, an FDA spokeswoman, said that an April 2009 U.S. Health and Human Services Department emergency declaration enables the FDA to authorize the use of unlicensed

---

[627] In 2012, it was confirmed the U.S. government lied to soldiers about their 1991 exposure to sarin gas. Kelly Kennedy, "Study: Wind blew deadly gas to U.S. troops in Gulf War," *USA TODAY*, 14 December 2012. U.S. military personnel were told chemical alarms that went off at U.S. bases in Saudi Arabia during the 1991 Gulf War were false alarms. In 2012, researchers Robert Haley and James Tuite and published in the journal *Neuroepidemiology* that troops were exposed to sarin gas from the January 18, 1991, bombings of Nasiriyah and Khamisiya. The plume of sarin gas reached Saudi Arabia.

[628] "Benefits Reconsidered for Ill Gulf War Vets," *Army Times*, 26 February 2010, online at www.armytimes. com/news/2010/02/ap_gulf_illness_ benefits_022610/. On September 25, 2007, *Reuters* reported that over 175,000 are still seriously ill. For more information on depleted uranium, go to www.teachpeace. com/depleteduranium101.htm.

[629] P B Asa, Y Cao, R F Garry, "Antibodies to Squalene in Gulf War Syndrome," *Experimental and Molecular Pathology*, March 2000. The findings are from a Tulane Medical School study, 1430 Tulane Avenue, New Orleans, Louisiana.

[630] Tom Randall and Gary Matsumoto, "Swine Flu Shot May Rely on Emergency Use of Additives," *Bloomberg*, 29 July 2009. The article is online at www.bloomberg.com/apps/news?pid=20601103&sid=a_ xObcaSxF2o.

[631] Ibid.

vaccines. These unproven experimental additives were feared to be part of at least 120 million flu vaccine doses.[632]

The NWO approach of manufacturing emergencies could deceive an anxious public into bypassing normal vaccine testing safeguards.[633] As explained in *Vigilant Christian I: The New World Order*, the NWO controls the drug companies supplying vaccines.[634] Anyone struggling to believe emergencies are manufactured need only remember the corporate media campaign to convince the public that Iraq was a weapons of mass destruction threat to the United States.

An amazing Swine Flu vaccine finding was reported in November 2009 in *The Atlantic*. An article titled "Shots in the Dark" states "the vaccine itself might not reduce mortality at all."[635] Indeed, ABC News reported the Swine Flu vaccine may carry increased risk, with data outside the U.S. showing that people vaccinated appeared to have twice the risk of getting Swine Flu.[636] In 2006, the *International Journal of Epidemiology* published research questioning influenza vaccination effectiveness, stating, "Numerous observational studies have reported that seniors who receive influenza vaccine are at substantially lower risk of death and hospitalization during influenza season than unvaccinated seniors, but these estimates could be influenced by differences in underlying health status between the vaccinated and unvaccinated groups."[637] *The Atlantic* article went on to say that scientists found the healthy-user effect explained the entire benefit that other researchers were attributing to the flu vaccine.

While vaccines have saved many lives and have the potential to help billions of people, when we start to look at the questions being raised by some medical experts and compare it to the

---

[632] Ibid. University of Rochester researcher John Treanor said, "The question is, do you really feel comfortable throwing this new thing into the mix and do you really need to?"

[633] On a related note, President Barack Obama declared the swine flu outbreak a national emergency on October 24, 2009 and empowered his health secretary to suspend federal requirements. Online at www.spokesman.com/stories/2009/oct/24/obama-declares-swine-flu-national-emergency/.

[634] Anthon Fauci, Director of the National Institute of Allergy and Infectious Diseases in Bethesda, Maryland said the U.S. has contracts with five companies to provide flu shots. Novartis is responsible for 45 percent of the supply, Sanofi 26 percent, CSL 19 percent, with the remaining doses from Glaxo and AstraZeneca Plc.

[635] Shannon Brownless and Jeanne Lenzer, "Shots in the Dark," *The Atlantic*, November 2009, page 48.

[636] Annie Guest, "Vaccines may have increased swine flu risk," *ABC News*, 4 March 2011 and online at www.abc.net.au/news/stories/2011/03/04/3155750.htm and reports from Finland online at www.hs.fi/english/article/Hundreds+of+reports+of+harm+from+swine+flu+shots/1135264564296.

[637] Lisa A Jackson, Michael L Jackson, Jennifer C Nelson, Kathleen M Neuzil and Noel S Weiss, "Evidence of bias in estimates of influenza vaccine effectiveness in seniors," *International Journal of Epidemiology, Volume 35, Number 2*, April 2006 pages 337-344. First published online on December 20, 2005 at http://ije.oxfordjournals.org/cgi/content/full/35/2/337?maxtoshow= &HITS=10&hits=10&RESULTFORMAT=&fulltext=Lisa+Jackson&searchid=1&FIRSTINDEX=0&resourcetype=HWCIT.

NWO agenda to eliminate over 6.5 billion people, there is a need to safeguard vaccines.[638] Other countries take the NWO threat seriously. The "Shots in the Dark" article ends with the ominous warning, "By being afraid to do the proper studies now, we may be condemning ourselves to using treatments based on illusion and faith rather than sound science."[639]

A sinister NWO vaccine program demands deniability; even a few million survivors who know the truth would make the world a dangerous place for the NWO leaders. This is why flu vaccination might become a multi-step program in which vaccines rushed past safeguards under the cloak of an emergency are combined years later with "proven safe" mandatory vaccines. In this scenario the mass deaths triggered by the combination of vaccines might be blamed on a swine influenza giving new meaning to Biblical warnings about pigs.[640]

A Dangerous Profession: Scientist

Scientists who frustrate the NWO by opposing pharmaceutical giants, governments, or other front organizations risk assassination. As explained earlier in the chapter, NWO agents often blackmail people, but the risk of murder is real. The following are examples of mysterious deaths of scientists who were working in areas directly related to the 2001 terrorism or in areas very important to the NWO.

Scientist Bruce Edwards Ivins worked at the United States Army Medical Research Institute of Infectious Diseases in Fort Detrick, Maryland. He died on July 29, 2008 of alleged suicide from Tylenol and two other drugs soon after learning the Federal Bureau of Investigation was preparing to indict him as the person responsible for the 2001 anthrax attacks. The problem with putting the blame on this microbiologist and vaccinologist is he did not have access to the anthrax that killed people.[641]

---

[638] Influenza viruses are identified as A, B, and C. Influenza A can infect a range of species, including humans and animals (e.g., pigs and birds). Only humans are infected by types B and C. Influenza A is responsible for most flu cases.

[639] Shannon Brownless and Jeanne Lenzer, "Shots in the Dark," *The Atlantic*, November 2009, page 54.

[640] One can imagine seeing the leaders and their children from many countries on television receiving the independently safe vaccine without having years earlier been exposed to the "unproved to be safe" vaccine.

[641] On July 25, 2011, U.S. District Judge Daniel Hurley blocked the government's attempt to change a court admission that proved Bruce Ivins could not be responsible for the 2001 anthrax attacks. He never had access to the special equipment needed to make the anthrax powder.
Greg Gordon, Mike Wiser and Stephen Engleberg, "Judge: U.S. must show 'good cause' to revise anthrax filing," *McClatchy Newspapers*, 27 July 2011 and online at www.mcclatchydc.com/2011/07/19/117864/justice-department-retracts-court.html#ixzz1TVIRL600.

British biological weapons expert David Kelly died on July 17, 2003 after allegedly slashing his own wrists. He was the Ministry of Defense's chief scientific officer and senior adviser on biological weapons to the UN biological weapons inspection teams in Iraq. Kelly told BBC journalist Andrew Gilligan the British government's dossier on weapons of mass destruction in Iraq was fabricated. Kelly's information was published and he was called to appear on July 15, 2003 before the parliamentary foreign affairs select committee. Two days after answering the select committee's questions, he was dead.

American John (Jack) Parsons Wheeler III was found dead in a Delaware landfill on December 31, 2010. Wheeler had served in the office of the Secretary of Defense and written a manual on the effectiveness of biological and chemical weapons. The Delaware state medical examiner reported on January 28, 2011 the cause of death was blunt force trauma. The alarming trend of scientists dying from suicide, physical assault, poisoning, a virus, or an airplane crash appears to far exceed mysterious deaths for the general public.[642] A few examples readers may want to research include Dr. Eugene F. Mallove, Dr. Steven Mostow, Dr. Jeong H. Im, Dr. Robert E. Shope, and Dr. Ian Langford. The number of scientists dying mysteriously led to the creation of websites that document these enigmatic deaths.[643]

American Hiroshima Programming

Predictive programming is a clever and subtle form of psychological conditioning using fiction as a precursor to fact. Statements from generals and intelligence officials are sometimes predictive programming messages. One example is the American Hiroshima warning by retired General Eugene Habiger.[644] The goal of the NWO is to present the public with information about a possible event so that should the event happen, such as an American Hiroshima false-

---

[642] Three additional examples include: Chitra Chauhan was 33 when she died on November 15, 2010. Potassium cyanide, the apparent cause of death, is suspicious because it was not used in her research projects. Chauhan, a molecular biologist and disease transmission expert, earned her doctorate from the Institute of Genomics and Integrative Biology in New Delhi, India.

Canadian Dr. Keith Fagnou was 38 when he died of complications resulting from an H1N1 influenza infection on November 11, 2009. His research focused on improving the preparation of complex molecules for petrochemical, pharmaceutical, or industrial uses. His work had overturned prior ideas of what is possible in the chemistry field.

Dr. David Banks was a foot and mouth disease expert trying to keep diseases affecting cattle, pigs, and fruit orchards out of Australia. He was 55 when he died in an aircraft crash in Queensland, Australia.

[643] Steven Qualye maintains a list of scientists who are dying called "Dead Scientists" and online at www. stevequayle.com/dead_scientists/UpdatedDeadScientists2.html.

[644] Bill Keller, "Nuclear Nightmares," *New York Times Magazine*, 26 May 2002. General Habiger, the four-star general who ran the anti-terror program until 2001, stated "it is not a matter of if; it's a matter of when." Keller noted "that, may explain why he now lives in San Antonio."

flag act of terrorism, the public will accept the planned changes. This is one reason why NWO fearmongering about nuclear terrorism is often accompanied with messages that freedom will have to be forfeited for security.

In the years since this book was first published, I have been able to obtain a more accurate understanding of the American Hiroshima threat by studying the predictive programming efforts of individuals in NWO front organizations, including the Council on Foreign Relations, the Trilateral Commission, and the Bilderberg Group.[645] Specific American Hiroshima predictive programming examples include:

- Graham Allison and his 2004 book *Nuclear Terrorism*
- Bill Keller and his 2002 article *New York Times Magazine* "Nuclear Nightmares"
- Nicholas D. Kristof and his 2004 *New York Times* article "An American Hiroshima"
- Former Congressman Curt Weldon and his 2005 book *Countdown to Terror*
- Lawrence G. Wright and his 2006 book *The Looming Tower*
- The Nuclear Threat Initiative's 2005 *Last Best Chance* film

All of the above sources of false information about the al Qaeda nuclear threat are members of the Council on Foreign Relations, Trilateral Commission, Bilderberg Group, or other NWO affiliated blood-oath secret societies.

One prime example of predictive programming by members of secret societies is the Hoover Institution's *Uncommon Knowledge* American Hiroshima discussion.[646] I recommend watching this video, published online by the Hoover Institution, that features Council on Foreign Relations (CFR) member Scott Sagan and Bilderberg, CFR, and Trilateral Commission member Graham Allison. The show begins with, "Today on Uncommon Knowledge, Preventing an American Hiroshima" and continues for another 26 minutes with a full suite of predictive programming messages.[647]

---

[645] A major improvement in this 2012 edition was to more carefully evaluate sources that are members of organizations known to be fronts for the New World Order. The earliest false reports about Osama bin Laden planning a nuclear attack on the U.S. are connected to Israel (e.g., the article "Bin Laden has Several Nuclear Suitcases" published in the *Jerusalem Report* on October 25, 1999).

[646] The video was published online by the Hoover Institution and can be viewed at www.youtube.com/watch?v=UZ3ploflj1s&feature=related.

[647] To read about more specific examples or watch videos of key NWO insiders delivering American Hiroshima predictive programming warnings, go to www.vigliantchristian.org/americanhiroshima.htm.

Bush's American Hiroshima Cloud

President Bush, who comes from a family that for generations have been NWO members, was highly effective in creating fear on October 8, 2002 when he said: "Don't wait for a mushroom cloud."[648] The predictive programming nuclear terrorism message deceived people to support the NWO-ordered Iraq War that Bush already knew would begin in 2003.[649]

In 2003 an Islamic justification for an American Hiroshima attack was reported to have been written by Sheikh Nasir bin Hamad. This document, "A Treatise on the Ruling Regarding the Use of Weapons of Mass Destruction Against Infidels," is cited by Daniel Benjamin and Steven Simon as the religious justification for an American Hiroshima attack.[650] Former U.S. Attorney General John Ashcroft contributed to conditioning and scaring the public when he falsely claimed al Qaeda or its sympathizers could have a nuclear bomb.[651] The Nuclear Threat Institute contributed to the public conditioning that al Qaeda was planning an attack on a nuclear facility by distributing *The Last Best Chance* video. The video claims to be based on U.S. government classified information and specifically warns of al Qaeda's American Hiroshima plan.[652]

Allison, Weldon, Wright and Al-Fad

Graham Allison is a dean at Harvard's Kennedy School of Government and author of *Nuclear Terrorism*.[653] His attendance at the May 31 to June 3, 2007 Bilderberg meeting in Istanbul, Turkey is noteworthy because Allison is the leading NWO voice warning the public about an American

---

[648] "Bush: Don't Wait for Mushroom Cloud," *CNN.com*, 8 October 2002. The complete text is online at www.cnn.com/2002/ALLPOLITICS/10/07/bush.transcript/.

[649] "Bush: Don't wait for mushroom cloud," *CNN.com*, 8 October 2002. President George W. Bush and his administration did not want to talk about the true threat of a mushroom cloud from terrorists because it would reveal how little was really being done to protect America. The complete text online address is www.cnn.com/2002/ALLPOLITICS/10/07/bush.transcript/.

[650] Daniel Benjamin and Steven Simon, *The Next Attack* (London: Hodder and Stoughton, 2005) 71. On a related note, al Qaeda documents are often available online. This enables a person to walk into an internet café in most cities in the Muslim world and participate in a virtual jihad training course.

[651] "Nuclear Terrorism Greatest Threat," *Associated Press*, 28 January 2005. Ashcroft also served the NWO by conditioning the public to believe Al Qaeda is the greatest danger facing the United States in the war on terrorism.

[652] *Last Best Chance* produced by Aaron Goddard and directed by Ben Goddard, 2005. To obtain the video, visit www.lastbestchance.org.

[653] Graham Allison, *Nuclear Terrorism: The Ultimate Preventable Catastrophe* (New York, New York: Time Books, Henry Holt & Company, LLC, 2004), 3. Graham Allison cites: David Johnston and James Risen, "Traces of Terrorism: The Intelligence Reports; Series of Warnings," *New York Times*, 17 May 2002.

Hiroshima.[654] Allison's presence at this Bilderberg meeting is one of many signals the NWO is actively considering nuclear terrorism as a means to advance their one-world agenda.

Allison greatly fueled the public's fears by claiming Osama bin Laden's official spokesman, Suleiman Abu Gheith, announced on a now-defunct web site, www.alneda.com, "We have the right to kill four million Americans, two million of them children, and to exile twice as many and wound and cripple hundreds of thousands."[655] Allison also wrote that Khalid Sheikh Mohammed, a chief patsy of 9/11, was claimed to have said Osama bin Laden was unyielding in his opposition to crashing airplanes into nuclear power plants because Osama bin Laden wanted nuclear facilities to be left alone "for now."[656] The "for now" is significant and comes from the NWO because Osama bin Laden was not involved in attacking the U.S. on 9/11. The NWO disinformation of "for now" sets the stage to blame al Qaeda for a future nuclear facility attack. Allison sells the NWO conditioning by estimating that there is a 51% likelihood an American Hiroshima will happen.[657]

Former Congressman Curt Weldon was the source for creating fear that a Muslim nuclear act of terror was imminent. He published a book disagreeing with U.S. intelligence officials who he claimed were refusing to inform the public that an al Qaeda cell was captured in Canada in 2003 as the terrorists plotted to fly a plane into the Seabrook nuclear power plant in New Hampshire. The Seabrook nuclear power plant is approximately 40 miles from Boston, and the false story warned that millions of people were almost exposed to radiation poisoning. Weldon also promoted the story that al Qaeda hijackers originating from Logan airport in Boston considered crashing into the Indian Point nuclear power station 40 miles north of Manhattan.[658]

---

[654] Allison's NWO front memberships are provided in *Vigilant Christian I: The New World Order*. See Appendix B, C, and D in book one to learn more about Allison and other secret society members. When a terrorist attack occurs, instead of chasing people in the caves of Afghanistan, the "what happened" investigation should begin by with the NWO members identified in book one.

[655] Graham Allison, *Nuclear Terrorism: The Ultimate Preventable Catastrophe* (New York, New York: Time Books, Henry Holt & Company, LLC, 2004), 12.

[656] Ibid., 19. Graham Allison notes that Khalid Sheikh Mohammed was interviewed by Al Jazeera about his leadership role in the 9/11 attacks.

[657] Nicholas D. Kristof, "An American Hiroshima," *New York Times*, 11 August 2004. Available at www.nytimes.com/2004/08/11/opinion/11kris.html? ex=1249963200&en=81ff0a19e469c48a&ei=5090&partner=rssuserland.

[658] Congressman Curt Weldon, *Countdown to Terror* (Washington, DC: Regnery Publishing, Inc., 2005), 9 and 83.

Lawrence Wright wrote a book with false information about Jamal al-Fadl, claiming he walked into the American Embassy in Eritrea in June 1996 and sold the CIA secrets.[659] The story Wright published was based on testimony al-Fadl made in February 2001 and included details making al Qaeda appear real. Some of the details include that Jamal al-Fadl was caught stealing $110,000 from al Qaeda and begged for Osama bin Laden's forgiveness. Wright wrote that Osama bin Laden said al-Fadl could not be forgiven until he returned the stolen money. Jamal al-Fadl decided not to return the money but to leave al Qaeda and help the CIA. From Eritrea al-Fadl was sent to a U.S. military base in Germany and questioned by FBI agent Dan Coleman. He revealed he was a Sudanese citizen who worked in Khartoum as al Qaeda's treasurer. He claimed he was the third person to pledge alliance to al Qaeda and provided detailed information about past and proposed operations.

Jamal al-Fadl offered the most detailed account of Osama bin Laden's interest in nuclear terrorism. His testimony in the trial of the earlier World Trade Center bombing helped place the blame on al Qaeda and was a centerpiece for the U.S. prosecution in 2001.[660] He was credited as the source who revealed the plans for what was called the Planes Operation and Operation Big Wedding.[661] The specific details provided by al-Fadl, especially the nuclear threat, helped convince people that the fictitious al Qaeda was real.[662] Evidence he made up his story about al Qaeda with substantial government assistance was available even before September 11, 2001, but statements by lawyer Sam Schmidt and others were ignored.[663]

---

[659] Lawrence Wright, *The Looming Towers: Al Qaeda and the Road to 9/11* (New York: New York: Alfred A. Knopf, 2006).

[660] United States of America v. Usama bin Laden, et al. (S(7) 98 Cr. 1023) and transcripts are online at http://cryptome.org/usa-v-ubl-dt.htm.

[661] Sander Hicks, *The Big Wedding: 9/11, The Whistle-Blowers & The Cover-Up* (Brooklyn, New York: Vox Pop), 2005.

[662] Carey Sublette, "Could al Qaeda go Nuclear?," *Nuclear Weapon Archive*, 18 May 2002 and online at http://nuclearweaponarchive.org/News/IslamicTerrorBombs.html. Also see Jamal al-Fadl's February 6, 2001 testimony in United States of America v. Usama bin Laden, et al. (S(7) 98 Cr. 1023) are online at http://cryptome.org/usa-v-ubl-02.htm and the false al Qaeda American Hiroshima threat appears on February 7, 2001 see http://cryptome.org/usa-v-ubl-03.htm.

[663] Additional information about Schmidt and the Embassy bombing trials is in a documentary written and produced by Adam Curtis. The documentary, *The Power of Nightmares: Episode 3 - The Shadows in the Cave*, originally aired on *BBC 2* on November 3, 2004.

Sam Schmidt, a defense lawyer in the trial for the Kenya and Tanzania embassy bombings on August 7, 1998, said: "And there were selective portions of al-Fadl's testimony that I believe was false, to help support the picture that he helped the Americans join together. I think he lied in a number of specific testimony about a unified image of what this organization was. It made Al Qaeda the new Mafia or the new Communists. It made them identifiable as a group and therefore made it easier to prosecute any person associated with Al Qaeda for any acts or statements made by bin Laden -- who talked a lot." The transcripts for United States of America v. Usama bin Laden, et al. (S(7) 98 Cr. 1023) are online at http://cryptome.org/usa-v-ubl-dt.htm.

Operation Big Wedding Deception

Operation Big Wedding was a clever disinformation effort promoted after 9/11 to fool people to believe the 19 hijackers were real. Major media outlets told the world the "big wedding" story that the hijackers thought they would die as martyrs and as a result each had a wedding with 72 virgins in heaven.[664] The fourth Vigilant Christian book explains that many of the alleged 19 hijackers are still alive and all were falsely blamed. I once incorrectly concluded Jamal al-Fadl was credible. I missed the earlier evidence that he had lied and identified my error only after I noticed that the people reporting about al-Fadl were members of NWO front organizations. I apologize for this mistake, and recommend watching the BBC documentary *The Power of Nightmares* to learn more about al-Fadl.[665]

An example of how Jamal al-Fadl's statements did not line-up with other credible sources is his account of how the name al Qaeda was selected. During the U.S. District Court New York January 2001 trial, al-Fadl stated that the name al Qaeda was coined at a meeting in Khost, Afghanistan in 1989. He claimed 10 people attended the meeting including Osama bin Laden. The purported meeting was chaired by an Iraqi, Abu Aoyoub, who provided a mission statement to wage jihad beyond the borders of Afghanistan.

Jamal al-Fadl claimed al Qaeda was the name used by the organization since 1989. The story sounds good, and a trail beginning with the first CIA al Qaeda reference in 1996 does appear to show al Qaeda existed before September 11, 2001, but repeatedly we find the trail has been manufactured. The disconnects include public statements by Osama bin Laden and the fact that he never used the name al Qaeda to refer to his handful of supporters before October 20, 2001

The entire Jamal al-Fadl testimony took on a new light when his testimony responsible for convicting four people in 2005 led to the revelation that hours of U.S. government videotape recordings with al-Fadl, believed to be helping him prepare for his testimony, were illegally withheld by the U.S. Marshals Service (more information is available at www.rotten.com/library/bio/crime/terrorists/jamal-al-fadl/).

[664] *The Miami Herald* and *Christian Science Monitor* are two of the many examples of 2003 publishers of articles with the disinformation: "In the weeks before Sept. 11, Jordanian intelligence had warned U.S. counterparts that bin Laden terrorists were planning a major attack using aircraft inside the continental United States. The Jordanians had intercepted a crucial al Qaeda message that dubbed the operation 'the big wedding.'"

[665] "The Power of Nightmares: Baby It's Cold Outside," *BBC News*, 14 January 2005 and the portion of the documentary is online at www.youtube.com/watch?v=mztfFdpd1Rk&NR=1. The full documentary is online at http://polidics.com/cia/top-ranking-cia-operatives-admit-al-qaeda-is-a-complete-fabrication.html.

(this is the date on which Osama bin Laden used the al Qaeda name in response to a question by al-Jazeera's Taysir Alluni).[666]

Jamal al-Fadl was and is a false centerpiece of the entire al Qaeda fabrication. It is possible he never really defected to the CIA in 1996 but returned to the CIA to serve his NWO disinformation role.[667] On another interesting note, al-Fadl received over $1 million from the U.S. government for his information, and while living as a protected government witness he won the New Jersey Lottery.[668] By making up the story that al Qaeda is real, al-Fadl became very rich.

Disinformation about al Qaeda and predictive programming is delivered frequently by the major media outlets. The ruling elite promote disinformation from people they pay, such as Jamal al-Fadl and reporters working for "credible" news sources. Often reporters believe they are simply involved in honest reporting. A 2005 *Washington Post* article by Shankar Vedantam is one example.[669] Vedantam probably did not know that his employer, the *Washington Post*, was one of the key newspapers selected by the NWO to help redefine current events and history.[670]

After Osama bin Laden's assassination in 2011 the predictable NWO "nuclear hell storm if Osama bin Laden is killed" warnings following the 9/11 attacks replayed.[671] The false warnings were intended to scare people, and they did. As with all previous reports about a planned nuclear attack by al Qaeda, the post-assassination "nuclear hell storm" claims are carefully constructed propaganda orchestrated by the NWO.

---

[666] Bruce Lawrence, *Messages to the World*: *The Statements of Osama bin Laden*, (London and New York: Verso, 2005), 108.

[667] Lawrence Wright, *The Looming Towers: Al Qaeda and the Road to 9/11* (New York: New York: Alfred A. Knopf, 2006), 5 and 191. Wright's discloses Jamal al-Fadl worked in Brooklyn prior to his claim that he joined al Qaeda.

[668] Ibid., 197.

[669] Shankar Vedantam, "Nuclear Plants Are Still Vulnerable, Panel Says," *Washington Post*, 7 April 2005, A12. He reported in the *Washington Post* that nuclear facilities remain exposed to an al Qaeda attack.

[670] In 1933 *The Washington Post* (founded in 1877) was purchased by NWO member Eugene Meyer. Meyer had joined the Council on Foreign Relations (CFR) in 1929 and was a partner of Federal Reserve Board governor Bernard Baruch. Meyer's daughter, Katharine Graham, was a frequent Bilderberg and CFR supporter. Her husband Philip Graham led *The Washington Post* starting in 1946 when Meyer left to head the World Bank. Katharine Graham led the paper for more than 20 years; she died on July 17, 2001. Her son, Donald Graham, is the current Chairman and CEO. Therefore, when Vedantam and other reporters are assigned to write articles for *The Washington Post*, they sometimes contribute to the false belief that al Qaeda exists without realizing that they are being subtly influenced by the newspaper's ownership.

[671] "9/11 Mastermind Reportedly Warned of 'Nuclear Hell storm' if Bin Laden Killed," *Fox*, 2 May 2011.

After studying all the American Hiroshima claims for about a decade, I have discovered a repeating pattern. With Graham Allison leading the way for the NWO that an al Qaeda American Hiroshima threat is real, members of secret society front organization continue to advance the NWO agenda by publishing false information.[672] Over time the reports prove to be false, but these false reports have deceived many people to believe that Islamic terrorists were responsible for the 9/11 terrorism and serve to condition people for an American Hiroshima.

Concrete Reasons to Care

In the first Vigilant Christian book, concrete evidence was provided that the NWO is both real and is seeking to start a third world war. The Georgia Guidestones and the Denver Airport are two examples that the NWO seeks to eliminate billions of people. The potential for future generations to be increasingly sterile from one or a combination of factors including Bisphenol A, Aspartame, Chemtrails, electromagnetic radiation, genetically modified foods, and other harmful ingredients deserves serious consideration.[673]

Revelation 9:20 informs us that plagues will kill many people. A vaccination or other scientifically engineered plague is also explained here because the NWO needs to have a plausible reason for rounding up people for mass inoculations, and it needs to be convincing enough that future generations will conclude the action was necessary. A manufactured deadly virus has the potential to accomplish the mass murder objectives and be dismissed as unintentional. For this reason, anytime a scientist connected to the NWO exhumes a flu victim's body, as recently happened with a person who died in 1918, we need to be vigilant.

To prevent World War III from happening during our children's lifetimes, four things must happen. The first is people have to learn about the NWO. Second, NWO control of the

---

[672] Graham Allison and Gregory F. Treverton editors, *Rethinking America's Security: Beyond Cold War to New World Order* (New York, New York: W. W. Norton & Company, 1992).
Graham Allison, *Nuclear Terrorism: The Ultimate Preventable Catastrophe* (New York, New York: Time Books, Henry Holt & Company, LLC, 2004), 3. Graham Allison cites: David Johnston and James Risen, "Traces of Terrorism: The Intelligence Reports; Series of Warnings," *The New York Times*, 17 May 2002.

[673] The claim that the NWO is seeking to replace many people with machines and modify human DNA is also very real. An example of potential human DNA change is explained by S. Matthew Liao, a professor at New York University. Liao is advocating changing DNA to give people cat eyes. He said the reason is "cat eyes see nearly as well as human eyes during the day, but much better at night. We figured that if everyone had cat eyes, you wouldn't need so much lighting, and so you could reduce global energy usage considerably." Ross Andersen, "How Engineering the Human Body Could Combat Climate Change," The Atlantic, 12 March 2012 and online at www.theatlantic.com/technology/archive/2012/03/how-engineering-the-human-body-could-combat-climate-change/253981/.

U.S. monetary system must be terminated through the abolishment of the Federal Reserve. Third, people must become vigilant about NWO attempts to infiltrate government agencies. And finally, the hiding ground of tax-exempt corporations and for-profit corporations must be transformed by denying corporations the legal rights of human beings.

If most of humanity continues to fail to see the NWO writing on the wall, or even the NWO writing on the Georgia Guidestones, dark times will fall upon humanity. Is it possible that Christians, resisting the powerful NWO, could be defeated? No. While the NWO will have some victories on earth, God gives us eternal peace. Blessed are the peacemakers who fight the spiritual and non-violent fight. Every person can be victorious over evil, regardless of what happens in the future, by accepting Jesus as our Lord and Savior.

11

Preventing Disaster

"And ye shall hear of wars and rumours of wars: see that ye be not troubled: for all these things must come to pass, but the end is not yet." Matthew 24:6

A world without wars may be impossible, but a world without nuclear wars is possible. We can prevent an American Hiroshima when we defeat the New World Order. We must persevere in our work for justice because in cowardice lies defeat, and it is in fighting for justice that we live with Christ.

How to Defeat the NWO

We can defeat the NWO in our lifetimes, though future peacemakers will have to continue the good fight because this is a spiritual battle, and as such, the struggle against evil is constant. The good news is that the Bible provides a clear message that in the end, God wins.

I ask you to turn to the front cover as a reminder that Christianity in Japan was targeted for destruction in World War II. In more recent years, the NWO Georgia Guidestones were constructed with ten guidelines for society; but they are deceptive and not as benign as they seem. The real messages of the Ten Commandments of the Antichrist are presented here:

1. Mass-murder billions of people.
2. Routinely kill babies regardless of fitness and diversity.
3. Abolish governments and most world languages.
4. Abolish Abrahamic religions under the guise of "rule passion—faith—tradition—and all things with tempered reason."
5. Establish a single rule of law for the world that will be legal but unjust.
6. Replace local justice and "jury of the people" courts with a world court.
7. Avoid laws that protect the minority from the majority.
8. Strip liberty and personal rights as mandated by NWO rulers.

9. Seek harmony with an abstract infinite or the NWO leaders' false god.
10. Deem people who oppose the NWO to be "a cancer on the earth" who will be killed for the false benefit of humanity.

Prayer and Education

With so many opportunities to work for peace, where do we start? A great way to start is oppose the one-world reign of terror with prayers and share that the NWO threat is real. The underdog can win eternally.[674] Today, the NWO has ill-used the U.S. through building it into the greatest absolute military power in history. If absolute power corrupts, have we become corrupted? Our failure to see how the U.S. government is being used by the NWO, combined with our lack of concern, strongly suggests the answer is yes.

People need to understand that terrorism is an NWO tool to erode the image and moral authority of a nation. Terrorism gives birth to people seeking the destruction of the U.S. We greatly undermine NWO terrorism when legitimate injustices are addressed. Justice is the ultimate medicine for terrorism. Justice prevails when people who use violence are prosecuted for their crimes.

Defeating terrorists necessitates defining terror as anyone, regardless of religion or country of origin, who kills an innocent person. To be blind to this reality guarantees ongoing acts of violence. Organizations that value human life differently and hold others to a different standard create terrorists. The world's law enforcement services must be freed from NWO infiltration and control. When members of secret societies affiliated with the NWO are fired, law enforcement professionals can serve as an important arm of justice.

Protect the Constitution

Most Americans still resist attempts to undermine the Constitution. A constitutional convention requires a two-thirds vote of both houses of Congress or two-thirds of the state legislatures. Colonel Edward M. House, the highest placed NWO insider during the Woodrow Wilson administration, unsuccessfully sought to have the U.S. Constitution "scrapped and rewritten."[675] NWO funded tax-exempt foundations have attempted several times in the last

---

[674] Jean Vanier, *Becoming Human* (Mahwah, New Jersey: Paulist Press, 1998), 34. On the notion of why underdogs are often supported, "Weakness carries within it a secret power. The cry and the trust that flow from weakness can open up hearts. The one who is weaker can call forth powers of love in the one who is stronger."

[675] James Perloff, *The Shadows of Power: The Council on Foreign Relations And The American Decline*, (Appleton, WI: Western Islands, 1988), 28. Colonel Edward M. House was a key person responsible for

century to win support for a constitutional convention. Protecting the Constitution from the NWO is a duty of every U.S. citizen.

The Constitution must be protected in order to help defeat all threats both foreign and domestic. The stage for the death blow to the Constitution is already decades in the making. Few Americans understand the Patriot Act or realize that Senator Ron Wyden revealed there is an even more draconian classified version of the Patriot Act.[676] The fear of nuclear terrorism is a smokescreen that helps mask the true intentions of the NWO who already have been successful in tricking people into willingly forfeiting some of their civil rights. The hope of the NWO is that a major catastrophe will drive people to abandon the Constitution in favor of a world government.

No False Allegiances

I am convinced that in heaven there are no national flags. The saying "my country right or wrong" is itself wrong and can lead to terrible abuses of power. Just saying that phrase makes me think of experiences in my life when my country prevented children from obtaining lifesaving medicine. Certainly it is never right and always wrong to deny children medicine. This statement may be hard for many Americans to believe so I will provide an example.

In 2009, I had to renounce my U.S. citizenship at the U.S. Embassy in Cairo in order to help save lives. I never expected this to happen, but the U.S. and Israel were enforcing a blockade of medical supplies to Gaza. The Egyptian ruling elite had promised to obey Israel's border crossing restrictions in return for uninterrupted U.S. financial support. After trying to go into Gaza for over a week, I and other volunteers were finally permitted to bring medicine, but only after being required to provide the U.S. government with a notarized document renouncing our citizenship for the period of time that we were in Gaza.

If you support the concept "my country right or wrong," think about how wrong this statement would have been in Germany during World War II. A reading of *Inside the Third Reich* by Albert Speer would decisively hammer home this crooked nail.[677]

This same kind of ultranationalist sentiment can be found in the United States. Consider for a moment the U.S. war in Vietnam. Many Americans now realize that Vietnam was one of

---

orchestrating the votes in 1912 that were needed for the Federal Reserve Act to become law.

[676] Spencer Ackerman, "There's a Secret Patriot Act, Senator Says," *Wired Magazine*, 25 May 2011, online at www.wired.com/dangerroom/2011/05/secret-patriot-act/.

[677] Albert Speer, *Inside the Third Reich: Memoirs by Albert Speer* (New York, New York: Simon & Schuster, 1997). The first edition in German was published in 1969.

our most painful lessons that "my country right or wrong" is misdirected. Robert McNamara, a NWO insider, explained how national ego, disregard for the positions of traditional allies, detachment from the soldiers in the field, and a failure to understand the enemy resulted in many people supporting the illegal Vietnam War.[678]

Another way to look at the question of unchecked ego and the broader issue of patriotism is to reflect on the statement, "God Bless America." I feel God would prefer we say, "God Bless Us All." All life is equally valued in God's eyes, therefore why limit God's blessing to a single nation? Rampant patriotism can result in a disconnect between how we value the lives of Americans versus how we value the lives of others.

Abolish Nuclear Bombs

Achieving a world without weapons of mass destruction is possible in our lifetimes. The majority of all Americans already believe that no nation, including the United States, should have nuclear bombs.[679] Should Americans provide the leadership to oppose the NWO, we could make a nuclear-bomb-free world possible. The combined reduction of weapons of mass destruction and the necessary trust-building measures may take many years to accomplish, but even accomplishing half of this goal would be wonderful. Bringing the total arsenal of weapons of mass destruction to half, a third, or perhaps a thousandth of the current levels would help position a future generation to achieve a nuclear-weapons-free world.

Top NWO agents, including Henry Kissinger, George Schultz, Sam Nunn, and William Perry, have a hidden agenda when they call for a nuclear-free world.[680] The NWO sees nuclear bombs in the hands of individual countries as frustrating their ability to achieve a one-world government. The NWO wants to be the only group in possession of nuclear bombs as part of their plan to prevent resistance as they enslave humanity. When Kissinger is writing about abolishing nuclear bombs, he really is saying abolish nuclear bombs except for the bombs the NWO will control.

---

[678] Errol Morris director, *Fog of War* (The studio is *Columbia Tristar* and the release date was 19 December 2003). In 2005, the National Security Agency files were declassified proving Lydon B. Johnson and Robert McNamera fabricated the Tonkin Bay incident to start the Vietnam War. Both men served the NWO.

[679] "No nations should have nukes, most in USA say," *AP-Ipsos poll*, 31 March 2005. Two-thirds of respondents say no nation should have nuclear bombs, including the United States.

[680] Henry Kissinger, George Shultz, William Perry, and Sam Nunn, "Toward a Nuclear-Free World," *Wall Street Journal*, 15 January 2008 and online at http://online.wsj.com/article/SB120036422673589947.html.

"Kissinger Joins Call for Global Nuke Ban," *CBS News*, 11 February 2009 and online at www.cbsnews.com/stories/2007/01/04/politics/main2330865.s html.

David Krieger said, "Each of us by our daily acts of peace and our commitment to building a better world can inspire others and help create a groundswell for peace too powerful to be turned aside."[681] Do you believe kindness begets kindness and violence promotes additional violence? If you do, help the U.S. pursue kinder and gentler policies. Do you believe that dialogue leads to understanding and secrecy promotes mistrust? If you do, call for open dialogues to resolve differences. Do you believe in loving your neighbor? If you do, stand up for peace and oppose the NWO.

The principles of a justifiable war are generally: having just cause, possessing right intention as declared by a proper authority, having a reasonable chance of success, and the end being proportional to the means used. Another way of looking at the concept of a just war is that in a just war, life is taken only to save life. In a world with weapons of mass destruction, weapons that kill millions of innocent people never pass the just war doctrine test. Jesus teaches us to turn the other cheek, not vaporize people who seek to harm us.

It takes courage to oppose the NWO and eliminate weapons of mass destruction. I ask you to imagine that you are at the gate to heaven and to enter you are asked, "Did you help oppose the NWO?" Perhaps it takes less courage to oppose Satan and his agents when you consider that your soul is more important than your life. Jesus taught us we must be prepared to die for our beliefs in order to live eternally.[682]

In a world where billions of people do not have clean drinking water, it really is a crime against humanity to spend our resources building and maintaining weapons of mass destruction. History shows that increased weapons in one country results in other nations increasing their weapons.

Jimmy L. Spearow has created Diagrams A and B to illustrate a few of the factors driving the nuclear and conventional arms race.[683] Notice on the following diagram that Nation A has a perceived threat from Nation B. The perceived threat generates insecurity, and the natural reaction for Nation A is to develop weapons and build nationalism. This helps Nation A feel more secure. Nation B becomes fearful of Nation A and as a result develops more weapons and fuels additional nationalism. The diagram concludes that war is the outcome of this cycle.

---

[681] David Krieger is a founder of the Nuclear Age Peace Foundation.

[682] Followers of Jesus are forever sheltered from death because God offers eternal life. John 12:24-25 - "Verily, verily, I say unto you, Except a corn of wheat fall into the ground and die, it abideth alone: but if it die, it bringeth forth much fruit. He that loveth his life shall lose it; and he that hateth his life in this world shall keep it unto life eternal."

[683] Jimmy L. Spearow, Ph.D., "Factors Driving Nuclear and Conventional Arms Race," Physicians for Social Responsibility presentation, 7 April 2005.

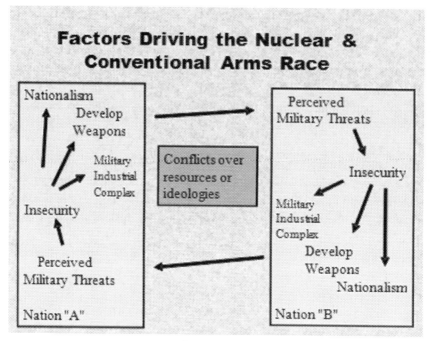

Diagram A

Without the education, such as the book you are reading, the cycle continues producing endless and ever increasingly deadly wars. For Christians, we are required to step outside this cycle of death and destruction. The truth is that the cycle of violence is dramatically lessened when we turn the other cheek. Albert Einstein once said, "You cannot simultaneously prevent and prepare for war."[684]

Imagine a new way of thinking. Citizens in independent nations control the issuance of money. Corporations are not allowed to have the same rights as human beings. Self-governing nations fund a multilateral police force to help prevent the spread of weapons of mass destruction. Diagram B illustrates this new way of thinking; specifically the key factors that help drive peace and goodwill. In the diagram, Nation A perceives no threat from Nation B. This leads to security in Nation A. Nation A is able to invest in foreign aid, improve its domestic services like health care, and in general help others. Nation B, receiving kindness from Nation A, is also secure. Nation B uses its peace dividend from not having to buy weapons to improve domestic programs and help others around the world. The natural outcome of this repeating cycle is endless peace.

---

[684] Albert Einstein, US (German-born) physicist (1879 - 1955). This quote is online at www.brainyquote. com/quotes/quotes/a/alberteins137744.html.

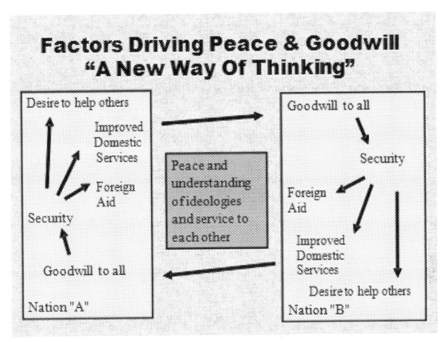

Diagram B

Many people have a false sense of security and think nuclear war is unlikely to happen. History has already proven that atomic weapons were almost used at several points after 1945. We know that during the Kennedy administration a first strike on the Soviet Union was recommended by members of the U.S. Joint Chiefs of Staff. The military leaders made this recommendation as a way to prevent a future nuclear war when the Soviet Union was projected to possess a substantial arsenal of weapons. Fortunately, a first strike on the former Soviet Union never occurred, and after his meeting with the Joint Chiefs of Staff where nuclear war was recommended, President Kennedy said, "And we call ourselves the human race."[685]

Perhaps another analogy can provide some insight into why doing the right thing yields ongoing benefits for future generations. As military officers, unlike CIA officers of that same era, we were taught not to torture captured prisoners during interrogations. I found myself asking the tough question: "Would I restrain myself from torturing a prisoner if the knowledge from a prisoner would save my unit?" As I wrestled with this question, I came to the same conclusion that the U.S. military would teach until September 11, 2001. If a soldier tortures another person,

[685] James K. Galbraith, "Did the U.S. Military Plan a Nuclear First Strike for 1963?," *The American Prospect*, 21 September 1994, Volume 5, Issue 19. President Kennedy was briefed on the net assessment of a general nuclear war between the two superpowers. As he walked with Dean Rusk from the cabinet room to the Oval Office President Kennedy said: "And we call ourselves the human race."

the immediate unit might be saved—but, in general, many more people will die in this war and in future wars because enemy soldiers will continue to fight when they know they cannot safely surrender. Doing the right thing may cost lives in the short run but will save lives in the long run. One only need look at the mass surrender of Iraqis during the Gulf War for proof that treating prisoners well will save lives.[686] The price of the Abu Ghraib torture is paid for in current wars, as many combatants fear what would happen to them if they surrender more than they fear fighting to the death.

The Abu Ghraib tortures can be understood when you know al Qaeda is not real. Waterboarding people 83 and 183 times, as we now know happened, is done only to ruin the mind of a person.[687] Since al Qaeda did not exist, the goal of the NWO was to use CIA torturers to brainwash people to believe they were part of an organization that did not exist. Overall, the NWO was unable to convince people that they were terrorists because of their faith in God. Often, the tortured men were eventually killed or quietly returned home.

The key point in these stories is that finding ways to stay true to a value system of right and wrong pays off in the long run.

Oppose Attacking Iran

We face an unassailable fact: the NWO is already in control of how history is written, the issuance of currency, the media, and most major corporations. The answer to defeating terrorists is not pre-emptive wars but understanding that the real terrorists are NWO insiders implementing false-flag attacks to advance a one-world government agenda.[688]

Iran is the big, early 21st century obstacle to the NWO's plan for securing ten world government economic zones as defined by the Club of Rome in 1974. The Club of Rome was founded in 1968 at David Rockefeller's estate in Bellagio, Italy. This NWO global think tank is advancing a one-world government by making the case for population reduction and ten economic zones. Iran frustrates the establishment of ten dependent economic zones because it

---

[686] The mass surrenders were likely to have been also facilitated by a classified weapons system that appears to have been used to disorient Iraqi soldiers.

[687] Scott Shane, "Waterboarding Used 266 Times on 2 Suspects," *The New York Times*, 19 April 2009 and online at www.nytimes.com/2009/04/20/world/20detain.html?sq=Waterboarding Used 266 Times on 2 Suspects&st=cse&adxnnl=1&scp=1&adxnnlx=1328517487-/xWm5HsE/ZcvHNBjBIso9w.

[688] "Israel Approves Plan to Attack Iran," *Sunday Times*, 13 March 2005. London's *Sunday Times* published a report saying that Prime Minister Ariel Sharon's security cabinet gave "initial authorization" to attack Iran if negotiations failed to persuade the Islamic republic to halt its nuclear program.
Seymour M. Hersh, "The Coming Wars: What the Pentagon Can Now Do in Secret," *The New Yorker*, posted on 17 January 2005. Available online at www.newyorker.com/fact/content/?050124fa_fact.

has a monetary system independent of NWO control. This means regime change in Iran will remain a top NWO priority.

The "packaging of an Iran regime change" for the American public started years ago and communicates the following four deceptive supporting reasons to begin what has the potential to become World War III:

1. Eliminate a rogue state's weapons of mass destruction.
2. Promote democracy in the Middle East by using force.
3. Aid allies by eliminating an enemy threatening Israel and Saudi Arabia.
4. Attack terrorists in their country before they attack in the U.S.

These four messages have been promoted for public consumption; however, none are true. What is true has been proven by Iraq and Libya. Any nation that is seeking to offer an alternate monetary system threatening the U.S. dollar ahead of schedule will be attacked if regime change is unsuccessful.[689]

Iran has not initiated a war with any country in over two centuries. Iran has some of the best universities, writers, painters, poets, and musicians in the world, but so far, no suicide bombers. Before the CIA overthrew Iran's government in 1953, Iran was America's best friend in the Middle East. Iran's government has no incentive to attack a nuclear bomb powerhouse such as Israel or any nation receiving protection from the U.S. The constant flow of media reports stating that Iran is seeking war with Israel has never been true.[690] Using force, even if World War III is averted, will help the NWO advance world government. Contrary to propaganda messages now frequently broadcast on television, attacking Iran will greatly weaken both Israel and the U.S.

Support a U.S. Department of Peace

A Department of Peace is needed to counter the NWO controlled Department of War. Many Americans forget that the Department of War was renamed the Department of Defense after World War II.[691]

---

[689] The NWO is in the process of devaluing the U.S. dollar and will eventually have it demonetized as part of their plan for a one-world currency.

[690] A comprehensive listing of media reports showing the march to war with Iran is online at www.teachpeace.com/Iran2012Timeline.pdf.

[691] The National Security Act of September 17, 1947, replaced the separate War and Navy departments with a unified military establishment called the Department of Defense.

George Washington introduced a Department of Peace bill into Congress in 1793. The African-American freeman Benjamin Banneker, a brilliant astronomer and mathematician, wrote in his 1792 Almanac about a Department of Peace to "balance" the Department of War. Banneker's friends, Dr. Benjamin Rush and Thomas Jefferson, supported the idea. Yet over 200 years and over 100 legislative bills later, we still do not have the Department of Peace. How many wars like Vietnam and Iraq would have been prevented if the NWO's hidden hand was exposed by this balancing force to the War Department?

Here is how a Department of Peace could immediately help. Secret society members would be prohibited from participating in the Department of Peace. As soon as possible, secret society members would be prohibited from serving and fired from all government position. The Secretary of Peace would be a mandatory presidential cabinet level position. A cabinet level position is required in order to position the Secretary of Defense and the Secretary of Peace as equals. Presidents would establish a common practice of consulting the Secretary of Peace before authorizing any arms sale or weapons shipment. In peacetime, both budgets would be equivalent. The power of authority as a cabinet level department with an equal budget would help prevent the Department of Peace from being sidelined with no real muscle to offset the Defense Department. On the international level, the Secretary of Peace would work to reduce international conflict, sponsor regional conflict prevention, and be a watchdog agency for U.S. military, CIA, and other U.S. organizations working in other countries.[692]

Since the U.S. has nuclear bombs, an argument can be made that no foreign threat beyond the NWO has existed since 1945. Having the courage to turn the other cheek means you need a police force but not a military to invade other countries. If a military is deemed necessary, a two-year tour of duty in the Department of Peace or a teaching assignment at the U.S. Peace Academy could be part of U.S. military career development. This rotational assignment for military personnel would help develop leaders of the military who have a broader perspective than one that constantly focuses on the use of force to solve problems.

The mission of the U.S. Peace Force would include assisting people who are suffering and delivering education programs to enable self-sufficiency. The current Peace Corps would naturally continue and could help lead this arm of the Department of Peace. Specifically, this would include building bridges, sewage treatment plants, clean water facilities, hospitals, and other infrastructure projects around the world. When you build a bridge or a hospital, people think more favorably of you, especially when they use the bridge or hospital. We will build friendships and frustrate efforts to fuel hatred of the United States. Approximately one-half of

---

[692] The NWO infiltration of the CIA is so extensive that the entire organization should be disbanded and employees should be prohibited from ever again serving in the U.S. government. The same is true for the Department of Homeland Security and the Treasury Department.

the Department of Peace would be the U.S. Peace Force; its mission would be to feed the hungry, aid the sick, remove land mines, clean contaminated areas from depleted uranium weapons, rebuild infrastructures, and encourage sustainable development. Fighting hunger, malaria, AIDS, and lack of clean water would be top priorities.

The other half of the Department of Peace funding should be focused on education. The Department of Peace could promote alternatives to violence with programs designed to educate from kindergarten through graduate school. In a positive twist of history, we would close down the Western Hemisphere Institute for Security Cooperation at Fort Benning, better known as the School of the Americas, and use the buildings to start the U.S. Peace Academy.[693]

A Department of Peace with the U.S. Peace Force and U.S. Peace Academy components dedicated to opposing the NWO would save lives and help take the profit out of war.[694] Innovative ideas, like enabling citizens to opt out of paying taxes that go toward weapons of mass destruction, could be spearheaded by a Department of Peace.

But heed this cautionary note: a Department of Peace infiltrated by NWO secret society members would be a disaster. The NWO-influenced Congress has always opposed creating a Department of Peace. Ironically, now that the NWO has firm Congressional control it could pass a corrupted Department of Peace initiative that would further their hidden agenda to frustrate peace efforts. The only way a Department of Peace could be valuable is if it is created after the Federal Reserve has been abolished and replaced with a monetary system that is free from NWO control.

Join Forces for Peace and Innovative Thinking

Becoming a force for peace requires individuals to be informed. To learn more about what is happening in the world and obtain ideas for a more peaceful world, I recommend joining the Teach Peace Foundation.

The Teach Peace Foundation is a non-profit, non-partisan organization focused on helping make our world better via acts of kindness and education. The Teach Peace team believes a more peaceful world is possible when the NWO becomes exposed.[695]

---

[693] An alternative and better site is the CIA headquarters in Langley, Virginia to make good use of the facilities when the role of the NWO is understood and Americans abolish the CIA.

[694] No one should profit financially from making weapons just like no fire department should profit from starting fires.

[695] Teach Peace Foundation, see www.teachpeace.com.

Stopping Harmful Behaviors is Transformational

Why not create an alternative and more prosperous future for everyone? We can transform ourselves and potentially our country if we start asking why not. Consider the difference between a to-do list and a not-to-do list. To-do lists are good, but not-to-do lists can be transformational. To illustrate this point, you may have a dozen or so tasks on a to-do list. Putting a check mark next to each to-do list task that is completed feels good and helps accomplish objectives. Putting a check mark next to a list of not-to-do behaviors changes your life. Whether it is stopping smoking, stopping swearing, or some other negative behavior, you are transforming who you are. Consider the transformational changes that are possible when people are educated about the NWO.

Hopefully you are now asking, "Why not stop missing opportunities for a more peaceful world?" The why not questions below are listed to facilitate reflection and promote group discussions. Why not:

- prohibit members of secret societies from holding public office?
- abolish the privately owned Federal Reserve and issue U.S. government money?
- teach students about the New World Order and show the money trail that has funded wars to advance their one-world agenda?
- implement safeguards to encourage safe vaccinations and prevent NWO corrupted vaccinations as a global security threat?
- restrict storage of U.S. nuclear bombs to America's borders?[696]
- abolish nuclear bombs?
- end all foreign wars?
- stop selling weapons to other countries?
- make space free of weapons? [697]
- eliminate our dependence on oil via clean alternatives?
- recognize that addressing human suffering is always in our best interest?

---

[696] David Espar, *War in the Nuclear Age: Part IV, Europe Goes Nuclear* (Annenberg/CPB Project, 1988). The online address is http://alsos.wlu.edu/information.asp?id2=863. Nuclear bomb distribution information is highly classified. Turkey, Germany, England, Belgium, Italy, and the Netherlands are widely believed by research experts like the Natural Resources Defense Council to be current launching points for U.S. nuclear bombs. Declassified information confirms the United States began deploying nuclear bombs in Europe in the 1950s.

[697] Chris Floyd, "Dark Matter," *Space.com*, 9 April 2004. The "Near Field Infrared Experiment" or NFIRE will be the first time in history that any nation has put a weapons platform in space.
Jeffrey Lewis, "Programs to Watch: Near-Field Infrared Experiment (NFIRE)," *Arms Control Today*, November 2004, 12.

These actionable questions can produce actionable answers that strengthen our democracy and leave our children with a legacy of a world with less hunger, suffering, and violence. The current financial crisis would not exist if the U.S. eliminated nuclear bombs. The over six trillion-plus dollars that the United States has already spent on nuclear bombs was literally wasted. The thought of how much more peaceful our world would be if the majority of these funds had gone to help educate and care for people makes me sad. The good news is that it is possible to stop wasting future trillions of dollars for weapons that only the NWO needs, and in the process improve our economy and the world.

Why Presidents Never Oppose the NWO

Almost all presidents have been a member of Freemasonry or another NWO-affiliated secret society. Presidents officially acknowledged as Freemasons include George Washington, James Monroe, Andrew Jackson, James Polk, James Buchanan, Andrew Johnson, James Garfield, William McKinley, Theodore Roosevelt, William Howard Taft, Warren Harding, Franklin Roosevelt, Harry Truman, Lyndon Johnson, and Gerald Ford.[698] The list of presidents closely affiliated with Freemasonry is longer. For example, on February 11, 1988, Ronald Reagan became an Honorary Scottish Rite Mason by the Grand Lodge of Washington, D.C.[699]

Presidents who have been members of other secret societies often communicated their support of Freemasonry by taking their oath of office using a Bible owned by the St. John's Masonic Lodge in New York City. This is the Bible used for the oath ceremony on April 30, 1789 by George Washington. Non-Masons who have shown their support of Freemasonry by using

---

[698] The Masonic Presidents of the United States is a permanent exhibit in the Masonic Library and Museum of Pennsylvania. The information in this exhibit is online at www.pagrandlodge.org/mlam/presidents/index.html.
Lyndon Johnson was an Entered Apprentice and received his first degree on October 30, 1937. On a related note, Abraham Lincoln applied for membership in Tyrian Lodge, Springfield, Ill., shortly after his nomination for the presidency in 1860. He withdrew the application and advised the lodge that he would resubmit his application again when he returned from the presidency. After Lincoln was assassinated, the Tyrian Lodge adopted a resolution on April 17, 1865 to say "that the decision of President Lincoln to postpone his application for the honours of Freemasonry, lest his motives be misconstrued, is the highest degree honorable to his memory."

[699] Ronald Reagan was made an honorary member of the Imperial Council of the Shrine. He participated in numerous Masonic functions throughout his career. Thomas Jefferson, James Madison, Zachary Taylor, Franklin Pierce, and William Clinton appear in some Masonic lists, but publicly Masonic officials usually claim their membership status is uncertain. For example, according to page 49 of the 1951 edition of the *Holy Bible, Masonic Edition*, Thomas Jefferson was a Mason.

the St. John's Masonic Lodge Bible include: George H. W. Bush (1989), Jimmy Carter (1977), and Dwight D. Eisenhower (1953).[700]

The extent of the NWO control of U.S. presidents and other people in top positions is explained in the first Vigilant Christian book. The below is a summary from book one of top leaders participating in at least one NWO front organization.

Presidents	Vice Presidents	Secretaries of State
Herbert Hoover	Richard M. Nixon	Henry L. Stimson
Dwight D. Eisenhower	Hubert Humphrey	Edward R. Stettinius, Jr.
John F. Kennedy	Gerald R. Ford	Dean G. Acheson
Richard M. Nixon	Nelson A. Rockefeller	John Foster Dulles
Gerald R. Ford	Walter Mondale	Christian A. Herter
James E. Carter	George H. W. Bush	Dean Rusk
George H. W. Bush	Richard B. Cheney	William P. Rogers
William J. Clinton	Joseph Biden	Henry A. Kissinger
		Cyrus R. Vance
		Edmund S. Muskie

Secretaries of War/Defense	Secretaries of the Treasury	Alexander M. Haig, Jr.
Henry L. Stimson	Andrew W. Mellon	George P. Shultz
Robert P. Patterson	Ogden L. Mills	Lawrence Eagleburger
James V. Forrestal	William H. Woodin	Warren M. Christopher
Robert A. Lovett	Henry Morgenthau, Jr.	Madeleine K. Albright
Neil H. McElroy	Robert B. Anderson	Colin L. Powell
Thomas S. Gates, Jr.	C. Douglas Dillon	Condoleezza Rice
Robert S. McNamara	Henry H. Fowler	Hillary Clinton
Melvin R. Laird	David M. Kennedy	
Elliot L. Richardson	George P. Shultz	**CIA Directors**
James R. Schlesinger	William E. Simon	Walter Bedell Smith
Donald H. Rumsfeld	W. Michael Blumenthal	Allen W. Dulles
Harold Bown	G. William Miller	John A. McCone

---

[700] The St. John's Masonic Lodge Bible was almost used by George W. Bush, but inclement weather resulted in a decision to protect the Bible from rain. The Bible was used in 1921 to swear in Freemason Warren Harding. Elite Masons believe this Bible is extremely significant, and it is used for special ceremonies, including Washington's funeral in December, 1799, the dedication of the Washington Monument in 1885, the re-laying of the U.S. Capitol's cornerstone in 1959, and the christening of the aircraft carrier USS George Washington at Norfolk, Va., in 1992.

Caspar W. Weinberger	Donald T. Regan	Richard Helms
Frank C. Carlucci	Nicholas F. Brady	James R. Schlesinger
Richard B. Cheney	Lloyd Bentsen	William E. Colby
Les Aspin	Robert Rubin	George H. W. Bush
William Perry	Lawrence H. Summers	Stansfield Turner
William S. Cohen	Henry M. Paulson, Jr.	William J. Casey
Donald Rumsfeld[700]	Timothy Geithner	William H. Webster
Robert M. Gates		Robert M. Gates
		R. James Woolsey
		John M. Deutch
		George J. Tenet
		Michael V. Hayden
		David Petraeus[701]

Americans are becoming more aware of the direct connection between the people leading the country and their membership in secret societies. As a result, many people are not surprised to learn that the Democratic and Republican candidates for president are members of secret societies. Occasionally, as was the case in the 2004 election featuring President George W. Bush and Senator John Kerry, the candidates are members in the same NWO secret society.[703]

Former President George H. W. Bush, Skull and Bones secret society class of 1948, joined the CIA that same year. President Barack Obama, "unofficial" CFR member, also has his allegiance first and foremost to the NWO.[704] Similar to George H. W. Bush, Obama's first job after graduating from Columbia in 1983 was with a CIA front company, Business International, Corporation.[705]

---

[701] Donald Rumsfeld was counted twice because he served as Defense Secretary in two separate administrations.

[702] Obama's first CIA Director, Leon Panetta is an NWO secret society insider but not a CFR member. Panetta was replaced by CFR member David Petraeus.

[703] George W. Bush and John Kerry are members of Skull and Bones. Rebecca Leung, "Skull and Bones: Secret Yale Society Includes America's Power Elite," *CBS 60 Minutes*, 13 June 2004, at www.cbsnews.com/stories/2003/10/02/60minutes/main576332.shtml.

[704] Barack Obama said on 3/31/08, in response to a question about his Council on Foreign Relations membership, "The Council on Foreign Relations, I don't know if I am an official member. I have spoken there before. It is basically just a forum where a bunch of people talk about foreign policy. There is no official membership page." The answer misleads the reader; the CFR is not "just a forum" for discussion and there is official membership with secrecy requirements.

[705] Business International Corporation (BI) was disclosed to be a CIA front company by *The New York Times* in the 27 December 1977 article "Established Many Links to Journalists in U.S. and Abroad." The firm's cover was further disclosed in subsequent years to the point that in 1986, the CIA made

Relatively few people know about Obama's CIA service because in 1982 the Intelligence Identities Protection Act made it illegal to disclose the identity of intelligence officers.[706] The closest Obama has come to acknowledging his true past is his 1995 memoir, *Dreams from My Father*, where without mentioning the CIA Business International by name, he disclosed he worked for a "consulting house to multinational corporations."[707]

When you understand the carefully guarded secret side of Barack Obama, you can understand his total support for the billions given to the NWO Federal Reserve owners during the 2008 global financial crisis. His NWO support also explains his $500,000 book advance for a children's version of *Dreams from My Father* and compensation even before the first edition was published.[708] Ask yourself, does it seem odd that a person only 34 years old is "paid" over a hundred thousand dollars to write his memoir?[709]

Obama Miracle Myth

The Obama miracle is really the story of the NWO placing another insider in the presidency. The Obama family NWO ties go back before 1959 and feature prominently in the lives of

---

the problem fade away by having the firm be acquired by The Economist Group and merged with The Economist Intelligence Unit. See http://en.wikipedia.org/wiki/Business_International_ Corporation for more information. In 1987, issue 14 of *Lobster Magazine* provided additional insights on the BI front company (www.lobster-magazine.co.uk/issue14.php).

BI as a CIA front company is also discussed in Carl Oglesby's book *Ravens in the Storm: A Personal History of the 1960s Antiwar Movement* (New York, New York: Simon & Schuster, 2008 page 201).

[706] *The Intelligence Identities Protection Act of 1982* is a United States federal law that makes freedom of speech a crime. The law passed because CIA agents were concluding a shadow power [the NWO] was guiding U.S. foreign policy. Arguably the best known CIA officer to disclose illegal activities is Philip Agee who wrote the *CIA Diary* and the *Covert Action Information Bulletin*. The law is rarely enforced in the courts because to prosecute a truth teller brings attention to the CIA officer being exposed.

[707] Sasha Issenberg, "Obama Shows Hints of His Year in Global Finance," *The Boston Globe*, 6 August 2008.

Barack Obama in *Dreams from My Father: A Story of Race and Inheritance* wrote, "Like a spy behind enemy lines, I arrived every day at my mid-Manhattan office and sat at my computer terminal, checking the Reuters machine that blinked bright emerald messages from across the globe." Sasha Issenberg of *The Boston Globe* noted Obama has acknowledged fictionalizing parts of the book and "those who worked at Business International say Obama's brief account contains inaccuracies or misrepresentations about the company."

[708] "Obama secures $500,000 book advance," *United Press International, Inc.*, 19 March 2009 online at www.upi.com/Top_News/2009/03/19/Obama-secures-500000-book-advance/UPI-82081237468228/.

[709] The book income helped provide cover and income for Obama to continue as a community organizer. In 2001 as the book funding depleted, Obama reported legal services income with $80,000 alone coming from the firm owned by Robert Blackwell, Jr. (see http://uspolitics.about.com/od/senators/a/barack_obama.htm).

his mother, father, stepfather, and grandmother.[710] NWO support in 2004 enabled Obama to successfully challenge the nominating petitions of all four Illinois U.S. Senate competitors.[711] James S. Crown, whose NWO family's investments include military contractor General Dynamics, donated at least $112,500 along with his family members, to help Obama become president.[712] NWO insider George Soros and members of his family donated $60,000.[713]

President Obama's reputation as a progressive reformer is myth. He is careful to serve the NWO, which is often framed as helping Wall Street. The one thing he is radical about is never deviating from the NWO agenda. He consistently betrays his supporters and explains his actions are a shrewd tactic necessary to achieve reform. When he sends troops to their deaths, he is making "tough decisions" for freedom. The real Obama can be seen in the secret deals he brokered with NWO fronts including the exposed pharmaceutical lobby meetings.[714] The truth is that Obama received more funding from NWO fronts Goldman Sachs and JPMorgan Chase than any candidate ever before.[715]

The NWO brainwashing efforts are so successful that most people do not realize the top candidates for president routinely serve the NWO. We are long past living in a country where the population elects its officials. Some people have realized this sad reality but erroneously believe

---

[710] Wayne Madsen, "Obama Family Ties to the CIA Revealed," *Rock Creek Free Press*, September 2010. Barack Obama Sr. met Stanley Ann Dunham, Barack Obama's mother, in a Russian language class in 1959.
Gregory Dail, "Spooks--Obama & Obama Mama Linked to CIA," *Orange County Conservative Examiner*, 24 August 2009 and online at www.examiner.com/orange-county-conservative-in-orlando/spooks-obama-obama-mama-linked-to-cia#ixzz1D2WGSb66.

[711] NWO agent David Axelrod is believed to be the source to leak information on 2004 U.S. Senate challengers resulting in their campaigns imploding.

[712] "After 2000 Loss, Obama Built Donor Network From Roots Up," *New York Times*, 3 April 2000 online at www.nytimes.com/2007/04/03/us/politics/03obama.html? pagewanted=2.

[713] Ibid. It is interesting to note the article title includes the words "From Roots Up" and then the article explains how Obama raised funds from the NWO elite.

[714] Timothy P. Carney, "Obama Transparency Fail: White House will keep secret Big Pharma-ObamaCare meetings secret," *San Francisco Examiner*, 8 March 2011 and online at www.sfexaminer.com/blogs/beltway-confidential/2011/03/obama-transparency-fail-white-house-will-keep-secret-big-pharma-o#ixzz1ogl8PpN2.
Brian Beutler, "White House Rebuffs GOP Investigation Of Secret Health Care Meetings," *Talking Points Memo*, 7 March 2011 and online at http://tpmdc.talkingpointsmemo.com/2011/03/white-house-rebuffs-gop-investigation-of-secret-health-care-meetings.php.

[715] Eamon Javers, "For Fundraising, Obama Relies Even More on Wall Street," *CNBC*, 22 July 2011 and online at www.cnbc.com/id/43854224/For_Fundraising_Obama_Relies_Even_More_on_Wall_Street. During Obama's 2008 presidential campaign financial service bundlers donated $16 million. In the 2012 reelection bid about one-third of Obama's elite fund-raising is from the financial sector.

corporations are the true ruling force. Only a smaller percentage of the population understands that the U.S. is controlled by NWO owners.

A Proposed Leadership Statement

The following is a recommendation of what a U.S. president should say to help prevent an American and Global Hiroshima.

The time has come to successfully end the war on terrorism and bring our soldiers home. I recognize that acts of terror are not perpetrated because people hate our freedom. Acts of terror are often because of a shadow elite that uses violence and fear to advance their one-world agenda.

Today, I reveal to you that a shadow government has been in control of our government for many years. The shadow government was proven to exist by Congress during the 1912 Money Trust Investigation. The cabal used their money and influence to put their agents in office and secure their power with the Federal Reserve Act of 1913. Sadly, most of my predecessors served the NWO. We can be free as a people only when we are free from the privately owned Federal Reserve. I call upon Congress to abolish the Federal Reserve and expose all other New World Order cabal infiltrations of our government.

We must decrease the escalating cycle of violence by working for justice around the world. I will therefore, on behalf of the United States:

- *Renounce our right to declare unilateral war and work passionately with other nations so that they do the same.*
- *Bring our brave and loyal soldiers home; aircraft, submarines and missiles have a global reach, therefore, no U.S. forces should be stationed outside our country in a time of peace.*
- *Protect our people from nuclear threat by beginning to eliminate all nuclear power and weapons in the United States.*
- *Free our nation from fossil fuels and end our willingness to support injustice overseas by putting our best scientists to work developing clean coal, fuel cells, solar, wind, geo-thermal, and other yet-to-be discovered efficient sources of energy.[716]*

---

[716] Fareed Zakaria, "Imagine: 500 Miles per Gallon," *Newsweek*, 7 March 2005, 27. We currently have the technology to develop vehicles that are powered by a combination of electricity and alcohol-based fuels, with petroleum as only one element among many.

- *Promise not to intervene in the political process of other nations or to seek the overthrow of democratically elected leaders.*
- *Stop military funding and arms sales to other nations.*
- *End hypocritical policies by no longer holding other nations to a standard different from that which we hold for ourselves; thereby regaining credibility as we seek to solve our most pressing challenges, especially stopping the proliferation of weapons of mass destruction.*
- *Protect future generations by safeguarding our environment and, champion a weapons-free space and ionosphere agreement.* [717]

Throughout our history the New World Order cabal has used us, as well as other governments, to fight many wars. Yet with the passage of time, these same countries that we once fought have become our friends. We need only think of our wars with England, Germany, Japan, Vietnam, and the Cold War with the former Soviet Union to realize that it is not a specific people that we must hate, but hate itself. If we kill in an attempt to achieve peace, we will have war forever. Martin Luther King, Jr., once said:

> *"A true revolution of values will lay hands on the world order and say of war: This way of settling differences is not just . . .*
>
> *A true revolution of values will soon cause us to question the fairness and justice of many of our past and present policies . . .*
>
> *A true revolution of values will soon look uneasily on the glaring contrast of poverty and wealth . . .*
>
> *A nation that continues year after year to spend more money on military defense than on programs of social uplift is approaching spiritual death."* [718]

Because we desire peace and justice we must ask for and give forgiveness. We must become the example we expect to see in return. We do this for ourselves and for our children.

God bless us all!

---

[717] "Strategic Master Plan FY06 and Beyond: Case 1," *Air Force Space Command*, 1 October 2003, 13. The Air Force already lists over $456 billion in projects required to weaponize space. The updated and top secret plan may show a far higher estimate that could in time exceed the six trillion dollars spent by the U.S. on nuclear bombs.

[718] Martin Luther King, Jr., statement at Riverside Church, 4 April 1967.

12

GOD WINS

"And the great dragon was cast out, that old serpent, called the Devil, and Satan, which deceiveth the whole world: he was cast out into the earth, and his angels were cast out with him." Revelation 12:9

The diabolical ancient plan for world government is designed to pave the way for the Antichrist. This final chapter reminds us that God has already won the battle against Satan and his forces. We fight the good fight against the New World Order as peacemakers because individuals can be saved and the rewards are eternal.

Prophecies Remain to be Fulfilled

The signs of the Apocalypse are happening now, and the proliferation of occult films, books, and music will only accelerate, resulting in more people supporting a one-world government. Many prophecies remain to be fulfilled, and no one but God knows if the Apocalypse will happen in the 21st century. One prophecy Christians and Muslims believe is that the Antichrist will enter the rebuilt Temple of Solomon and proclaim he is God.[719] The Antichrist's announcement in the rebuilt temple in Jerusalem will signal a period of time called the Abomination of Desolation.[720]

---

[719] Daniel 9:27 - "And he shall confirm the covenant with many for one week: and in the midst of the week he shall cause the sacrifice and the oblation to cease, and for the overspreading of abominations he shall make it desolate, even until the consummation, and that determined shall be poured upon the desolate." Many scholars in each of the Abrahamic faiths believe the Dome of the Rock, constructed on the site of Solomon's Temple, will one day be destroyed to make the prophecies of future events possible. Archaeological discoveries in recent years indicate Solomon's Temple was north of the Dome of the Rock where there is now empty space. It is possible the Dome of the Rock may not be destroyed.

[720] The term "Abomination of Desolation" is describing the Antichrist having an image of himself in the Jewish Temple, stopping the daily offerings to God, and declaring he is the leader of the world.

We are instructed not to fear the arrival of the Antichrist or the Abomination of Desolation. The Antichrist comes into power proclaiming world peace from the rebuilt temple in Jerusalem, but is secretly bringing global war.[721] The books of Daniel and Revelation inform us that people on earth during the Antichrist's rule will suffer greatly for three and a half-years.[722] The rule of the Antichrist will kill a third of the global population by three plagues.[723] At the end of the Antichrist covenant, Jesus returns to defeat the Antichrist at the Battle of Armageddon in the Valley of Megiddo.[724] The battle is not a military battle but won by the Lord with the spirit of his mouth and brightness of his coming.[725]

Jesus provided clear guidance on salvation when he was asked about the Hebrew Bible's 613 commandments.[726] Jesus replied to a question about what is the most important commandment by answering that there are only two rules: the first is to love God and the second is to love your neighbor.

Parable of Ten Virgins

An understanding of the Book of Revelation helps us see that a spiritual American Hiroshima may be on the horizon. Insights to prevent a spiritual American Hiroshima may come to you when you understand the parable of the ten virgins. The parable of the ten virgins tells us many people experience the Day of Wrath. Jesus said as reported in Matthew 25:1-12:

---

[721] Daniel 8:25 "And through his policy also he shall cause craft to prosper in his hand; and he shall magnify himself in his heart, and by peace shall destroy many: he shall also stand up against the Prince of princes; but he shall be broken without hand."

[722] Revelation 13:5 - "And there was given unto him a mouth speaking great things and blasphemies; and power was given unto him to continue forty and two months.

[723] Revelation 9:17-19 - "And thus I saw the horses in the vision, and them that sat on them, having breastplates of fire, and of jacinth, and brimstone: and the heads of the horses were as the heads of lions; and out of their mouths issued fire and smoke and brimstone. By these three was the third part of men killed, by the fire, and by the smoke, and by the brimstone, which issued out of their mouths. For their power is in their mouth, and in their tails: for their tails were like unto serpents, and had heads, and with them they do hurt."

[724] Megiddo is in northern Israel and the Antichrist and his false prophet are cast into a lake of fire.

[725] 2 Thessalonians 2:8-10 - "And then shall that Wicked be revealed, whom the Lord shall consume with the spirit of his mouth, and shall destroy with the brightness of his coming: Even him, whose coming is after the working of Satan with all power and signs and lying wonders, And with all deceivableness of unrighteousness in them that perish; because they received not the love of the truth, that they might be saved."

[726] The 613 commandments are statements and principles of law, ethics, and spiritual practice contained in the Torah. The commandments are also called the "Law of Moses" and "the Law."

"Then shall the kingdom of heaven be likened unto ten virgins, which took their lamps, and went forth to meet the bridegroom. And five of them were wise, and five were foolish. They that were foolish took their lamps, and took no oil with them: But the wise took oil in their vessels with their lamps. While the bridegroom tarried, they all slumbered and slept. And at midnight there was a cry made, Behold, the bridegroom cometh; go ye out to meet him. Then all those virgins arose, and trimmed their lamps. And the foolish said unto the wise, Give us of your oil; for our lamps are gone out. But the wise answered, saying, Not so; lest there be not enough for us and you: but go ye rather to them that sell, and buy for yourselves. And while they went to buy, the bridegroom came; and they that were ready went in with him to the marriage: and the door was shut. Afterward came also the other virgins, saying, Lord, Lord, open to us. But he answered and said, Verily I say unto you, I know you not."

My understanding of this parable is that the ten virgins in the stories are the people who acknowledge that they are Christians. The oil in the lamp is symbolic for the Holy Spirit. The Christians filled with the Holy Spirit enter heaven. To be filled with the Holy Spirit means loving God and loving your neighbor fully. Applying this understanding to now, if you support wars killing your Muslim neighbors because you have been fooled into believing they are responsible for the 9/11 attacks, is your lamp full or partially empty? To be filled with the Holy Spirit means you are not duped into lashing out at your neighbor even when you have been wronged.

Eternal Victory

The NWO totalitarian plan has been attempted throughout history and has always failed. Examples include Lenin, Stalin, Hitler, and Mao. More distant examples are Nimrod, Nebuchadnezzar, Genghis Khan, Alexander the Great, the Caesars, Ivan the Terrible, Charlemagne, and Napoleon. Not one of Satan's disciples has accomplished the Great Plan because God has not allowed it.

So speaks this author, confident in his Christian faith, the convictions of his belief structure buttressed in Holy Scripture. I would pause here, however, to remind my readers that we dwell always in a world in which some truths and purposes are shrouded, that God alone knows, and that therefore in all our dealings with others the utmost humility is appropriate. Who is to say other messages of love are not also Holy Scripture? As good Christians, it is not ours to judge other people, but ours to accept those who work alongside us in loving service to others as cherished friends, as God surely intends.

God will send four carpenters to help educate people about the NWO. The four carpenters will make darkness visible by exposing the NWO on a global scale. As a result, Satan's deceptive occult buildings, monuments, economic system, new age religion, and magical world will be increasingly exposed.

> "Then I raised my eyes and looked, and there were four horns. And I said to the angel who talked with me, 'What are these?' So he answered me, 'These are the horns that have scattered Judah, Israel, and Jerusalem.' Then the LORD showed me four craftsmen. And I said, 'What are these coming to do?' So he said, 'These are the horns that scattered Judah, so that no one could lift up his head; but the craftsmen are coming to terrify them, to cast out the horns of the nations that lifted up their horn against the land of Judah to scatter it.'" Zechariah 1:18-21

The end-time prophecies of Daniel, Ezekiel, Revelation, and the parable of the ten virgins remind us that we do not need to stop the one-world government in order to win the battle with the NWO. Defeating Satan and his agents starts with a prayer and continues each day as we love and serve everyone. All life is equally valuable, and Jews, Muslims, and Christians should never forget all three religions worship the God of Abraham. If a person feels less loved by you because he or she does not believe in God, you are miscommunicating what it means to be a Christian. God's love is unconditional, and we are all sinners. Holding people accountable for their bad behavior does not mean you stop loving them.

Scripture can interpret Scripture, meaning answers to biblical questions can be found in the Bible. Scripture is the ultimate authority for defining Christian faith. For this reason, the NWO needs to replace the centrality of Jesus in Scripture with anti-Christian teachings. Changing loving our enemies to killing our enemies is a prime example.

Sadly, the NWO is succeeding in convincing people to see killing others as necessary for national security reasons. No matter our differences, beliefs, or actions, we are all children of God. Actions that should result in one person or small groups being sentenced to prison are used by the NWO to falsely kill thousands of people. The NWO wants to distort Christianity into a religion more willing to use weapons that kill thousands of children rather than turning the other cheek. The Bible tells us the NWO will succeed in fooling most people, including many Christians, to welcome the Antichrist.

The truth is that loving God and loving your neighbor means there are no exceptions to the Ten Commandments. In a very important way, you can defeat the NWO with your daily acts of kindness by making sure they include people who reject your understanding of God.

God is unconditional love. Jesus' crucifixion on the cross is the ultimate act of unconditional love. We are created to love unconditionally. In 1 Corinthians 13:4-7 we learn, "Love is patient, love is kind. It does not envy, it does not boast, it is not proud. It is not rude, it is not self-seeking, it is not easily angered, it keeps no record of wrongs. Love does not delight in evil but rejoices with the truth. It always protects, always trusts, always hopes, always perseveres."[727]

If this book has helped you, please share it with another person.[728] If you share this book it may help save others. During the Tribulation many people will be convinced to follow the Antichrist, but Scripture informs us that a person who refuses the mark of the Beast and accepts God will be saved.[729] I recommend the following prayer to defeat the NWO and Satan's plan that is designed to deceive you into rejecting Christ.

I am truly sorry and I want to turn away from my sinful life toward You. Please forgive me, and help me avoid sinning again. I believe that Your son Jesus Christ died for my sins, was resurrected from the dead, is alive, and hears my prayer. I accept Jesus as my Lord and my Savior. Please send Your Holy Spirit to help me obey You, and to do Your will for the rest of my life.

Pure love has no fear. God has no fear. The presence of love is the presence of God. Fear is faith in Satan and gives the NWO power. We for whom the Bible is our rock and our guide are provided constant comfort and hope even through the Valley of the Shadow of Death because Satan's plan is defeated by God's plan.

Accuracy Guarantee

To support that everything I have written in this book is true, I offer to publicly debate anyone. Should anyone ever find a mistake in this book, please send an email to contact@

---

[727] The New International Version is provided because it is easier for most people to understand. The King James Version is, "Charity suffereth long, and is kind; charity envieth not; charity vaunteth not itself, is not puffed up, Doth not behave itself unseemly, seeketh not her own, is not easily provoked, thinketh no evil; Rejoiceth not in iniquity, but rejoiceth in the truth; Beareth all things, believeth all things, hopeth all things, endureth all things."

[728] People who are not Christians can better understand why a Christian would want to share their understanding of the Bible to save people from the horrors of the global Holocaust that comes with the arrival of the Antichrist.

[729] Revelation 13:8 - "And all that dwell upon the earth shall worship him, whose names are not written in the book of life of the Lamb slain from the foundation of the world."
Revelation 14: 11-13 - "And the smoke of their torment ascendeth up for ever and ever: and they have no rest day nor night, who worship the beast and his image, and whosoever receiveth the mark of his name. Here is the patience of the saints: here are they that keep the commandments of God, and the faith of Jesus. And I heard a voice from heaven saying unto me, Write, Blessed are the dead which die in the Lord from henceforth: Yea, saith the Spirit, that they may rest from their labours; and their works do follow them."

vigilantchristian.org. I will promptly publish the correction on the www.vigilantchristian.org/corrections.html page.

Thank you for considering the ideas in this book which make darkness visible. You can learn more about how the NWO is paving the way for the Antichrist by visiting www.vigilantchristian.org and reading the other Vigilant Christian books.

May the peace of the Lord be with you.

APPENDIX A

MAPS

The following maps may be helpful for sections of the book that discuss the ten economic zones for the one-world government, the Korea Peninsula, and the Middle East.

MAP 1—Ten Economic Zones

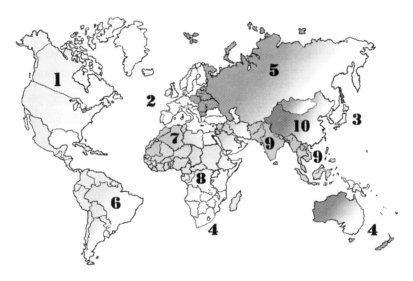

Legend

1. America, Canada, and Mexico
2. The European Union
3. Japan
4. South Africa, Australia, and New Zealand
5. Eastern Europe, Pakistan, Afghanistan, Russia, and the former countries of the Soviet Union
6. Central America, South America, Cuba, and Caribbean Islands

7. The Middle East and North Africa
8. The rest of Africa except South Africa
9. South and Southeast Asia, including India
10. China (Mongolia is now included with China)

The ten economic zones help explain hotspots around the world. One region of the world that illustrates this point is the Asia Pacific region. Taiwan and China are key hotspots with rising tensions between them that could result in a conventional or nuclear war.[730] The NWO influenced U.S. war plans in the 2017 timeframe indicate expected increased tension in this part of the world with China often portrayed as the enemy in these futuristic war simulations.[731] Current Middle East wars are linked to the establishing military bases to enable the NWO to region 10 (China and Mongolia).[732]

---

[730] Christopher Bodeen, China: Law Would Allow Action Vs. Taiwan, *Associated Press*, 8 March 2005. China unveiled a law authorizing military action to stop rival Taiwan from pursuing formal independence. Tension with the Bush administration increased as President Bush's weapons sales and statements of support for Taiwan contradicted the One China policy and prompted China to send a message that war was authorized. The Chinese government said an attack would be a last resort if peaceful means fail.

[731] *Arsenal of Hypocrisy, The Space Program And The Military Industrial Complex*, AOH Productions Inc., www.arsenalofhypocrisy.com, 2003.

[732] The One China policy endorsed in 1972 by President Nixon and Chairman Mao Tse-tung in the Shanghai communiqué is window washing. A unification of the China and Taiwan, similar to the July 1, 1997 unification with Hong Kong, has not happened because the NWO does not want it to happen.

MAP 2—The Korean Peninsula[733]

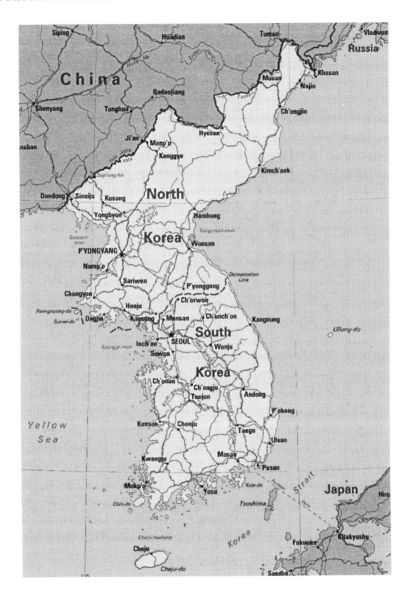

[733] Perry-Castañeda Library Map Collection, modified CIA produced maps, 2004. Permission notification received on 6 April 2005. The online addresses are www.lib.utexas.edu/maps/middle_east_and_asia/middle_east_ref04.jpg and www.lib.utexas.edu/maps/middle_east_and_asia/korean_peninsula.gif.

MAP 3—The Middle East

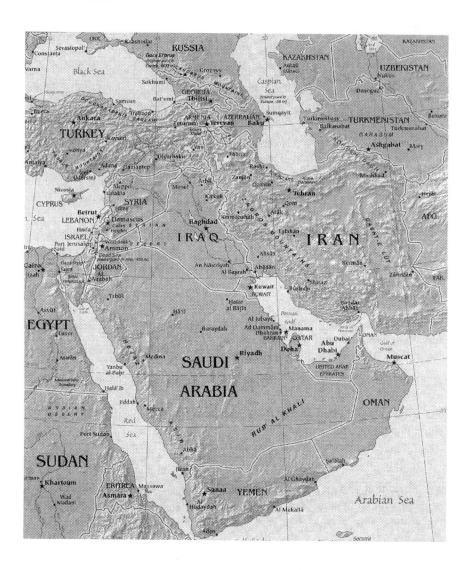

Appendix B

Vigilant Christian Book Series

The Vigilant Christian book series is innovative and paradigm changing. Each book is a tapestry of carefully explained events with each hair-raising assertion backed up with a thorough documentation of sources.

The five books in the Vigilant Christian series shine light on various dimensions of secret societies which are attempting to bring about totalitarian rule. The New World Order dimensions exposed includes its origin, modern development, occult beliefs, control of monetary systems, and plans underway to destroy the United States. Understanding different dimensions of the New World Order can help you make sense of world events, safeguard children, and deepen your faith in God.

Book Title	Purpose
Vigilant Christian I *The New World Order* VIGILANT CHRISTIAN I THE NEW WORLD ORDER DAVID J. DIONISI	*The New World Order* explains the origin and development of the New World Order. Concrete evidence is provided from authentic secret society sources. Book one explains how modern secret societies seek to establish totalitarian rule and are a continuation of what is also known as the Egyptian mystery religion.

Book Title	Purpose
Vigilant Christian II Preventing an American Hiroshima 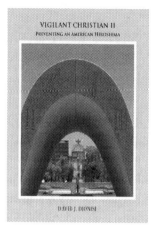	The New World Order agenda is advanced by planned chaos. From the chaos, fear is used to paralyze clear thinking and introduce incremental evil. A top New World Order focus is to destroy Christianity and the United States. *Preventing an American Hiroshima* explains the threat of New World Order terrorism and seeks to prevent an American Hiroshima.
Vigilant Christian III The Occult Religion of the 9/11 Attackers 	The 9/11 terrorism was a mass human sacrifice. This book includes over 100 images to show 9/11 was a religious ritual. Analyzing the 9/11 attacks from the New World Order religious perspective reveals that 9/11 was more about spiritual objectives than it was about exploiting oil-rich nations. With knowledge of the NWO religion for a "new age," you can also understand why productions from Hollywood are often promoting occult works, and how to protect children from these abominations.

Book Title	Purpose
Vigilant Christian IV *9/11—The Secret War* VIGILANT CHRISTIAN IV 9/11-THE SECRET WAR DAVID J. DIONISI	When people learn the truth that the New World Order is responsible for the 9/11 terrorism, clear thinking can return. The New World Order planned 9/11 as a religious ritual which would also divide Christians, Muslims and Jews. This is the first book ever published that has accurately explained how the NWO used multiple intelligence services to execute the 9/11 murders.
Vigilant Christian V *Perfect Money Planning* THE WALL STREET JOURNAL MONEY & INV Vigilant Christian V Perfect Money Planning David J. Dionisi	This book explains financial planning in the context of monetary systems controlled by the New World Order. The advice offered will help you achieve financial stability. Generous giving and socially responsible investing are key themes throughout the book. *Perfect Money Planning* will help you navigate how to use God's resources wisely as you provide for your family and future.

A discount is available at http://shop.teachpeace.com when ordering all five books at the same time.

INDEX

Fleischer, Ari 91, 104
Fluoride 134, 136, 137, 138, 144, 160
Ford, Gerald 37, 132, 203
France
  661 Committee 82
Fujimura, Yoshikazu 40

G

Ganser, Daniele 89
Garfield, James 203
Garofalo, Mary 142
Germany
  following World War II 193
  intervention 4
  Nazi nuclear program 35, 38, 39
Glaspie, April 102
Goebbels, Joseph 129
Gonzales, Alberto 75, 76
Gordon, Joy 81
Gordon, William 40
Graham, Donald 188
Graham, Katharine 188
Graham, Philip 188
Groves, Leslie 7, 20, 21
Gulf War
  Desert Storm goes into action 103
  eradicated diseases reappear 82
  health care available prior to 81
  mass surrender 198
  preventable Iraqi deaths 59
  started on January 17, 1991 97
  victory celebrations assassination attempt 103

H

Habiger, Eugene 182
Hamilton, Lee 102
Harding, Warren 203

Hatoyama, Yukio 18
Heisenberg, Werner 35, 36, 37
Helms, Richard 129, 130, 134, 135, 136
Herman, Edward 62
Hersh, Seymour 130, 131
Hideyoshi, Toyotomi 16
High Frequency Active Auroral Research Program
  147, 148, 149, 150, 154
Hiroshima 5, 13
Hiroshima Peace Park vii
  Atomic Bomb Dome vii
Hirschfeld, Wolfgang 39
Hitler, Adolf 57
Honduras
  Battalion 316 73, 74, 78
Hussein, Saddam
  aided by Ronald Reagan 97, 100
  assassination attempt of George H. W. Bush 103, 108
  assisted by the U.S. Centers for Disease Control 98
  collaboration with the United States 100
  creation of anthrax, botulinum toxin and gas gangrene weapons 98
  economic sanctions 80, 81
  evil alliances 97
  exploited the Oil for Food Program 81
  false British uranium claim 104
  given deadly ingredients by the Reagan administration 99
  Iran was a tempting target 98
  mass murderer 97
  meeting with April Glaspie 102
  not expected to remain in power 103
  no threat to the U.S. 107
  no U.S. commitments 102
  Ronald Reagan supported 67
  ruthless dictator 106
  Stephen Pelletieres investigation 107

228

www.vigilantchristian.org